THE LAST
GOOD JOB
IN AMERICA

Also by Stanley Aronowitz

False Promises

Food, Shelter, and the American Dream

Crisis in Historical Materialism

Working Class Hero

The 60s without Apology
edited with Sohnya Sayres, Anders Stephanson,
and Fredric Jameson

Education Under Siege
with Henry A. Giroux

Science as Power

Postmodern Education
with Henry A. Giroux

Roll Over Beethoven

Politics of Identity

The Jobless Future
with William DiFazio

Technoscience and Cyberculture
edited with Michael Menser and Barbara Martinsons

Death and Rebirth of American Radicalism

Dead Artists, Live Theories and Other Cultural Problems

Post-work
edited with Jonathan Cutler

From the Ashes of the Old

The Knowledge Factory

THE LAST GOOD JOB IN AMERICA

WORK AND EDUCATION IN THE NEW GLOBAL TECHNOCULTURE

Stanley Aronowitz

ROWMAN & LITTLEFIELD PUBLISHERS, INC.
Lanham • Boulder • New York • Toronto • Plymouth, UK

ROWMAN & LITTLEFIELD PUBLISHERS, INC.

Published in the United States of America by Rowman & Littlefield Publishers, Inc.
A wholly owned subsidary of The Rowman & Littlefield Publishing Group, Inc.
4501 Forbes Boulevard, Suite 200, Lanham, Maryland 20706
www.rowmanlittlefield.com

Estover Road
Plymouth PL6 7PY
United Kingdom

Chapter 2 originally appeared in *Social Text* 51, Duke University Press. All rights reserved.
Chapter 4 was previously published as the introduction in Paulo Freire, *Pedagogy of Freedom: Ethics, Democracy, and Civic Courage* (Lanham, Md.: Rowman & Littlefield Publishers, Inc., 1998).
Chapter 5 was previously published in Stephanie Urso Spina, ed., *Smoke and Mirrors: The Hidden Context of Violence in Schools and Society* (Lanham, Md.: Rowman & Littlefield Publishers, Inc., 2000).
Chapter 8 originally appeared in *Transition* 69, Duke University Press. All rights reserved.
An earlier version of chapter 10 appeared originally as Stanley Aronowitz, "Between Nationality and Class," *Harvard Educational Review*, 67:2 (Summer 1997), 188–207. Copyright © 1997 by the President and Fellows of Harvard College. All rights reserved.
Chapter 12 originally appeared in *Social Text* 58, Duke University Press. All rights reserved.

British Library Cataloguing-in-Publication Information Available

The hardback edition of this book was previously cataloged by the Library of Congress as follows:

Aronowitz, Stanley.
    The last good job in America : work and education in the new global technoculture / Stanley Aronowitz.
        p. cm. -- (Critical perspectives)
    Includes bibliographical references and index.
    ISBN 0-7425-0975-3 (alk. paper)
        1. Educational sociology--United States. 2. Career education--United States. 3.
    Labor--United States. I. Title. II. Critical perspectives series.
LC191.4 .A76 2001
306.43--dc21   2001019745

ISBN 0-7425-0975-3 / 978-0-7425-0975-7 (hardcover)
ISBN 0-7425-6026-0 / 978-0-7425-6026-0 (paperback)

Printed in the United States of America

♾™ The paper used in this publication meets the minimum requirements of American National Standard for Information Sciences—Permanence of Paper for Printed Library Materials, ANSI/NISO Z39.48-1992.

CONTENTS

PART I   ACCELERATED LIVES

1   No Time for Democracy?
Time, Space, and Social Change   3

2   The Last Good Job in America   29

3   The End of Bohemia   45

PART II   EDUCATON AND DEMOCRACY

4   Thinking Beyond "School Failure"
Freire's Legacy   59

5   Violence and the Myth of Democracy   73

6   Higher Education as a Public Good   89

7   Education for Citizenship
     Gramsci's "Common School" Today   103

PART III   CULTURE, IDENTITY, AND DEMOCRACY

8   The Double Bind of Race   113

9   Race Relations in the Twenty-First Century   125

10   Between Nationality and Class   137

PART IV   CHANGING THEORIES OF THE STATE

11   Globalization and the State   159

12   Capitalism and the State
     Marcuse's Legacy   177

13   Onto-history and Epistemology   197

PART V   JOBS IN A GLOBALIZED TECHNOCULTURE

14   On Union Democracy   209

15   Unions as a Public Sphere   225

16   *The New Men of Power*
     The Lost Legacy of C. Wright Mills   239

Notes   255

Index   261

About the Author   275

I

ACCELERATED LIVES

NO TIME FOR DEMOCRACY?

TIME, SPACE, AND SOCIAL CHANGE

1

Perhaps you know the joke: we are born, we go to school, we get a job (either for wages or unpaid work at home), we get married and have kids (or not), and then we die. The joke is about the life cycle and is meant to convey the utter banality of human existence. The banality is taken seriously by many biologists who hold that humans—like other life forms—have only one task from the evolutionary genetic perspective: reproduction of the species. Once achieved, we are better off dead. In the social significance of the concept, the notion of "reproduction" defines much of what we mean by the everyday. Like the labor process (which, for the most part, is organized around the repetition of predetermined operations based on a division of labor that reduces each participant's labor to a fraction of an elaborate continuum), the practices of everyday life resemble repetition more than they produce difference. We must eat to live, we usually prepare and eat three meals a day, and most of us habitually sleep a certain number of hours. We spend a great deal of time shopping for our daily bread and a certain amount of time cleaning—the house, the daily dishes, our clothes, and ourselves. Parents, usually women, spend a great deal of time raising their children; for the middle class at least, child-rearing activities tend to merge with the inevitable routines of homework and preparations for twenty years of schooling.

Etta Kralovec and John Buell have argued that homework "disrupts families, overburdens children and limits learning."[1] Its main purpose is to keep our collective noses to the grindstone. School homework is not coded as an intellectual adventure but has become closely integrated into the everyday life of households. From the point of view of the system, everyday life is the best discipline. In sum, we are habituated to system maintenance—a series of activities that freeze historical time.

The first line of Henri Lefebvre's study of the May 1968 uprising in Paris, "Events belie forecasts," tells us that while we are prone to prediction and control—indeed, this seems the very essence of modernity—the outcomes of human action are underdetermined by the conditions delineated by social scientists.[2] Seen from the bottom, making history entails a break in reproduction, the life processes by which, through their everyday activities, we maintain the prevailing system. A demonstration in Seattle "gets out of hand" and persuades both participants and onlookers that difference is possible and that the repetition of difference is better than the repetition of a social regime of atemporality. In that same city, a strike by engineers against overtime and speedup forges new spaces of contestation, and raises the question whether the proletarianization of qualified labor is an ineluctable feature of capitalism's conquest of all of social space. Throughout this book, *capitalism* designates a system while *capital* designates a social actor or agent.

In the following pages, one finds a piece on UAW Local 595, a labor union in the automobile industry that resists the prevailing model of pure and simple business unionism by preserving the union hall as a public sphere. Rank-and-file movements that insist the norm of democracy oversee the internal governance of their labor organizations, and that successfully challenge an entrenched leadership only to confront the practico-inert, are also discussed in the following chapters. The question arises—and it is a question about historicity—Will the insurgents in power reproduce the past or produce new social spaces? In short, will they make a real difference? It is *always* a question; unlike the practitioners of cynical reason, I assume the answer is indeterminate because forces are overdetermined by the self-perceptions of the actors and by the conditions they find already at hand. True, the odds are that the institutional features of established organizations—bureaucracy, "integration" into the dominant system, the logic of hierarchical power—are likely winners. The struggle addressed in some of these chapters is, how is another outcome possible?

What do I mean by the time and space in the title of this chapter? Social time consists of "clock time," the so-called objective measure of labor and leisure; what some have termed "subjective time" is how we experience duration. Clock time, a precursor, a condition of, and a consequence of postagricultural production, is well known: time is divided into seconds, minutes, hours, and so forth; for many, it is the basis for discipline, especially at the workplace and at school, for wage payment, and as a marker of social life—reservations or starting times for dinner, starting times for television broadcasts, movies, theater performances and concerts, or appointments to meet friends. Subjective time is a constellation of experience that stands in contrast to the clock. It expresses our feelings of boredom, the anxiety of being rushed, the sense as we grow older that time is fleeting, the sense of the young as much as the old that they have too much "time on their hands."

The interaction between clock time and the experience of duration is heavily conditioned by historical contexts and by social structures. Agricultural societies measured time by seasons, by the movements of the sun, and by watching and interpreting the motion of the heavens. The main timepiece was the sundial—a childhood toy of mine—which, under the sun, by the spatial geometric movement of a "hand," approximates the imprecise phases of a day—sunrise, midmorning, high noon, midafternoon, sunset, and finally night, the more or less undifferentiated condition of darkness. There was a time for planting, a time for harvest, and a time for maintaining, repairing, and improving the implements of work such as horses, carriages, and plows. Since these activities occupied between a third and a half of the year, the peasant or farm household was a space of human and animal repair. As urban industrial society encroached on the autonomy of rural life, the space/time of the household diminished as the laboring days grew longer and household time withered. Gradually, peasants and small farmers were obliged to spend their time away from working the soil by laboring in factories or workshops because their debt to landowners, banks, and merchants skyrocketed beyond the value of their crops. Eventually, everywhere on the globe, hundreds of millions of farm families were driven from their land into the cities. The structure of industrial labor overwhelmed the structure of feeling.

Industrial civilization brought objective time to its zenith of sovereignty but was, nevertheless, contested. Men, women, and children were obliged to sell their labor to employers "from the rising to the setting sun," but their work was measured by the relation of volume of production to the smallest units of time possible. Thanks to scientific management introduced by Frederick Winslow Taylor in the 1880s, the results of their labor were measured in seconds. The point of technological innovation, both in machinery and in management (a term we employ for industrial organization and supervision), is to reduce the time necessary for the production of the commodity. From the earliest years of the factory system in Britain to its later development in the United States, labor challenged the common sense of the twelve-hour day and resisted the rationalization of production, especially the Taylor and the Ford systems. From the last half of the nineteenth century to the mid-twentieth century, labor struggles were largely defined by the struggle for time. Labor advanced the slogan "8 hours of work, 8 hours of rest, and 8 hours to do what we will" and carried these sentiments to the picket line, into politics, and perhaps most importantly, into the sinews of industrial culture's common sense.

From the culmination of historic struggle for the eight-hour day by organized labor in the 1880s to the emergence of the "new economy" of information and communications in the 1980s, the hours away from labor—the dreamwork of rest as much as what became known as "leisure"—were spaces for the autopoetic experience of duration. Of course, these spaces were quickly filled by various incursions of consumer society, from television to shopping. With the advent of the one-family home as a characteristic domicile of the post–World War II era, men and women spent a great deal of their free time repairing their homes. The space of autopoesis became a counterweight to the constant pressure to extend the workday, to crowd out self-defined experience.

Dot.comism changes more than whether we produce material or immaterial goods. The new economy is more than a descriptive euphemism for the advent of the computer as a leading tool of the industrial and commercial workplace and the Internet as a space for obtaining information and engaging in communications. Dot.com signifies that many of us increasingly live our lives in many respects within the boundaries of the Internet. Many now work on computers, building and repairing the hardware, developing and using the software, using them as the basis for gathering information and sending work orders for the exchange of goods, shopping for personal items, or in business. Most of us caught up in the dot.com matrix do not make our living in the information business, but we are nonetheless caught in the information environment. It is not only a question of how much clock time we spend on the Net, it is also a question of whether the Net is a sign of the speeding-up of life—a sign system for the invasion of clock time into lived experience.

Habits—the routines that frame our daily lives—have been irreversibly altered and speeded up by information. Shortly after rising in the morning, many of us on this side of the digital divide turn on the computer and our first act is to check for e-mail. In my own case, in the late afternoon or early evening, I unlock the door, put my things down, and head for the computer to retrieve my e-mail. A half hour later or more, I rise from my chair—unless I have several messages that require an answer, in which case I may spend another fifteen minutes to an hour at the computer. Before I go to sleep, I check my mail again. At the end of an average day, I will have spent at least an hour and a half on the Net. If I am checking a book on Amazon.com, a bibliographic reference, or exploring the Net for some piece of random information, the time extends to two or sometimes three hours a day. When the machine freezes (as is the wont of the Windows series) or the e-mail program screws up, sometimes my evening is spent finding ways to unfreeze or restore my equipment. It's easy to say "walk away and read a book," but sometimes it seems that my blood is made as much of bytes as white and red corpuscles.

We are accustomed to hearing that older people experience time as a kind of express train or jet airplane, but this feeling now extends to large chunks of the professional managerial class and to students as well. Generations of computers, modems, and other engines of communications have become faster and faster. We can collect huge quantities of information, send and receive dozens—perhaps even hundreds—of messages in a single day. The cognitive processes that are the condition of reflection and individual and collective capacity to differentiate ideas are overrun by the speed of the machine that compresses time. If Taylorism was a way to reduce labor to repetitive operations which only management could coordinate and comprehend, the application of computer-based work and communication tends to inhibit the individual from discursive competence by framing communications in completely instrumental terms. Even our dreamwork sometimes appears in digital configurations. In short, in the new economy, the divide between labor and leisure tends to disappear as waking and sleeping become part of a continuum regulated by electronic processes, and individuality fades from view. In the process, the proudest achievement of the labor movement—the weekend—is consigned to memory. We yearn for "downtime" but it remains elusive. Paid and unpaid labor become an end rather than a means. As an end, labor tends to dominate our entire existence; it's not all about money, it is equally about what and who we have become.

One of the wiser mottoes of union organizers is that "the boss organizes the shop." This is a double entendre. On the one hand, the design and flow of production have the force of nature and many workers find it difficult to imagine a different process; on the other hand, despite its effort to achieve rationality embodied in a segmented division of labor, absolute authority tends to be arbitrary. If not inevitably, then frequently, the boss will violate his (or her) stated policy of justice by speeding up the work without explanation, firing a popular worker, showing arrogance and thereby demeaning the workforce, or cutting or freezing wages or benefits while taking profits in the form of higher executive salaries. As Louis Dumont and Barrington Moore discovered, people do not revolt because they are oppressed *in general,* but only when their conventional entitlements have been violated by those in power. In the current vernacular, they become attached to their culture, the sedimentary social practices by which they reproduce their place in the social hierarchy. They may be at its bottom, but it is *their* place. Thus did the Indian untouchables refuse the government's effort to improve their conditions by "liberating" them from their time-weary job of shoveling manure and dirt from the streets. They knew that once they lost this economic niche, the heavens would shake and their lives would be disrupted. Although the government promised them equality, all they saw was that they would face the insecurity of the marketplace. For them, the brave new world promised by the modernizers was a nightmare. The lesson is that however much they may grumble (since people are often habituated to their subordination), if the boss lets well enough alone, the chance of rebellion against the status quo is small.

The wager is that the vicissitudes of the economic and political system compel the employer, the government, or those at the commanding heights to violate the tacit social contract with those whose consent is a central precondition of their power. Clever or not, power will concede only those demands it deems necessary in order to maintain itself. When things are relatively quiet, pressure mounts from within the hierarchy to make a move against the contract. In labor agreements, the parties agree to a grievance procedure because it is expected that the boss will violate the contract in fairly small ways. Many employers make incursions against traditional work norms by unilaterally introducing new technologies, raising productivity requirements, trying to change work schedules so that they are not required to pay premium rates for overtime, or speeding up the operations. The larger social contract, which is tacit rather than explicit and is embedded in cultural expectations, is subject to impersonal forces over which the boss has little or no control. When the normal working procedures of the Boeing engineers were dishonored by management, the engineers reluctantly took to the streets to restore their professional expectations. It also works the other way. For example, most things being equal, only an incompetent businessman would refuse to move a plant or other workplace to take advantage of lower wages and concessions (such as tax abatements or a new plant built by local authorities without cost to the employer). The employer may regret that he is depriving employees of well-paying jobs, but if competitors are moving out of town, he is likely to follow.

Take the case of consumer expectations. As this chapter is written (fall 2000), farmers and truckers in France are blocking roads as a protest against higher fuel prices just as truckers undertook similar actions in 1995 to dramatize their wage claims and other grievances. Within three or four days, fuel shortages were reported throughout the country. In the United States, where direct action is (for most contests) not a cultural norm—even strikes often have a ritualistic appearance—blocking roads to express protest is considered extremely provocative, although farmers have occasionally taken to driving their tractors to state capitals and blocking traffic for miles to protest falling prices and reduced government subsidies. For this reason, the World Trade Organization (WTO) protests in Seattle were startling because they seemed to violate the beliefs that politics is local and that American politics is largely confined to the ritual of voting and lobbying elected representatives and agency officials. Perhaps, having caught the suing fever, we Americans have placed great faith in the courts to do what legislatures are prone to elide and which our movements are not powerful enough to force into existence.

For example, neither Congress nor the executive branch has been able to throttle the deleterious effects of industrial pollution; both have been reluctant to limit car and truck emissions. The power of big business lobbies, especially those of the oil companies, is widely acknowledged in the political and legislative process. Americans know that multinational oil companies have systematically blocked the development of alternative energy resources for home heating, automobiles, and mass transit, and have fought the imposition of higher gasoline taxes in order to finance these alternatives. Political discourse is tied to legislation and other legal remedies. The slogan that America is a land "governed by the rule of law" persists despite more than a century of bald evidence that the wont of giant, oligopolistic oil and energy companies is to violate regulations established to control their inordinate power—and then to purchase freedom from persecution by heavy financial contributions to both political parties.

Reproduction reigns when every four years half the adult population—but only half—troops to the polls to elect a new national administration and Congress that, for most of the past half century, are dedicated to staying the course. At best, they might adjust the law and its administration to ameliorate protest, consider complaints from smaller competitors against larger ones, and mediate relations among corporations themselves. The profile of the electorate reflects constituencies of highly organized groups that, to a degree, participate in the economic and institutional life of society. Those excluded from consumer society lack sufficient income and credit, a condition that generally corresponds to their nonparticipation in unions, PTAs, veterans' organizations, and other mainstays of civil society. Whatever their aspirations, they are in—but not of—mainstream political life and see no reason to change; they also see no reason to vote. They are the young who hold the preponderance of minimum and subminimum wage jobs, blacks, Latinos, and recent immigrants, people who live in poverty, most of whom work at the bottom, which, since the culture of neo-Smithian economics now flourishes as our dominant ideology, leaves them without the security enjoyed by Indian untouchables.

Of course, none of this would be possible without the adroit invocation of the rhetoric of freedom. We are doused in the conflation of freedom with the free market. The concatenation signifies the identification of freedom with the deregulation of capital, "free enterprise," and privatization of public goods. Consistent with seventeenth- and eighteenth-century English classical political economy and political theory, freedom is clearly connected to property, primarily productive property but also residential, transportational, and various other forms of personal property. The overwhelming fact that there really is no free market (and there has never been one) does not deter those in or seeking power. In the face of the abuses of the private management of the bulk of health services, a presidential candidate confidently asserts that private insurance companies and service providers can do the job better than a universal, publicly run service. The absurdity is compounded by the fact that nobody laughs.

The cognitive dissonance between what many know and what they accept as permissible political discourse may be explained by the aphorism that politics is the art of the possible; the reason that common knowledge is beyond the realm of the practical remains to be explained. I contend that the political agenda is framed by the configuration of the universal—but not denotative—concept of "freedom" with a series of anomalous metaphors that do not correspond with experience but resonate, instead, with desire. The market seems to provide a denotative referent to freedom when all other referents, including participatory democracy and individual autonomy, have lost credibility in the wake of the growing authoritarianism of everyday life. Perhaps market ideology works because it provides hope and perspective for the relatively affluent who, after all, constitute the most influential segment of the polity, itself a minority of the population. Reversing this dystopia is up to the anonymous majority to reassert its own political will.

2

In 1967, philosopher Herbert Marcuse returned to Germany, his homeland, to deliver a series of lectures on the theme "The End of Utopia." He did not return to Germany as an ordinary academic. The 1964 publication of *One Dimensional Man*, a gloomy statement of our inability to think critically and to achieve freedom due to the advent of technological society, had made this sixty-six-year-old scholarly professor an instant celebrity. By the "end of utopia," he meant that capitalism itself had generated most, if not all, of the material conditions for genuine freedom; humankind finally possessed the material means for solving the historical problems of scarcity, not only in the advanced industrial countries but also in the developing countries of Asia, Africa, and Latin America. Marcuse argued that humankind had achieved a unique moment in its history, the potential end of material scarcity, which would open the way for the full flowering of Eros. Potentially, we were no longer in the technical thrall of necessity that made work the primary human activity. We were on the cusp of a new age of freedom, if by freedom we meant our liberation (at least in a large measure) from the necessity to measure life by the time we spent in paid labor. Accordingly, the steady advance of "automation," including the computerization of many types of work and the consequent quantum leap in labor productivity, permitted us to anticipate the abolition of alienated labor in agriculture as well as in industrial production. Under proper circumstances, namely new political and social relations, society's collective technological might could be employed in the virtual eradication of poverty.

The burden of Marcuse's argument in the Berlin lectures was that there could be no more utopias, if by that term we meant an impossible dream of a qualitatively different and better life; utopias were impossible because the material conditions for emancipation were not yet in existence. Marcuse did not question that life could be better; nor did he repeat the by now hackneyed Panglossian claim (pronounced most famously by Francis Fukuyama) that the triumphant capitalist system is the best of all possible worlds. Marcuse had already asserted that, objectively, we no longer needed to earn our daily bread by working for long hours at routine, often backbreaking, jobs that might shorten our lifespan and deaden our senses. Moreover, science had so matured that we might envision the gradual end of epidemic diseases that regularly decimate whole populations—the latest is the effect of AIDS on perhaps a third of the people of the southern African countries. Abandoning the long-held socialist project of worker control of the production process, he offered the alternative of less necessary labor. Freedom begins with shorter labor time and greater time for the full development of individual capacities. Absent constraints imposed by the system of social domination, Marcuse declared we had the opportunity to enter the realm of freedom no longer consigned to a distant future but imbedded in the present.

In this respect, he claimed, we were at the "end of history," if history signified the more or less rapid transformation in the conditions of human existence, especially the unfettering of the productive forces as an absolute precondition for the "Good Life." The Good Life could be achieved here and now; for Marcuse, the remaining obstacle was the prevailing social arrangement. If labor's discipline and capital's ideological hegemony relied on the imperative of work based on scarcity, Marcuse argued, the stage had been set by capital itself for its own demise. Capital could no longer claim that work without end was intrinsically necessary, but this did not prefigure, at least in the short run, a new birth of equality and freedom. Even though the productive forces were developed under capitalism rather than awaiting a revolution to unchain them, to achieve the emancipation of labor from the thrall of alienation, radical action remained necessary—but it would not be easy. Although technological change systematically reduced the necessary time required for the production of goods, under capitalist relations, labor was still the measure of value of commodities in exchange. In the era of late or advanced capitalism, the state, its bureaucracies, and other institutions have as their defining task to hold back the imminent tendencies of present-day society for human liberation. Most of us in advanced societies, Marcuse declared, live in a condition of relatively comfortable "unfreedom." We may own a private home or an apartment as well as a late model car, and be free of the privations associated with hunger, but we are increasingly deprived of the ability to shape our own lives. We have exchanged power for comfort.

If a revolutionary futurity depends on our capacity to imagine difference and to act on the hope that we can really make life over, this comfortable unfreedom subverts the intensities of desire and of hope. Miraculously, in the midst of material plenty, capital has reimposed scarcity as a social and psychological category; it has filled the hearts of millions with the fear of obliteration. In recent years, women and men work harder and longer to stay in the same place. Marcuse calls the failure of most advanced countries to severely reduce working hours in the wake of the existing technological possibilities "surplus repression" because most labor has become socially unnecessary and hence, surplus. By these formulations, Marcuse foresaw the termination of "social time" (the distinction between past, present, and future) and the possibilities of difference and of indeterminate change—indeterminate because the pace and direction of change depend on human agencies. In Henry Ford's felicitous words, "history is bunk" because modernity nullifies all tradition. Marx was no less direct.

> Constant revolutionizing of production, uninterrupted disturbance of all social conditions, everlasting uncertainty and agitation distinguish the bourgeois epoch from all earlier ones. All fixed, fast-frozen relations, with their train of ancient and venerable prejudices and opinions, are swept away, all new-formed ones become antiquated before they ossify. All that's solid melts in air, all that is holy is profaned.[3]

The cultural significance of the bourgeois epoch is that—amid the turbulence of buying and selling, the powerful labor displacements wrought by technological innovation, and the sovereignty of the new and the wholesale casting away of the old—all that matters is the present. If capital has an overriding agenda since the rise of the labor movement, it is to foster, however unconsciously, historical amnesia in order to preserve social relations. Oppositional classes and social groups that have forgotten the past may be doomed; contra Santayana, they cannot relive it. Marcuse may be the preeminent critic of what might be termed the struggle for time because he poses most forcefully the question of whether society itself and each of its members is inextricably bound to its own technology and its reproduction. In the societies in which we live, change is almost exclusively measured by technological innovation; social institutions are viewed as eternal, a thing of nature.

Therefore, every social problem is subject to the technological fix. Since capital has aggrandized the vast complex of machinery and technical knowledge, it becomes the only possible agent of social relationships. Of course, from capital's perspective, the only institutions to be dismantled are those that constrain the freedom to exploit all of the continents, and to dominate both the human body as it has dominated lower animal forms and all of "outer" space. Its putative oppositional forces are impelled to address their own constantly evolving needs by demanding access to science and technology while, as Donna Haraway has persuasively argued, becoming "cyborgs"—humans who have internalized and integrated the technological apparatus into the constitution of the self so that humanity is inseparable from the information processing machines it has created.[4]

The productive forces are sufficiently developed to accomplish the tasks associated with emancipation from the realm of necessity that, for Marx, was the precondition for human freedom. Marx believed that a proletarian revolution would be needed to overcome the obstacles presented by the system of domination, and he had reason for optimism. In his own lifetime, he experienced what R. P. Palmer termed "the century of revolution," from the rebellions of 1830 to the virtual continent-wide revolutions of 1848, especially in Germany and France, and the Paris Commune of 1871, which witnessed the advent of the first (temporarily) successful struggle for power by the workers.

Capitalism has proven more resilient than Marx and his followers could have predicted. While the forces of capitalism did not manage to avoid periodic economic crises in the twentieth century, those same forces invented mechanisms such as state regulation and a generous credit system to develop mass consumer society, which enabled a substantial fraction of the working classes of advanced capitalistic societies to enjoy some of the fruits of their own productivity. In fact, continuously enlarged mass consumption became a condition for the further expansion of the economic system. As a result, a major function of the state is the use of these regulatory powers to prevent what Marx calls the "anarchy of production" from spilling over into inherent market limitations and the institutional capacity for absorbing the surpluses. In the wake of the decline of the powers of organized labor since the 1970s, neoliberals mounted an assault on the welfare state and dismantled most state regulations—themselves the result of the historic compromise between an insurgent labor movement and capital. The state maintains its interventionist role by, among other measures, using the Federal Reserve to manipulate interest rates in order to stimulate investment and consumption. Thus, even if the "objective" conditions have matured for ending the dominance of the realm of necessity over the realm of freedom, the "subjective" conditions (a self-organized and politically conscious proletariat) have opted out of their "historic" mission to end capitalism and its repressive social relations.

The irony of the postwar era is that a highly organized working class of the most advanced capitalistic societies has become so successful within the system's framework that it no longer entertains, let alone embraces, ideologies of emancipation from capitalism. Indeed, in every capitalist country, the working class has entered into a series of compromises. The most important of them was the working class's renunciation of its claim to social rule after World War II, in return for which it gained a highly elaborated social wage (welfare state). Facilitated by a generous credit system and by fairly high wages for a substantial minority, workers acquired a purse by which to engage in a level of private consumption approximating that traditionally reserved for the middle classes. These compromises neither abolished exploitation at the workplace nor eliminated alienation from civil society, the sphere in which citizens engaged in the debates that determine the direction of their public life. Workers were still obliged to stage strikes, mass demonstrations, and other disruptions of production in their fights against speedup (management's arbitrary exercise of power) and sometimes against a union leadership that increasingly identified with the interests of the employer and, for this reason, signed long-term collective bargaining agreements, according to which strikes and other job actions were prohibited. In turn, as work-without-end for nearly every woman, man, and (illegally) many children as well, displaced civic life, citizenship was reduced to the ritual of voting—which the organs of mass propaganda assured us made a real difference. Meanwhile Labor, Socialist, and Communist Parties, and in the United States, the liberal wing of the Democratic Party, conceded more ground to the parties of capital. In all Western countries, these parties fashioned themselves as parties of government rather than as oppositional parties, which left their constituencies with only the tools of direct action to express their rejection of mainstream policies.

By the mid-1960s, in Europe as well as the United States, labor's "integration" into society seemed complete. For the relatively few remaining critics of capitalist society, such as Marcuse, the American sociologist C. Wright Mills, and a handful of other radical intellectuals, the question was no longer *when* fundamental social transformation might occur and under what circumstances but *whether* it was still possible. Marcuse went a step further than most. Although he firmly believed that revolutionary consciousness does not precede practice but emerges alongside, and in consequence of, social struggles that often begin with a relatively modest set of demands (and escalate only if power refuses to bend), he was convinced that the precondition for the development of struggles that might lead to setting the terms of a new series of social relationships was a working class in a position of radical opposition to the existing state of affairs. That is, he embraced the Marxist evaluation that the working class, whether or not it was fully conscious of its situation, was both the subject and the object of capitalist social relations. The chance that a qualitatively different future might actually emerge depended upon its ability to understand and act on its situation.

Marcuse's evaluation of the contemporary situation of the late twentieth century was that the working classes of all advanced capitalistic societies were no longer a class in radical chains; they were in—but not of—society. They had accepted the terms and conditions of the prevailing system of domination. Although still subordinate to the rules of capital, many had won substantial benefits from the system; their collective thought was ensconced in its intellectual frameworks, dictated in a great measure by technological rationality. They could no longer imagine an alternative, let alone possess the desire for fundamental change. Even if, as Mills opined in his study of the ruling circles, *The Power Elite,* the labor unions were "dependent variables" of the political economy (or in the popular vernacular, junior partners), workers' organizations were often at the tables of power. They often bargained the conditions of their own subordination.

If many critical intellectuals had given up the possibility for genuine emancipation from the thrall of arbitrary power, a relatively small group of Italian and French social theorists disagreed. In Italy, Mario Tronti argued that the workers' movement was a perennial threat to the capitalistic system not so much because it adopted the socialist alternative but because workers understood labor as the theft of free time. Their lives were increasingly eaten up by a workplace that offered nothing but endless subordination under the whip of arbitrary managerial control. Rather than raising the traditional socialist demand for "workers control" of the terms and conditions of production, the workers' rebellion in the auto factories of Northern Italy was conducted over the "refusal to work." Wage strikes were accompanied by struggles over what Andre Gorz later termed the "prison" factory. Beyond traditional forms of labor protest, the 1960s witnessed the emergence of a new social type: the slacker. Young workers were prone to take Mondays and Fridays off, to walk off the job if pressed too hard by line supervision, to quit onerous factory jobs, or to engage in infor-mal sabotage as a form of protest. Following Tronti's lead, reading what he called the "unknown" Marx (the work embodied in the notes to *Capital*, *The Grundrisse*), the political theorist Tony Negri observed the transformation of the "mass" worker—the laborer who is stripped of all craft because the machine has displaced his or her knowledge; for this reason, he stands naked before the capitalist marketplace and is transformed into the socialized worker who com-bines knowledge and skill in the new automated workplace. Negri suggests that this new worker is more likely to resist subordination and to recapture time, since he or she is qualified to operate the productive system. Among Marx and Engels's many other insights that were more fully realized in our time rather than theirs, in 1848 they observed:

> The bourgeoisie has stripped of the halo every occupation hitherto honored and looked up to with reverent awe. It has converted the physician, the lawyer, the priest, the poet, the man of science into its paid wage laborers.[5]

Anticipating by nearly forty years the current mania over the "new" econo-my in the wake of the broad application of automation and cybernation to the industrial and service workplaces, Andre Gorz and Serge Mallet similarly announced the birth of a new working class of qualified knowledge producers. They argued that in the wake of capitalism's ability to overcome its crisis ten-dencies, new qualitative demands were appearing, especially among the waged technical intellectuals (scientists, engineers, technicians, computer program-mers, and others) who produced the knowledge that increasingly drove the industrial machine. On the basis of Mallet's empirical studies at the Thomson corporation, a leading French computer maker, they detected the contradiction between the fact that the automated labor process required a worker who could comprehend the entire process rather than a particular cog in its wheel, and the centralization of management and control in corporate hands. Unlike the assem-bly-line worker, the knowledge worker was fully qualified to run every aspect of the production process, from design to execution. What prevented this was sim-ply the arbitrary authority of management and the power of capital. As Tronti and Negri argued, the "mass" worker wants less alienated labor, while the new qualified and educated worker demands not only a living wage but autonomy in the workplace. The struggle against the efforts of managers and investors to sub-ject scientific and technical knowledge to the priority of profits defined the new terms of class combat.

Tronti, Negri, Gorz, and Mallet were visionary thinkers. Decades after their provocative writings, it appeared that the new working-class thesis was destined to be consigned to "poetry," the resting place of much utopian thinking, and not to politics. The May 1968 French and the autumn 1969 Italian uprisings, upon which Negri's ruminations were largely based, remain powerful components of radical mythology, but until recently utopian hope, on the ground, suffered its inevitable tie to the grim realities of Soviet-style state socialism, and even before the collapse of communism in 1991. Moreover, neoliberal economics had all but replaced the Keynesian welfare state as the dominant paradigm of politics, economics, and social policy by the 1980s, and even before the collapse of communism in 1991, scientists and engineers seemed safely ensconced on the side of capital.

After years in the suffocating environment of the pit mines, coal miners routinely contract a disease known as black lung, just as textile workers suffer white lung as a result of the sedimentation of lint from the loom in their respiratory systems. Stress is the black lung of the technical classes. Of course, the event that signaled to the technical class that the powers-that-be would not concede their demands for relief against stress and fatigue was President Ronald Reagan's unceremonious firing of eleven thousand air traffic controllers in 1981, after they conducted perhaps the first major strike against stress in the history of the American labor movement. Having lost its commitment to solidarity—and more importantly, its nerve—the AFL-CIO responded to the president's provocation by holding out the tin cup of mercy. Reagan had no change to spare and he ushered in the new era of sanctioned scabbing with its consequent concession bargaining. Indeed, for a decade thereafter, the defeat seemed to confirm the bad utopianism of those who would reassert the possibility of historical time. With the collapse of the Soviet Union in 1991 and most of the communist governments of Eastern Europe shortly thereafter, any hopes for what Arthur Schlesinger Jr. posited as thirty-year cycles of great social movements (the last having peaked in the late 1960s) seemed dashed. Although democratic governments around the world exulted at the end of that corrupt, brutal, and authoritarian empire, many saw these events as confirmation that history had, indeed, ended (in the Marcusian way of thinking).

For most of the 1990s, there was scant evidence of a qualitatively different future from the all-too-visible present. As the decade wore on, battered by runaway capital and rapid technological change resulting in the loss of millions of relatively well-paid industrial jobs in advanced countries, labor movements everywhere in the West continued to slip in power and numbers. The once-buoyant ecology movements of Germany, France, and the United States seemed safely subsumed under social-democratic and social-liberal tents as well. Having lost on many points of their radical social agenda, many feminists settled for more access to professional and managerial jobs and, buffeted by a conservative cultural backlash in the United States, were preoccupied with saving abortion rights. Although the professional and technical classes constituted the core of the ecology and consumer movements, they gave few indications of uprising at the workplace. For nearly two decades, they quietly suffered from corporate downsizing, causing many to move from their homes to more modest surroundings or even to leave the region.

Most disappointing to those who, in the face of the apparent collapse of the opposition in the West, followed the formula that only in the East and South were revolutions possible and alive, China led the way among developing countries in adopting the neoliberal program of privatization. Less-endowed nations, such as Vietnam and the new black-led governments of South Africa, were similarly caught in the embrace of the International Monetary Fund and the World Bank, leading institutions of the new global capitalist empire. In the 1980s and 1990s, many poor countries were obliged to pay back World Bank loans at interest levels rivaling their gross national incomes. By the turn of the twentieth century, more than a billion and a quarter people on the globe were unemployed or underemployed, real wages in the United States and third world countries actually declined, infant morality increased in about one hundred of the poorest countries, and pestilence—most notably malnutrition and AIDS—afflicted wide areas of Africa and Asia, leading to millions of deaths.

Perhaps one indication that the conflation of the present and the future was temporary, at best, was the demonstration of more than fifty thousand protesters at the much-heralded Seattle meeting of the World Trade Organization in December 1999. The meeting was intended by its sponsors, the leading transnational corporations and the most powerful nation-states, as one more nail in the coffin of the already weakened labor movement, a major turning point in their twenty-five-year effort to reduce living standards in the most developed countries and to open labor and capital markets in the rest. More than thirty thousand trade unionists (mainly from steel, apparel, and transportation sectors) joined environmentalists, student antisweatshop activists, and feminists in a bold attempt to disrupt the meeting. The demonstrators perceived the treaty as an invitation to large transnational corporations to seek countries that offered plentiful low-wage workers and child labor to pour goods across national borders, regardless of their effects on domestic industries or whether they met decent labor or environmental standards. Ostensibly, the goals of most of the demonstrators were fairly modest. The unions wanted restrictions on investments that did not meet an international fair labor standard and, in order to protect jobs in the major industrial countries, demanded that unfair price competition be regulated by the WTO. Others boldly focused on the characteristic secrecy and elitism in the leading global institutions. They demanded open proceedings and broader democratic participation in decision making by nongovernmental organizations. The demonstrators all but shut down the WTO meeting and seriously crippled everyday business activity in the city for almost a week. At the same time, the progressive International Longshore and Warehouse Union (the organization of West Coast dockworkers) shut down ports from Puget Sound, Washington, to San Diego, California. For an entire day, no cargo moved in or out of the coast's cities.

Much has been written about this event. Recognizing the limits of national politics and genuinely impressed by the unprecedented participation of organized labor, the most optimistic assessments forecast a new global alliance of labor, environmentalists, and other social movements with enough power to set a new agenda for economic and political life. In the year that followed, however, American unions proved somewhat shy of taking on the major institutions of global capital, the International Monetary Fund, and the World Bank. Their primary task in a presidential election year was to elect the Democratic candidate, Al Gore, whose position on world trade is a carbon copy of the Clinton administration's neoliberal policy. Labor agreed with Gore to disagree over this issue and promptly fell in line behind his campaign. Except for some local groups, unions were noticeably absent in a follow-up march in Washington, when parts of the coalition that organized the Seattle events attempted to disrupt a meeting of the International Monetary Fund. This time, the police were ready; the far smaller demonstration was successfully contained within a few blocks of the Capitol. Needless to say, demonstrations at the Democratic and Republican conventions were conducted without labor's participation.

An emerging global movement marked the first public presence of a new phenomenon in the history of contemporary radicalism, the anarchist wing, mainly composed of young intellectuals and activists whose main contribution to the movement was to advocate and to practice direct action. Civil disobedience in the streets of Seattle certainly succeeded in making the issues visible, especially because the civil authorities were apparently caught napping. When they attempted to counter the effects of the demonstrations, they reacted crudely and elicited widespread criticism from both the Right and the Left. The adroit tactics of the anarchists provided a refreshing departure from the usual arsenal of march, speak, and go home that has characterized recent political protest.

Beyond their passion for direct action, their disdain for social reform, and their scorn for electoral action, the anarchists have contributed few new ideas to the movement. More interesting than their lack of new ideas, however, is that a new generation of political activists has disdained the traditional Left's reliance on the electoral process and other institutional forms of protest. This new refusal to "play the game" often takes the form of elevating the "streets" to the main site of contestation. The anarchists are generally supportive of the recent efforts by some trade unions to organize the working poor, especially in New York and Los Angeles. In their battle to disrupt the ordinary reproductive life of the cities, they find themselves confronting the police and the courts more often than some would wish. It remains to be seen whether, as with the militants of the German Greens, the stability of the political system may force many to reconsider whether they should engage in a long march through the institutions rather than attempting to evade them.

Some pro-free-trade commentators criticized the WTO protests as evidence of shortsightedness and of crass self-interest. Defenders countered by reminding critics that, in the current economic climate of untrammeled transnational corporate power, free trade was tantamount to a program of reducing global living standards, sanctioning bald labor exploitation, and endangering the physical environment beyond its tolerance. The nation-state, still a potent actor in world as well as local politics, no longer remains the only arena of social contestation. Finally, social movements, including unions, are beginning to confront the leading institutions of international business—the World Bank, the International Monetary Fund, and the World Trade Organization—and are challenging their sovereignty over much of the world's economic life. Together with parallel protests in Paris, Berlin, and Prague, labor is painfully joining with largely "middle-class" ecologists to demand a voice in global economic and social policy. In sum, the Seattle events and the subsequent demonstrations in Washington, Philadelphia, and Los Angeles have taken the first steps in defining new political space.

Closing the yawning gap between economic globalization and traditional political localism strikes to the heart of the historic limits of citizenship. In my view, the significance of the WTO event is not confined to the specific questions it raised. Perhaps more important is that, primarily through direct action, new political space is being produced. More people see themselves as having dual citizenship: the nation-state and the globe. Mired in secrecy and committed to spreading neoliberal doctrine, the great institutions of international capitalistic regulation and enterprise continue to try to narrow political space even as they fiercely pursue opening new economic markets. They can no longer hide, however, behind pious statements of concern for the poor. Recent protests in Washington, D.C., Seattle, and other sites have done much to expose the tension between the democratic pretensions of these institutions and their authoritarian practices.

The year 2000 saw another major breakthrough: doctors discovered that even if they themselves were ostensibly self-employed, they were actually the wageworkers of managed care corporations, and consequently, new unions of salaried physicians sprang up in several cities. For the first time, the American Medical Association, a historic opponent of professional unionism, sanctioned unions among physicians. The main doctors' unions became affiliated with Service Employees, although psychologists joined the AFL-CIO teachers' union and podiatrists became members of the Office and Professional Employees Union. Protesting the reluctance of America's largest air carrier, United Airlines, to meet growing demand by new hiring, pilots refused to work overtime and brought the huge corporation to a virtual standstill. After protracted negotiations, United settled and agreed to hire new employees rather than continuing to rely on its existing workforce to meet rising demands.

Overworked and systematically excluded from access to the "new economy," wireless industry technicians and telephone operators for the newly merged Verizon, members of the Communications Workers of America, and the Brotherhood of Electrical Workers staged a two-week strike against compulsory overtime, to obtain access to jobs in the growing wireless sector, and to force the company to remain neutral in the union's organizing efforts among that sector's workers. As controllers of the repair and maintenance of the vast Northeastern and Midsouthern telephone systems, the line workers used their knowledge and access to the system's nerve center—the telephone lines—to subdue the largest regional communications company in the United States. In another case, the least-heralded but perhaps the most interesting vindication of the thesis that the future belonged, at least in part, to the rapidly expanding qualified and educated workers, Boeing engineers walked off their jobs in a remarkable protest against speedup and other management policies designed to subordinate them to a conventional industrial regime. In both the Verizon and Boeing strikes, the issue of time framed the dispute. Despite all the talk of the "new" economy of immaterial production, management still insisted on controlling the labor process and arrogated to itself control of employees' time. The strikers emerged victorious because they used their considerable power at the workplace.

The Boeing strike revealed the contradictions of professionalism. Although they had a collective bargaining agreement, only about seven thousand of the sixteen thousand engineers had joined the union; the majority believed their professional training and credentials would be sufficient to protect them against abuse and further believed they did not need a union. Constantly pressured to work faster and according to prescribed procedures, despite its minority strength, the union decided to risk a strike to ameliorate or end these onerous conditions. To the union's—and the company's surprise—nine thousand nonunion engineers joined the strikers. Through its policies, the company itself had persuaded the engineers that they were mere workers, in essence, and that they would have to prove their professional standing by force, not by credentials. It took only a few days for the company to realize it was facing a united workforce and Boeing yielded to most of the workers' demands.

These are still straws in the wind. Most doctors and lawyers have not recognized themselves as well-paid wage laborers even though, on an hourly basis, many of them earn little more than a highly skilled plumber or electrician. Nor have the preponderance of engineers in the private sector chosen the path of unionization. When these professionals form associations, they are the professional kinds that rarely address the growing tendency of corporations to treat them as knowledge producers and evaluate them on productivity criteria.

The great exception to the still-scattered appearance of unions among intellectual workers over the past decade has been the veritable explosion of organized graduate assistants in some of the nation's major universities. In virtually all cases, the main issues were salaries and the graduate students' belief that their time for study and for writing was being taken up by the university's insistence they teach nearly full work loads in exchange for "stipends" or "fellowships" that were barely enough to live on. The nine thousand assistants at the University of California and thousands in a number of Big Ten schools, such as Iowa, Wisconsin, and Michigan, have won union recognition; there are active campaigns in Illinois and Indiana. Rutgers and several community colleges have separate adjuncts' unions and New York's City and State Universities have had adjuncts in their faculty and staff unions for three decades. In the private schools, active campaigns were under way in the year 2000 at NYU and George Washington University, following an earlier unsuccessful effort at Yale. There are now more than thirty union contracts for graduate assistants and adjuncts in American universities.

For decades, the National Labor Relations Act has afforded few protections for workers wishing to form unions of their own choosing. The Taft-Hartley Amendments (1947) and a series of Supreme Court decisions have allowed employers wide powers to thwart union efforts by intimidation, firing employees for union activity, conducting speeches in the workplace that threaten to move the plant or office if the union wins an election, and so forth. In the case of professors at private colleges and universities, administrations and boards of trustees have resorted to crass flattery and the spurious argument well known to industrial workers of yesteryear that unions will bring a "third party" into the close relationship between faculty and administration, thereby sundering the collegiality of the community. Most full-time faculty enjoy tenure, a position that reduces the effect of employer efforts to dissuade them from unionization in the state schools.

The revival of the previously abandoned demand for the repeal of the Taft-Hartley Act may lead to genuine labor law reform or, as Staughton Lynd has argued, to a reappraisal of the concept of labor law itself. Lynd insists that the enactment of the National Labor Relations Act in 1935 was the Roosevelt administration's response to rank-and-file strike activity without the law that, in 1934, had exploded throughout the country. The law accelerated unionization by sanctioning government-supervised elections for bargaining representation, but it established the principle that, like the market, unions needed to be regulated and their freedom to strike and undertake other types of direct action to advance their interests needed to be restricted. Needless to say, most union leaders praised the labor relations law; like employers, most of them were happy that the government took responsibility for thwarting the rank and file. The relationship between a fairly restrictive labor law and union democracy remains a relatively unexamined question in labor studies today. This is particularly evident in the labor relations laws dealing with public employees. Unions of federal and many state or local employees have been denied the right to strike as a condition of collective bargaining. In effect, unresolvable disputes are subject to third-party arbitration, which deprives unionized employees of their most potent weapon and tends to render collective bargaining a form of collective begging.

3

In the past decade, human rights have become an explosive foreign policy issue in American politics. American military and diplomatic participation in Rwanda, Bosnia, Kosovo, and the Persian Gulf as well as the trade status of China are debated on human rights criteria more than any other. The Clinton administration waffled on these issues. It declared that the Yugoslav government was an outlaw in the international community for its near genocidal policies in Bosnia and its massive expulsion of a million Kosovans while, at the same time, insisting that U.S. economic interests were too compelling in China to apply prohibitions against trade and investment in that country—despite the Chinese government's atrocious record on human rights.

Nor was the Clinton administration vigilant in the wake of mounting evidence that the North American Free Trade Agreement had resulted in massive job losses at home because employers were able to pay substandard wages and impose putrid working conditions on Mexican workers. The fact that American corporate investments in the apparel industry (especially shoes) resulted in the large-scale deployment of child labor seemed to deter the U.S. government not at all. Only under pressure from labor activists and UNITE (the needle trades and textile union) has the government even acknowledged the problem. However, throughout the 1990s, the Clinton administration insisted that job losses would be balanced by greater job gains and that human rights abuses would eventually be corrected.

Given the accumulation of labor's grievances against the neoliberal policies of a Democratic administration, it is a wonder that the WTO demonstration took so long to be initiated. The picture becomes much clearer when we take into account the fact that, during the Clinton years, labor law enforcement—with respect to the right to organize and issues of occupational health and safety, child labor, and corporate violations of environmental standards—has been weak. Neoliberal economics requires that its proponents disdain all regulations that might impede growth, including those that protect workers. There is little doubt that, pro-union rhetoric aside, Democrats and Republicans are united in their determination to continue their policy of maintaining a flexible labor market in which contingency, rather than job security, is the watchword. If some companies are obliged to hire full-time workers again after two decades of "flexibility," a September 11, 2000, report in the pro-business *Financial Times* questions whether these trends will continue in an economic downturn.[6] In the face of such considerations, organized labor—at least at the top echelon—is curiously complacent. Its passion for the lesser evil overcame any lingering doubts during the 2000 U.S. presidential election. Apparently, the fight for human rights begins at the border.

This raises the question of rights-based discourse, which has dominated "progressive" politics since the beginning of the Reagan-Thatcher era of the last quarter century. The demand for "rights" usually signifies that the protagonist seeks some form of distributive justice but accepts the prevailing relations of power. Thus, grievances are confined to access to existing opportunities within the system rather than making such claims on it that might alter relations of power. The mass strikes of the period before the Supreme Court's 1937 sanction of labor's rights embodied in the National Labor Relations Act (NLRA) were, perforce, claims on power that had no rights basis. With the notable exception of the failed national textile strike (betrayed by its own leadership, which called off the strike when it was assured by President Roosevelt that he would settle it in their favor), three local struggles—in Toledo, Minneapolis, and San Francisco—all culminated in labor victories without a legal framework that guaranteed labor's rights. Autoworkers, truckers, and dockworkers respectively were able to mobilize all of organized labor and a substantial section of the city's nonunion labor force as well to support their demands, including recognition by employers.

The historic function of the New Deal was to channel protests of many types, preeminently those of workers, into carefully regulated and sanctioned activities that left space to punish violators. Violators were those who engaged in acts of civil disobedience, such as factory occupations (sit-down strikes) and disruptions of production in the forms of strikes and selective job actions during the life of a collective bargaining agreement, and in the sphere of civil society, broke racist laws by sitting at lunch counters and other public accommodations or refusing to accept military race segregation. Always sensitive to both the commanding heights of political and economic power (which wooed them shamelessly even as courts and the executive branch imposed fierce discipline on the labor movement) and the threat posed by their own constituents (whose demand for democratic sovereignty over union affairs they brazenly opposed), key American labor leaders eagerly embraced the Roosevelt coalition in which rights and justice were the watchwords. One of the more remarkable achievements of the coalition was its successful incorporation of the leadership of the newly formed industrial unions, many of which underwent literally and linguistically a baptism of fire. Having gained power over organizations that recruited millions of new union members, the new leaders—among whom were a fair number of communists and socialists—were eventually pleased to take their places in the pantheon of the New Deal. After the 1937 sit-down strike, the battering ram of militant industrial unionism was declared illegal by the courts and all but abandoned by the unions themselves.

Until the direct-action phase of the black freedom movement (1955–1965), no significant social movement was willing to confront power directly. Even if the aims of the Montgomery bus boycott and the subsequent sit-ins were to secure access, the road to social justice entailed a program to smash the white supremacist hold on public institutions. However, the Civil Rights and the Voting Rights Acts of 1964 and 1965 may be seen as parallel to the NLRA nearly thirty years earlier. As in the 1933–1937 period, the movement was divided between those who relied on the law and the courts to achieve desegregation and those who relied on direct action. As in the earlier struggles, the resolution of the conflict was to persuade the movement to forsake civil disobedience for the law.

The last thirty-five years have witnessed a shift in the emphasis of the leading civil rights organizations from concerns with issues of inequality to issues of access by blacks and other excluded groups to opportunities for social (that is, middle-class) mobility—that is, opportunities to achieve unequal status and position. Erstwhile militant civil rights figures exemplified by Jesse Jackson, former SNCC (Student Nonviolent Coordinating Committee) chair John Lewis, and Julian Bond have chosen to focus, chiefly, on whether blacks are hired by corporations, are provided bank and insurance company loans to start businesses, and have chances for elective office. The main strategy to achieve these objectives is to lobby, cajole, and otherwise beseech corporate America and the Democratic Party to make room for "minorities." Since the object is to strengthen the black middle class rather than black labor, civil disobedience is shelved.

Meanwhile, the economic and social gap between the black working class and the professional and managerial class, black and white, widens.

The incorporation of the once-vibrant feminist movement into the American political and social systems is among liberalism's stunning achievements. Emulating the early civil rights and labor movements, feminists marched, demonstrated, and engaged in acts of guerilla theater and civil disobedience to advance their programs of abortion "on demand," equal pay for equal work, and in its most radical form, sharing with men all the tasks associated with the reproduction of the household—cooking, shopping, cleaning, and especially child rearing. As Arlie Hochchild and others have argued, this occurred in an era when, for feminist reasons as well as for those of economic necessity, women entered the paid labor force in large numbers, and most were subject to the "double" shift. Contestation over these questions rose in the late 1960s and early 1970s to a level that matched the earlier labor and civil rights movements and, in some respects, posed even more fundamental questions. What was the substance of full equality? How can women achieve citizenship beyond the vote if they work from dawn to midnight? What are the implications of time-sharing in the home as well as paid labor for the constitution of working hours?

In the clamor of the women's struggle, the United States Supreme Court stepped into a space that neither the Congress nor the executive branch of government was prepared to fill. In *Roe v. Wade,* it deployed the privacy argument under the Constitution to grant women the right of abortion. Feminists and their supporters greeted this decision as an unexpected but great victory. In the intervening years, religious and other social conservatives have been unable to rescind abortion rights but have chipped away at the local level by sponsoring legislation that, among other things, restricts its practice. Moreover, Congress has consistently refused to fund abortions for poor women and remains a serious obstacle to its universal application. In many states, physicians have performed abortions despite threats of violence, boycott, or severe harassment. While advocates have shown considerable power to mobilize tens, even hundreds, of thousands of demonstrators when abortion rights were directly challenged—as in the 1989 *Webster* decision—the leading feminist organizations have mainly emulated the civil rights movement in redirecting the thrust of their activities towards issues of educational and employment access. Like the NAACP, they have become fully integrated as junior partners into the leading circles of the Democratic Party.

We can see the role of law in taming the oppositional fervor of large social movements. In the instance of the feminists, the movements were partially disarmed by the courts and came, for this reason, to rely on them. However, the Reagan-Bush years have been marked by a sharp rightward turn in the courts.

Although the Supreme Court remains reluctant to overturn the nearly three-decades-old *Roe* decision, state legislatures and state courts continue to challenge the decision. There is more than an even chance that, given a slight shift in the Court, it can be overturned. Moreover, even in a Democratically controlled Congress, women's organizations have been unable to secure funding for abortions for poor women. The radicalism of the early feminist movement lives on, but only in the collective memory of a handful of its activists and their younger historians. No feminist political figure would seriously propose that household tasks be equally shared among conjugal partners or that working hours be adjusted by law to require these arrangements. Instead, scholars as much as women's organizational leaders prattle on about the "glass ceiling" in the executive suite, even as the chasm between women's and men's wages appears stuck at about 80 percent, the improvement having as much to do with the deterioration of male wages as advances in women's economic status.

Labor organizations, most of the social movements that have engaged in the fight to preserve the social wage, and the feminist and the civil rights movements have become securely fastened to liberal democratic institutions such as the legislature and the two-party system. It may not be too bold to speculate that these affiliations may experience more tension in the years to come. Despite the show of dexterity in the new millennium by neoliberal Socialist and Democratic centrists in the face of growing anticorporate feeling in all advanced capitalist societies, including the United States, few can doubt that once victorious they will be obliged to return to the same old stand. Under these circumstances, at least a fraction of the centrist coalition (which now includes the leaders of many social movements) will, under the force of their own base, be obliged to shift in the direction of making history. With the collapse of social democracy, in both its communist and labor-socialist forms, there is no place for young people to go except to left-libertarianism, such as those calling themselves "anarchists." Whether the severe antistatism of the largely youth protest against globalism remains operative over the long run, in the near future we can anticipate not more of the same, but a return to a politics of direct democracy and direct action. The reinvigoration of the Left depends upon this.

THE LAST GOOD JOB IN AMERICA

There's a wonderful museum of eighteenth- and nineteenth-century material culture in Shelburne, Vermont. Last summer, our family joined thousands who marveled at exhibits of toys, miniatures of soldiers and battle scenes, and the many transported authentic artifacts or replicas: of living rooms, kitchens, pantries, and other objects of everyday life. The Shelburne museum has two purposes: to help in the current revival of the Vermont economy by attracting tourists and to remind us, through reenactments of popular material culture, as well as representations such as artworks, how rural and small-town people once lived and worked. My favorites were the working blacksmith and print shops. The print shop reminded me of old movies about courageous small-town editors crowded into a single room with their presses. The Shelburne presses were more industrial but the technology was the same. Amid the clanging hammers hitting the forge, the fire, and the heat, one had a vivid picture of what skilled manual work might have been like before the automobile displaced the horse and buggy, cold type all but destroyed the old printer's craft, and modern techniques eliminated the need for the blacksmith's endurance.

These were good jobs. They paid well and, perhaps equally important, engaged the mind and the body of the worker. Apart from the laborious task of typesetting done by hand, the printer had to carefully set the controls on the machine just right. It was a time-consuming but supremely intellectual activity.

The blacksmith enabled our daughter, Nona, to participate by forging a metal hook. Walking through the museum's sprawling acres, I could not help drawing in my head an analogy with the disappearing professoriat. One day, some academic entrepreneur—a future *Lingua Franca* publisher such as Jeffrey Kittay, for example—will hit on the idea of exhibiting mid-twentieth-century academic material culture. There will be replicas of a professor's study. On the desk will sit an old Olympia typewriter and some yellow pads filled with notes for an article, book, or the next day's lecture. Another ornament of the bygone time is the inevitable ashtray. The study will be lined with books, many volumes surfeited with dust. A leather jacket and denim work shirt will hang on the door's hook. The magazine rack will be filled to the brim with scholarly journals: the *New York Review* and *Lingua Franca,* those quintessentially academic *feuilletons* that went out of business about 2010 because there were too few professors around to read them.

By this near-future time, most of us will have been retread as part-time discussion leaders, freeway or turnpike flyers, and will manage only to scan the day's video of the famous scholar's lecture on whatever subject we've been assigned before meeting the fifty students at the local American Legion hall where the group meets. The actual postsecondary faculty member of the future might still own a desk but the shelves will contain as many videocassettes and DVDs as books, and there might or might not be a magazine rack.

Thoughts on Daily Life

It's Wednesday, one of my writing days. Today, I'm writing this piece for which George Yudice and Andrew Ross have been nudging me for a couple of days. Our daughter, Nona, will return home about 3 P.M. and it's my turn to get her off for her after-school music class and prepare dinner. As it turned out, she brought a friend home so I have a little extension on my writing time. I couldn't begin working on the piece yesterday because I go to CUNY (City University of New York) Graduate Center on Tuesdays. Even so, after making her breakfast and sending Nona off to school every other day, reading the *Times* and selected articles from the *Wall Street Journal* and the *Financial Times,* and checking my e-mail, I usually spend the morning editing my Monday writing. But yesterday our Nona was home with a stomach bug and because Ellen, her mother, had umpteen student advisements at NYU, it fell to me to make her tea, minister the puking, get some videotapes, and commiserate. Anyway, Monday morning after my usual reading routine, I finished an op-ed for *The Nation* on the future of the Left. Otherwise, I would have started this article a day earlier.

Monday was somewhat out of the writing mode because I had a second (oral) exam to attend. I'm chair for a candidate who was examined in cultural studies (me), psychoanalysis, and feminist theory. She knew her stuff but took some time to get rolling, after which it was quite good. After the exam I answered my calls, wrote two recommendations for job applicants in the early evening, attended a colloquium given by Elizabeth Grosz and Manuel De Landa, and arrived home about 9 P.M., after which Ellen and I prepared dinner (Nona eats earlier).

On Tuesday afternoons I meet with students. At this time of year (mid-December), many sessions are devoted to discussing their papers that are due at the end of January. This semester I preside at a seminar on Marx. We are reading only four texts but a lot of pages: the early manuscripts, *A Critique of Hegel's Philosophy of the State*, *Capital*, and the *Grundrisse*. There are about twenty-five students in the group, who form three study groups that meet weekly to address the critiques and commentaries as well as study the texts more extensively than the two-hour session with me could possibly accomplish. Sometimes after class I meet with one of the study groups to help with the reading. Yesterday I did some career counseling in the early evening for a friend who is thinking about quitting his job to try to work for the labor movement.

Tonight I'll read *Economic and Philosophical Manuscripts* because tomorrow one of the groups is making a presentation. Yesterday, a few of them met with me individually to discuss, among other things, the merits of Althusser's argument for an epistemological break between the early and late Marx, the state/civil society distinction, and whether Marx's *Capital* retains the category of alienation in the fetishism section of Volume 1. Tomorrow, after checking my e-mail, I will edit some of this stuff I am writing and arrive at school about noon to meet with a student about last semester's paper for a course called "Literature as Social Knowledge." Then I'll try to work on the piece until my office hours, which is simply a continuation of what I do on Tuesdays, except some of my dissertation students may drop in to give me chapter(s) or to talk. At 4:15, I'll meet my seminar, after which a small group of students has asked to meet about the publication chances of a collective paper they wrote on what the novels of Woolf, Lessing, and Winterson tell us about the gendering of social life. I'll probably get home by 9 P.M.

Friday is committee and colloquium day in the sociology Ph.D. program within which I work. I serve on no departmental committees; all of my committees, more than twenty of them this year, are as dissertation advisor or chair of a CUNY-wide committee that raised some money to help the faculty do interdisciplinary curriculum planning, but I will try to attend the colloquium. I often invite my advisees to meet me at home because life is too hectic in my office. My

office is a place where students hang out, there are myriad of telephone interruptions, and I am called upon to handle a lot of administrative business such
as change of grade forms, recommendation letters, and so on.

Over the weekend I'll have time for my family, having hopefully finished a
draft of this piece. I also have to finish a longer collectively written article for a
book called *Post-work*, which came out of a conference sponsored by the Center
for Cultural Studies, of which I am director. The group will meet on Monday
evening to go over my collation. I may get it done on Sunday or Monday. Next
week, Jonathan Cutler, the coeditor of the volume, will work with me on writing
an introduction.

I am one of a shrinking minority of the professoriat who have what may be
the last good job in America. Except for the requirement that I teach or preside
at one or two classes and seminars a week and direct at least five dissertations at
a time, I pretty much control my paid work time. I can't say that everyday life—
shopping, cleaning, cooking, the laundry, telephone calls, and taking care of the
car—my unpaid work time—is entirely thrilling but since we share most of these
tasks, the routines are not as onerous as they could have been. I carve out some
time for frivolous enjoyment: at night I watch the 10 P.M. crime slot on television and the 11:00 news. Otherwise, evenings are taken up with the pleasure I
derive from talking to Nona and Ellen, and reading.

I work hard but it's mostly self-directed. I don't experience "leisure" as time
out of work because the lines are blurred. For example, I read a fair amount of
detective and science fiction, but sometimes I write and teach what begins as
entertainment. The same goes for reading philosophy and social and cultural
theory. I really enjoy a lot of it and experience it as *recreation* but often integrate
what I have learned into my teaching and writing repertoire. What is included
in academic labor anyway? In any case, much reading is intellectual refresh-
ment. Even though I *must* appear for some four hours a week at a seminar or
two, I don't experience this as institutional robbery of my own time. It's not
only that I like to "teach" (or whatever you call my appearance in the classroom). I'm not convinced that even the best of my lectures has genuine pedagogic content, and I hardly ever give a "talk" in class that lasts more than ten
minutes without student interruptions, either questions or interventions. Most
of the time I work from texts; I do close with readings of particular passages,
inviting critique and commentary, and offering some of my own.

When I meet with study groups, it's always of my own volition. Needless to
say, the job description really doesn't require it; few of my colleagues encourage
such groups to form. My assent to serving on so many dissertation committees,
about a quarter outside the sociology program, and my agreement to a number
of tutorials and independent studies are by no means "required" by some man-

dated workload. Whatever I take on, it's for the personal and intellectual grati-
fication or obligation which I have adopted.

As a professor in a research school and a teacher of Ph.D. students, I feel I
should also raise money to help support students, in addition to doing whatever I can to help them find jobs and getting their dissertations published. As
director of a center, I need to find money for its public life: talks, conferences,
and postdoctoral fellowships. I don't *have* to do any of this work, but I feel that
I should go back to undergraduate teaching if I won't or can't contribute to
meeting these urgent student needs. So I raise between $15,000 and $50,000 a
year for student support and for conferences and research projects.

Finally, for all practical purposes, my career is over; none of this work is
motivated by the ambition or necessity of academic advancement. I am a full
professor with tenure and have reached the top of a very modest salary scale, at
least for New York. I earn $5,000 or so more each year than an autoworker who
puts in a sixty-hour week, but less than a beginning associate in a large New
York corporate law firm or a physician/specialist in a New York HMO. But most
of them work under the gun of the managing partner(s), and in the case of the
law firm, only five out of a hundred attorneys have a prayer of making partner.
If they don't, they're out. With a two-paycheck household, we can afford to eat
dinner out regularly, send our kid to camp, give her the benefit of piano lessons,
fix the car, and own and maintain a couple of early- and late-model computers
and a decent audio system. We pay a mortgage on an old, ill-heated farmhouse
in upstate New York where we spend summers and some autumn and spring
weekends. Because in my academic situation I have nothing career-wise to strive
for, I'm reasonably free of most external impositions. Before every semester, my
chair asks me what I want to teach. What's left is the work, and even with the
warts—administrative garbage, too many students (a result of my own hubris),
taking on too many assignments, writing, and otherwise—I enjoy it.

What I enjoy most is the ability to procrastinate and control my own work
time, especially its pace: taking a walk in the middle of the day, reading between
the writing, listening to a CD or tape anytime I want, or calling up a friend for a
chat. I like the intellectual and political independence the job affords. I can
speak out on public issues without risk of reprisal from the administration or
from my program. I am able to participate in many different kinds of "outside"
intellectual and political activities, including union-related activism; starting,
writing for, and editing radical journals; and working with educational and
social movements. In its original intent, organizations such as the AAUP
(American Association of University Professors) fought for tenure because contrary to popular (even academic) belief, there was no particular tradition of academic freedom in the American university until the twentieth century, and then

only for the most conventional and apolitical scholars. On the whole, postsecondary administrations were not sympathetic to intellectual, let alone political, dissenters, the Scopes of the day. Through the 1950s, most faculty were hired on year-to-year contracts by presidents and other institution officers who simply failed to renew the contracts of teachers they found politically, intellectually, or personally objectionable.

Well into the 1960s, for example, the number of public Marxists, open gays, blacks, and women with secure mainstream academic jobs could be counted on ten fingers. Contrary to myth, it wasn't all due to McCarthyism, although the handful of Marxists in American academia was drummed out of academia by congressional investigations and administrative inquisitions. The liberal Lionel Trilling was a year-to-year lecturer at Columbia for a decade, not only because he had been a radical but because he was a Jew. The not-so-hidden secret of English departments in the first half of the twentieth century was their genteel anti-Semitism. For example, Irving Howe didn't land a college teaching job until the early 1950s and then it was at Brandeis. Women fared even worse. There's the notorious case of Margaret Mead, one of America's outstanding anthropologists and its most distinguished permanent adjunct at Columbia University. Her regular job was at the Museum of Natural History. She was a best-selling author, celebrated in some intellectual circles, but there was no question of a permanent academic appointment. Her colleagues Gene Weltfish and Ruth Benedict, no small figures in anthropology, were accorded similar treatment.

It's not surprising that in these hard times the University of Minnesota's administration decided to try to turn back the clock forty years and rescind tenure. Only the threat of an AAUP-conducted union representation election caused the board of trustees and the president to (temporarily) withdraw the proposal. In the absence of a powerful enough Left, there is little other than market considerations to prevent university administrations from abrogating the cardinal feature of academic work: the promise that, after five or six years of servitude, mainly to the discipline and to the profession, a teacher may be relatively free from the fear that fashion will render their work obsolete and, for this reason, not worthy of continuation of employment. The irony of the present situation is that many who win tenure still work under the sword of no promotions for dissenting intellectual work, harassment, and probably most painful of all, utter marginalization. For those who have been incompletely socialized into their professions, tenure turns out to be a chimerical reward. With some notable exceptions, by the time a teacher has achieved tenure, at least in the major schools, internalized conformity is often the condition of long-term survival.

In this respect, in addition to protecting genuine political dissent in conventionally political terms, tenure can protect academic dissidence—scholars and intellectuals who depart, sometimes critically, from the presuppositions of conventional science, literature, or philosophy. But tenure is job security only in the last instance. Typically, the successful candidate must demonstrate their *lack* of independence, originality, and hubris. Peer review is often used as a way to weed out nonconformity. It works at all levels: to get tenure and, in many systems for which pay raises depend almost entirely on "merit," climb the pay scale often entails publishing in the "right" journals (in the double-entendre sense) and prestigious academic presses. For example, I know a wonderful younger scholar coming up for tenure in a quasi-Ivy League college who decided to accept a publishing offer from Stuffy University Press rather than one from an aggressive hotter house. He admitted his book might end up in annual sales, but going with the prestigious academic press would do the tenure trick. It's hard to say whether the more aggressive choice would have been as efficacious in his ultimate goals, but he felt in no position to take a chance. The second question is, how much will this decision affect his chances to become an intellectual rather than a professional clerk of the institution?

It must be admitted that most faculty have long since capitulated to the strictures of the conservative disciplines and to the civility and professionalization demanded by academic culture. Many define their intellectual work in terms of these strictures and, in the bargain, measure their contribution not by the degree to which they might be organic intellectuals of a social movement, but at best by how they might make piecemeal, incremental changes in the subfield to which they are affiliated. The overwhelming majority does not aspire to genuine influence. Moreover, they disdain any discourse or activity that cannot be coded as civil; the idea of confrontation as a means of clarification is beyond the bounds of acceptability. Insofar as institutional power continues to reward conformity, tenure is quite beside the point for the overwhelming majority of the professoriat.

For the time being, I write what I please without the sword of unemployment or ostracism hanging over my head. If I were on the job market, most sociology departments would not hire me because I follow neither the discursive nor the methodological rules of the discipline; first and foremost, I'm a *political* intellectual whose views occasionally are in public view. Although some at UC-Irvine were sympathetic with my political views in 1977, it is doubtful I would have gotten a tenured professorship there if the program into which I was hired grasped that my work in labor was informed by cultural studies and what that has come to mean. They did and they were stuck with me, just as the CUNY Graduate Center's program hired me for the same reason. I have been relatively well treated at CUNY, although like anybody who speaks her or his mind, I cannot say I am universally admired.

I work hard, but only peripherally for the institution. In this period of galloping reaction, some of which is coded as populism, these privileges may appear to some to be luxuries, our writing and our teaching merely the ruminations of a narrow academic elite. Some are even moved to attack my working conditions as evidence that the last good job should be ended. It's subversive for a labor regime that is working overtime to close the doors to a democratic workplace and to freedom, and to pose endless paid work as the ideal to which we should all strive. For this tendency, I am one of a (thankfully) diminishing fragment of the professoriat whose privileges must be rescinded, the sooner the better. After all, if hardly anyone else enjoys these conditions, why should I? Accordingly, the task is to reach an equality of misery. I want to suggest a different perspective on academic teacher work.

At its best, the chief characteristics of academic teacher work are that (1) work is largely self-directed, (2) much of it is useful, in the direct sense, neither for the economy nor for the political system and may even be opposed to the institutions, and (3) the work entails little compulsory labor either in teaching or in administration. Rather than proposing an equality of alienated labor, we should fight to universalize throughout society the autonomy and shorter working hours of the senior professoriat at research universities, not just for those in higher education. We should resolutely oppose the tendencies within higher education that have created a large academic proletariat of adjuncts and that have subordinated most of the full-time faculty and staff to near-industrial working conditions by piling increased course loads and administrative assignments on them. To the claim that state systems of postsecondary education "cannot afford" to pay people to do their own work, including reduced teaching and administrative loads, we should defend the idea that the best teachers are in the first place *intellectuals* possessed of wide knowledge and excited about their writing and reading. Then we must learn to aggressively state the cultural value of the goal of shorter working hours for all. In short, to save the last good job in America, we need to stand for a wholly different philosophy and practice from that of the prevalent ideology.

A Little Political Economy of Teacher Work

Most of us who work for wages and salaries are subject to external compulsion throughout the workday. Signifying one of the most dramatic shifts in work culture, the ten- and twelve-hour workday has become almost mandatory for many factory, clerical, and professional employees. Forty years ago, looming automation was accompanied by the threat of unemployment and the promise of shorter hours. It was also a time when the so-called mass culture debate exploded in universities and in the media: Would the increased leisure made possible by technological change be subordinated to the same compulsions as paid labor? Would television, for example, crowd free time? Or would the late twentieth century become an epoch of such innovations as lifelong education, the recreation of civil society (imagine all the cafés filled with people who have the working lives of full professors), a flowering of the participatory arts, a golden age of amateur sports?

One of the predictions of that period has been richly fulfilled. World unemployment and underemployment reached a billion in 1996, 30 percent of the working population. And this is the moment when part-time, temporary, and contingent work is threatening to displace the full-time job as the characteristic mode of employment in the new millennium. The part-timers have little space for individual development or community participation. You may have heard the joke: the politician announces that the Clinton administration has created ten million jobs in its first four-year term. "Yeah," says the voter, "and I have three of them."

This is a time of work without end for many Americans and work shortage for many others, especially youth, blacks and other "minorities," and women whose jobless rate is higher by a third than men's. Behind the statistics lies a political and cultural transformation that has already wiped out the gains of three generations. A hundred years ago, the dream of the eight-hour day animated the labor movement to a new level of organization and militancy. Today, for many, it is but a dim memory.

In the main, unions embraced technology because, if its benefits were distributed to producers, it could provide the material condition for freedom from the scourge of compulsory labor and the basis for a new culture where, for the first time in history, people could enter into free associations dedicated to the full development of individuality. In the aftermath of the defeat of the Paris Commune (where for a brief moment workers ran the city), Marx's son-in-law railed against the dogma of work and insisted on the "right to be lazy." Some workers, imbued with the protestant ethic, vehemently disagreed with this utopian vision—many of the best labor activists were temperance advocates— but did not dispute the goal of shortening the workday so they could fix the roof or repair the car. Whether your goal was to spend more time fishing, drinking, or at "productive" but self-generated pursuits, nearly everyone in the labor movement agreed, mediated for some by the scurrilous doctrine of a "fair day's pay for a fair day's work," to do as little as possible to line the bosses' pockets.

As everyone knows, we are having our technological revolution and the cornucopia of plenty is no longer grist for the social imagination; it is a material possibility. As Robert Spiegelman, Herbert Marcuse, Murray Bookchin, and others have argued, scarcity is the scourge of freedom and, from the perspective of the rulers, must be artificially reproduced to maintain the system of domination. Hence, working hours are longer, supervision—call it surveillance—more intense, accidents and injuries more frequent, and wages and salaries are lower. The poor may inherit the earth and God must love them because he has made so many of them; for the present, Marx's metaphor—that the more the worker produces, the more he or she is diminished, enriching only the owners—seems more relevant than in 1844 when first he wrote these ideas.

Technology is deployed as management's weapon against its historic implication of freedom. It permits radically shorter working hours but, instead, has been organized to produce a three- or four-tier social system. At the bottom, millions are bereft of the "Good Life" because computer-mediated work destroys jobs faster than the economy creates them. Many are fully unemployed; some still receive government support. Others are casual laborers who "shape up" everyday at the docks of companies such as United Parcel Service and Fed Ex for a day's work or are migrant farm workers. You can see the shape-up any morning in the South Bronx or Chicago's West Side where mostly Latino workers await a furniture or vegetable truck for a day's hard labor.

At the pinnacle of the working class, a shrinking elite—industrial workers in the large enterprises, craftspersons, and technical employees—still have relatively well-paid, full-time jobs and enjoy a battery of eroding benefits: paid vacations, health care (with the appropriate deductibles), and pensions. In between are the at-risk categories of labor: laid-off workers rehired as "contractors" or "consultants," both euphemisms for contingent workers; workers in smaller enterprises with lower paying, full-time jobs and fewer benefits; and, of course, the bulk of college teaching adjuncts.

As capitalism reorganizes and recomposes labor, the idea of a *job* in contrast to paid labor is increasingly called into question. I won't dwell on the political economy of capital's offensive. Many of its salient features are well known: sharpened international competition, declining profit rates, global mergers and acquisitions. But it is important to underline the crucial fact of the decline, even disappearance, of the opposition and alternatives to capitalism. The socialist project has fallen into disarray; powerful national labor movements find themselves unable to confront global capitalism with more than sporadic resistances.

Corporate capitalism and its fictions, especially the "free market," have become the new ideological buzzword of world politics and culture. Corporate capitalism penetrates every itch and scratch of everyday life. Under the sign of privatization, public goods are being disassembled: health care, environmental protection, and, of course, state-sponsored culture, signified by, among others, the legislative evisceration of the National and State Endowments; the Councils on the Arts and Humanities and their replacement by corporate-sponsored arts programs, notably those aired by PBS (the Petroleum Broadcasting System); countless corporate-funded museum exhibits; and the reemergence of corporate sponsorship of all kinds of music, especially middle-brow classical music. Sixty million Americans obtain their health care from health maintenance organizations (HMOs)—private consortia of hospitals, managers, and owners. The mission of these groups is to get rid of patients, not disease. All of these institutions operate under the sign of cost-containment; ultimate success is measured by the number of subscribers turned away, not the number served.

No more startling change has occurred than the growing tendency by local school boards to use their funds to outsource instruction, curricula, and other educational services to private contractors. Meanwhile, the drumbeat of vouchers gets louder as the public perception that elementary and secondary schools are "failing" prompts an orgy of straw-grasping. As a recent report using standard measures indicated, these arrangements do not seem to have a noticeable effect on improving school performance, but it is seems clear that panic will overcome reason. Teachers' unions have resisted privatization but the propaganda campaign on behalf of "free choice" (the euphemism for privatization) appears, at times, overwhelming.

It was perhaps inevitable that the steamroller should have arrived at the doorstep of America's universities and colleges. By 1990, in contrast to the general decline of the labor movement's density in the work force, faculty and staff were joining unions in record numbers. By the 1990s, some two hundred thousand faculty and staff (exclusive of clerical workers) were represented by the three major unions in higher education: the American Federation of Teachers (AFT), the AAUP, and the National Education Association (NEA). Thousands of college and university clerical workers organized into a wide diversity of organizations, including the AFT, but mostly others such as the UAW and, in public universities, the AFSCME (American Federation of State, County, and Municipal Employees). To pay for rising salaries for clerical workers and faculty and to compensate for falling revenues for research, many administrations imposed tuition increases that exceeded the inflation rate and were beefing up their endowments with—you guessed it—large donations from corporations and the individuals who headed them.

The growing influence of corporate donations to private and public research universities has been supplemented by a cultural corporatization of higher education. Once limited to community and technical colleges, vocationalization has become a virus infecting the liberal arts undergraduate curriculum. In many institutions, social science and humanities departments have been reduced to service departments for business and technical programs. Many colleges have agreed to offer degrees, majors, and specially tailored courses to corporate employees in return for company reimbursements of tuition and other revenues, and have accepted money from corporations to endow chairs in vocationally oriented fields. In some cases, notably the Olin Foundation, not only are chairs offered to universities but also the right-wing professors to sit on them.

This configuration is not confined to technical and managerial areas; it has become one of the solutions for the sciences, which have progressively lost public funding for research in fundamental areas. Many scientific departments must now justify their faculty lines by raising outside money to perform (mostly) product-oriented research. Most famously, MIT molecular biologists entered hotly contested Faustian bargains with drug companies that, in return for patent ownership, have subsidized research. This model has been reproduced in many other institutions and has, to some extent, become the norm. Of course, American scientists are accustomed to subordination to higher authorities; their involvement with the defense establishment is a sixty-year marriage.

Faculty unions are not entirely a solution to the conditions that generate them: an acute power switch from the faculty to administration and to government and corporations over some hiring, curricula, and academic priorities; sagging salaries except for the high-profile stars and top administrators; and, at least in the public universities, legislatively mandated budget cuts which, in most instances, buttressed the power switch and resulted in some layoffs, a much tighter market for real jobs, increased workloads for those who have them, restrictions on promotions, and pay raises calibrated to the inflation rate. In sum, the faculty sees their unions as a means to restore their lost autonomy and shrinking power as well as to redress salary and benefits inequities.

Academic labor, like most labor, is rapidly being decomposed and recomposed. The full professor, like the spotted owl, is becoming an endangered species in private as well as public universities. When professors retire or die, their positions are frequently eliminated. Many universities, as we have recently learned in the Ivy Leagues, convert a portion of the full professorship to adjunct-driven teaching—whether occupied by part-timers or by graduate teaching assistants. At the top, the last good job in America is reserved for a relatively small elite. Fewer assistant and associate positions leading to professorships are being made available for newly minted Ph.D.s. As the recently organized Yale University graduate teaching assistants discovered, they are no longer—if they ever were—teachers-in-training. Much of the undergraduate curriculum in public and private research universities is taught by graduate students who, in effect, have joined the swelling ranks of part-timers, most of whom are Ph.D.s. Together, they form an emerging academic proletariat. They make from $12,000 to $20,000 a year, depending on how many courses they teach and where, whether they teach summers, and whether they are hired as adjunct instructors or assistant professors. Except for those termed "graduate teaching assistants," most do not get benefits or have offices or, indeed, any of the amenities enjoyed by full-time faculty.

It reminds me of my semester teaching at the University of Paris at Saint Denis. Only the chair of the department had an office. The rest of the faculty, from part-timers to full professors, crowded into a single large room where they deposited their outer clothing and some papers while they taught. After class, they picked up their belongings and headed home. In most French universities, the university as a public sphere is simply unthinkable, a situation which once described the American community or technical colleges. The postsecondary scene of the future may, unless reversed by indignant and well-organized students and faculty, resemble more the second-tier European and third world universities than the "groves" celebrated in the popular press.

Administrators offer contradictory accounts of this emerging configuration of academic teacher work. They claim teaching is merely part of the academic apprenticeship of graduate students and a means to support them through school. On the other hand, they are wont to claim that the proliferation of adjuncts is a sad but necessary aspect of the imperative of cutting costs. According to this line of reasoning, they would create many new full-time positions leading to professional status if only they could—but they can't. At City University of New York, where the number of new full-time lines has slowed to a slow faucet leak, approximately half of all courses in the undergraduate curricula are taught by adjuncts; in community colleges, the proportion is 60 percent. Even in schools such as New York University, which has made substantial efforts to rebuild its full-time faculty, some key programs such as the school of continuing education and the lower division, undergraduate offerings of many traditional departments are largely taught by adjuncts; NYU has five thousand adjuncts.

In the largest middle-level state systems, such as California State University and CUNY, the research function is not genuinely encouraged except for the natural sciences but remains a sorting devise to get rid of faculty by denying tenure to those who fail to meet the criterion of producing the requisite quantity of publications. Many full-timers teach four and five courses a semester and have dozens of student advisees. In some instances, the professor who defies gravity's law by remaining intellectually active is labeled a rate-buster by the exhausted or burned-out majority of her or his colleagues. When combined with committee work, many faculty members have been transformed into human teaching machines while others, in despair, desperately seek alternatives to classroom teaching, even stooping to accept administrative positions, and not just for the money or power. The old joke that the relationship between a tenured professor and a dean is the same as that between a dog and a fire hydrant became one of the anomalies of the waning century. Now the administrators are the cat and the faculty the cat box.

A Margin of Hope?

In *The Jobless Future,* William DiFazio and I argued that academic teacher work is heteronomous. Salaries, working conditions, and expectations are crucially shaped by where the teacher is employed and in what capacity. I have already alluded to the heavier teaching loads in middle- and lower-tier colleges. In community colleges and state nonresearch four-year institutions, teaching loads and student advisements have been rising in the 1990s. Many more professors are teaching introductory courses where texts are prescribed by the department, especially—but not exclusively—in the community colleges that enroll half of the fifteen million students in postsecondary education. As teacher/student ratios skyrocket, class size increases; at one campus of CUNY, an introductory course enrolled eighty students. The graduate assistant told me that she had no teaching assistant or grader. This narrative is fairly typical of many public four-year colleges. When the course load was three classes for full-time faculty, and no more than thirty students enrolled in each class, the professor had time to read and write. It was at least one of the better jobs. Today, many institutions of postsecondary education have an industrial atmosphere, especially with the increasing vocational curricula in the liberal arts.

Research universities have smaller classroom teaching loads in order to facilitate faculty research, especially raising the money, at least in the social and natural sciences. Apart from composition and other required introductory courses, which have increasingly become the meat and potatoes of English departments in community colleges and middle-level universities, philosophy, criticism, and history are activities treated as ornaments by many universities. The leading figures in these disciplines enhance the institution's prestige, which has implications for fund-raising, and in some instances, provide administrative leaders for elite schools. Deans, provosts, and presidents are frequently recruited from the humanities in high-prestige liberal arts colleges and private research universities; the public universities lean towards natural scientists or professional managers.

Many faculty members maintain their intellectual and social distance from students, even from graduate students. It's not only that they are busy with their grant-funded research, their writing, and their celebrity—even if in rather narrow circles. The distance is produced by the growing gap between the professoriat, who in the elite universities have almost completely identified with the institution, and graduate students, who increasingly recognize that collective action rather than individual merit holds the key to their futures. For example, when I was invited to address a meeting of hundreds of members of the recently organized Yale Graduate Assistants Union in spring 1995, I was dismayed but not surprised to find only three senior faculty in attendance, one of whom promptly resigned his job in the sociology department to return to the labor movement. The other two (David Montgomery and Michael Denning) and a few others who could not make this particular event are union stalwarts in this otherwise snow-blinded community of scholar-managers. Critics and scholars of the Left, along with more conservative faculty, were prominent by their absence. A year later, I was informed that a distinguished historian at the school renounced a graduate assistant who had participated in an action to withhold grades as a protest against the administration's refusal to recognize the union.

The formation of an academic proletariat, even in the elite universities, must be denied by the professoriat that has gained richly from the labor of their "students." The professors must continue to believe that those who teach the bulk of the undergraduate classes are privileged crybabies destined to become the new privileged caste. Strikes, demonstrations, and other militant activity are expressions of graduate students' flirtation with outworn ideologies of class and class struggle and not to be taken seriously. It is not only that the professors are indifferent to the new graduate assistants unions; they are hostile to them. In effect, they take the position of the administration and its corporate trustees because they identify themselves as its supplicants.

Some who are acutely aware they hold the last good job in America believe their best chance to preserve it lies in becoming what the infamous Yeshiva decision alleges: that faculty in private schools are managers and therefore ineligible for union protections under the law. It is not merely that they are highly paid and enjoy the prestige of institutions standing at the pinnacle of the academic system. Their identities are bound up with their ornamental role. To break with the institution on behalf of graduate students would acknowledge that higher education *at all levels* is being restructured and that they may be the last generation of privileged scholars. This admission would prevent them from playing their part in closing the gates.

The Yale struggle is only the most publicized of a growing movement whose main sites are in state research universities. Iowa, Michigan, UC-Berkeley, UCLA and San Diego, SUNY-Binghamton, and the parent of them all, Wisconsin, are among the dozen major universities with graduate assistant unions, many of them affiliated with conventional blue-collar organizations such as the UAW and in Iowa, the UE, and the AFT. In many cases, the AFT or AAUP contract covers adjunct faculty but graduate assistants must organize separately.

Academic unionism has, in general, not yet addressed the very core of the crisis: the restructuring of universities and colleges along the lines of global capitalism. Most of us are situated in less-privileged precincts of the academic system. We have witnessed relatively declining salaries and the erosion of our benefits. Like many industrial workers, we have been driven into an impossibly defensive posture and are huddled in the cold, awaiting the next blow. We know that full-time lines are being retired with their bearers, and that more courses are taught by part-timers at incredibly low pay and with few, if any benefits. We are aware of the tendency of elite as well as middle-tier universities towards privatization, towards aligning the curriculum with the job market, and towards experiencing the transformation of nearly all the humanities and many social sciences into service programs for business, computer technology, and other vocational programs.

In short, although more highly unionized than at any time in history, academic labor has not yet devised a collective strategy to address its own future. We know the charges against us—that university teaching is a scam, that much research is not "useful," and that scholarship is hopelessly privileged, emanating from a right-wing position which wants us to put our noses to the grindstone just like everybody else. So far, we have not asserted that the erosion of the working conditions for the bulk of the professoriat is an assault on one of the nation's more precious resources, its intellectuals. Guilt-tripped by mindless populism whose roots are not so far from the religious morality of hard work as redemption, we have not celebrated the idea of *thinking* as a full-time activity and the importance of producing what the system terms "useless" knowledge. Most of all, we have not conducted a struggle for universalizing the self-managed time some of us still enjoy.

3

THE END OF BOHEMIA

Kate Millet is unpatriotic. The author of one of the defining books of feminism, *Sexual Politics*, has for years enjoyed a large Bowery loft and pays the un-Manhattan rent of $500 a month. So what else can a red-blooded landlord do other than to throw her out? Nobody should pay that kind of rent for so much space in this day and age unless it is in Mount Olive, Illinois. If everybody adopted Millet's attitude of fighting to stay put, slackers would again dominate Lower Manhattan and money would be crowded out. After all, hordes of young professionals and businesspeople are coming to the East Village neighborhood and are happy to pay $2,000 a month for a one-bedroom railroad flat; if he succeeds in evicting Millet, the landlord is likely to get $4,500–$5,000 for her loft. Millet has been living off the past for too long. It's time to declare the Bohemia to which she came thirty years ago dead and buried. If Kate wants to live cheap, she might consider Jersey City. Or better yet, South Orange. And as for loft living for a writer of modest finances, forget about it. As the conservative ideologue and city planner Peter Salins wrote in his 1975 deadpan piece "New York in the Year 2000," Manhattan (meaning almost every inch of real estate below 125th Street) is reserved for the rich, not even for the famous.

My first reflection on the end of New York's Bohemia came when, in the late eighties, my friend and former editor Joyce Johnson published a memoir and postmortem of her life with the Beats, *Minor Characters*. It won the

National Book Award and I suspect the recent film documentary on the same bunch will be a strong contender for an Oscar. Whether clear or blinky-eyed, these recollections established that Bohemia was then. Johnson's book followed a plethora of early eighties paeans by and about the group known as the New York Intellectuals who, while not exactly bohemians in the traditional meaning of the term, often lived on the margins in the service of their writing just like artists and musicians. Before the 1960s, most of these writers were freelance, employed for substandard salaries by little magazines or, like theater people and musicians, working occasionally at temporary or part-time jobs while waiting for their breaks. As always, bohemian and other marginal lives look better in retrospect, but there are good reasons to wax nostalgic about this almost vanished breed.

Bohemians are the gypsies of late capitalism. For a century, they set down their tents at the heart of the cities only to be upbraided as exemplars of sloth, then celebrated as the new signs of romantic heroism, and then finally uprooted. Recently, some have pulled up stakes and moved to the periphery of the global city—from New York to Williamsburg, Greenpoint in Brooklyn, and other unlikely sites in the metro area. If the South Bronx and Jersey City are temporary havens for those who have stared into the heart of professionalism and the job machine and declared "the horror" and refuse to seek steady work, the question is whether these outposts can be defended against the encroachments of residential capitalism. The history of Bohemia since Baudelaire has signified art's rejection of its commercial uses, but it has also been the unwitting tool of the renewal and reconfiguration of urban space.

The tradition of Bohemia is closely tied to the periodic rebellions, chiefly by artists and intellectuals, against the values of industrial and commercial capitalism. Unlike political revolutionaries who set about to transform society, bohemians seek social space to enable themselves to pull out of established social practices like steady work. Bohemians reject status and material rewards as long as its price is that you must enter the nine-to-five grind to perform in a job and, if a writer or an artist, selling your soul to the commercial magazines or ad agencies. Bohemia feeds on the limits of capitalism. The bohemian communities are the unintended consequences of residual housing space in working-class neighborhoods and of the creativity of those who make a personal and collective decision to live an alternative and often adversarial life in styles made possible by a trademark of the so-called free market, the select sites of inequality.

In consideration of the elementary need to eat and pay the rent, some acquire the skills of table waiting or office work, or are adjuncts in the metro area's many colleges and universities, but contrive to sell their services on a temporary basis because they believe full-time jobs are deterrents to their ability to perform real work. The point is not to fit your own work or pleasure into the job machine but to fit the demands of the market into your life. For them, paid labor remains a concession dictated by necessity. Mostly—but not always—young, they prefer to be condemned as slackers and live in semisqualor to suffering subordination that is the condition of most wageworkers in the straight world. Meanwhile, some ply their various trades: writing, painting, crafts, music, sloth for almost no recompense except the enjoyment of their audiences, and work for wages only when the stomach growls and the landlord appears at the door with the marshal in tow. Sometimes they make part of a living by selling their work on the street—pottery, paintings, broadsides—or start magazines and publish chapbooks on a shoestring budget, which they distribute on the streets and, on consignment, to the few remaining independent bookstores that, like the saber-toothed tigers, are an endangered species. For example, two of my friends, Robert Roth and Arnie Sacher, publish an occasional journal of fiction, poetry, and politics, *And Then,* whose costs are defrayed by the editors and some of their friends. Robert distributes one of the NYU newspapers around Washington Square and Arnie lives on what remains of a modest inheritance. Both are always on the edge but seem to keep their balance.

The everyday life of a bohemian is a monumental struggle to capture as much time as possible from the "system" by winning and reconfiguring urban space in ways that are simply unavailable to those caught in the job machine. Bohemians attempt to enter the realm of freedom—life without (much) wage labor and without the material means. When it works, you arise when the spirit moves you, do your own creative work until all hours in the morning, and have plenty of time to spend with friends or alone at coffee houses or bars. The bohemian life is self-generated and self-controlled. It is not important to have fancy furniture, a late-model car, or to hit the in-clubs (in any case, who can afford these goods?); what counts are the pleasures to be derived from freedom to be with your friends and from the streets. There are things available in concentrated geographies that the Internet cannot hope to supply: personal contact when you are feeling blue, some butter or margarine or a spare can of beer, for example. Neighbors help each other out when they are strapped for cash or need someone to watch their kids, their cat, or their apartment.

Greenwich Village is the echt Bohemia of the twentieth century and now mostly lives on in the collective imagination of its former residents, scholars, and tourists. At the turn of the twentieth century, it bordered on the old Canal Street Irish ghetto whose residents worked on the bustling West Side docks and as lorry drivers, and the Village's inhabitants were chiefly the Italian immigrants who came to sweat in Lower East Side garment shops, in other production industries, and in construction. These working-class precincts were the models for bohemian enclaves—shabby housing, mean streets, and cheap rent. In this era, Bohemia was defined by sex and politics. From about 1900 to World War I, the Village was a haven for intellectual and artistic radicalism—writers and painters, political activists of the anarchist, socialist, and progressive stripes, and for their patrons, the class traitors and refugees from the corporate establishment, such as Mabel Dodge. Her salon on Fifth Avenue, which regularly featured the oratory of labor leaders such as Big Bill Haywood as much as writers like *Masses* editor Max Eastman and political artist John Sloan, still infuses our collective memory of that period. It was a time when novelist Floyd Dell and many others advocated "free love" and feminist Margaret Sanger, also a Dodge regular, provided the technology and the politics needed to make it feasible. It was the moment of Isadora Duncan's display of the sensuality of the Victorian-shrouded human body through dance.

In the 1920s, the Village was discovered by the philistines who, armed with pocketfuls of money, bought their way into *chic*. They converted the old working-class boarding houses into townhouses and built large apartment buildings above Eighth Street where, even in the Great Depression, rents were out of the reach of most bohemians. Most were forced to leave, but through the 1950s the Village remained something of a model for similar neighborhoods in many large cities: artists continued to arrive and made gathering places of the old Irish bars despite the gradual decline of the Manhattan docks. As a few artists and writers made a little more money, they were able to remain in the neighborhood until well into the 1970s. The longshoremen and truck drivers did not go away until gentrification was in full bloom in the 1980s and automation resulted in the closing of nearly all Manhattan piers for cargo. Until then, you could go into the Cedar Bar on University Place, the Lion's Head on Hudson Street and then on Sheridan Square, and the White Horse and enjoy the crush of working men and literary types who swilled their pints, and talked politics and art, even as they snubbed the gawking tourists.

Until the appearance of the phony co-ops and condos—phony because they violated the first principle of a real co-op, when you leave you must sell your apartment back to the co-op, not to a private owner—Bohemia was assisted by the monumental tenants' movements that forced the city to enact rent control and, until the last decades eroded its fundamental provisions, maintained it against the best efforts of the real-estate lobby to water it down. Although rent control is not entirely dead, it suffers from chronic, maybe fatal, weaknesses. The law now allows landowners to convert rent-controlled and rent-stabilized apartments into co-ops and condos, and even decontrol some units when a tenant leaves or the occupant is shown to be an illegal squatter; it exempts buildings with fewer than six units from coverage of the law, decontrols units that rent for more than $2,000 a month, and permits landlords to co-op a building and maintain a two-headed system with co-operators and tenants, which often results in the capitulation of the latter. Bohemians have been slow to recognize their solidarity with the long-time tenants who do not necessarily share their cultural proclivities. Under these conditions, the arrival of the bohemians had been perceived by long-time tenants, often correctly, as a harbinger of the destruction of the neighborhood, of their own eviction. Tenants knew that if the bohemians were there, could the gentrifiers be far behind?

The Greenwich Village bohemians did what bohemians often do. By the late 1940s, the Village's reputation was already out of step with its everyday existence. Having created exotic bars and restaurants, galleries, and coffee houses, the old Bohemia laid the conditions for its own demise. The still-numerous community of artists and other intellectuals provided the panache needed by local brokers to offer tiny, cramped quarters for exorbitant rents to newly arrived young professionals and, before the co-ops, gave developers the chance to convert some of these buildings into suitable apartments or townhouses for the truly affluent. Today, Greenwich Village's reality is a high-rent district populated by the few remaining Italians and some others fortunate enough to hold on to rent-controlled apartments; as a residential area, it has largely become the bedroom community for Wall Street brokers, media executives, business people, and the growing number of young men and women with sumptuous trust funds.

In the wake of the arrival of the postwar liberal intelligentsia and the civic virtue of the well-off came the *Village Voice*. Founded in 1955 by ex-GI Dan Wolf, the weekly newspaper was, from the beginning, not mainly a vehicle for the bohemians but for political reformers, many of them part of the new affluent population who fervently sought to upgrade the neighborhood and to replace the old Tammany machine headed by Carmine DiSapio with clean government officials. People like Ed Gold, a journalist at Fairchild Publications, shoe fortune heir Stanley Geller, the high-strung, ambitious attorney Ed Koch, Sarah Schoenkopf, like Koch a migrant from Essex County, New Jersey, and others who had found in the losing races of Adlai Stevenson hope that a new politics was possible within the Democratic party, laid the groundwork for the ultimate reform victory, and the *Voice* became their mouthpiece.

But these relatively staid types could not a lively newspaper make. Shrewdly, Wolf realized he had to recruit real writers and reporters to make the enterprise successful. Soon Norman Mailer, Michael Harrington, jazz critic Nat Hentoff, poet Joel Oppenheimer, and political cartoonist Jules Feiffer, who were part of the dwindling Village bohemians, joined the paper and gave it a more radical cast than Wolf contemplated, at least at the beginning. Reporters Stephanie Harrington, Jack Newfield, Susan Brownmiller, and Mary Nichols played an enormous role in helping the reform movement by exposing the shady dealings of city and state governments. Equally important, the *Voice* became the newspaper of record for countercultural art movements: the exploding off-off Broadway theater, independent film, the downtown galleries that were rapidly challenging Fifty-Seventh Street, and the remnants of a severely hobbled but still vital jazz scene that, after being run off Fifty-Second Street, gradually settled in the Village, only to migrate several times more, first to the east, then uptown to the edge of the Upper West Side.

As it turned out, it was not the already gentrified Greenwich Village that made the *Voice* a meeting ground for artists, writers, and the emerging cultural radicals but a portion of the Lower East Side which had acquired the name East Village, and those who migrated west of Hudson Street. Responding to the emergence of the new Bohemia in Lower Manhattan by the early 1970s, the *Voice* became hydra-headed; for the next fifteen years, more than half the paper was downright countercultural, much to chagrin of the staff populists, many of whom were premature social conservatives and wanted the paper to stick to its narrow economic and anticorruption political agenda, which still dominated the front of the book.

The flight of the bohemians at first took the form of the colonization of the West Village, an old working-class slum. When I moved from Newark to New York in 1962, my first stop was an unbearably decayed one-bedroom apartment at 69 Bank Street, just west of Greenwich Street. My rent was $82—about the same as my estranged wife, two children, and I had paid in Newark for a large, well-kept two-bedroom apartment in the Clinton Hill section. The West Village was slowly being cleared of its small factories and workers as the artists, writers, and a growing community of academics, activists, and a few lawyers crept in. My partner and I did what artists and intellectuals have done since the nineteenth century. We spent hundreds of dollars making this sewer into a suitable dwelling and prepared the apartment for its eventual tenants.

The West Village was home to the urbanist Jane Jacobs, whose *Death and Life of Great American Cities* became the virtual manifesto for those who were fighting the gentrifiers, and to artist-activists like Rochelle Wall. Jacobs's claim was that neighborhoods like the West Village which, in the early 1960s, still had not a few factories, a working dock, several truck terminals, warehouses, and was the site of the larger of New York's two meat-packing districts, were safer and more interesting than exclusive residential enclaves because people were on the streets at all times of day and night. Jacobs's formula: you want to fight crime and promote conviviality, construct neighborhoods of "mixed" uses. What value, she argued, to reproduce the suburban desolation in the heart of the city, the program of the current and many former mayors. The emerging artistic community heartily agreed and set about to join with the remaining working-class tenants to fiercely oppose conversions, co-ops, and other development schemes designed to make a playground for investors of this narrow-streeted area. Together with the residents of the Lower East Side and the remaining South Village Italians, they beat back, in successive struggles, David Rockefeller's plan for a Lower Manhattan Expressway and its twin, the proposed beltway. As a result of their obstinate resistance, these diverse forces managed to hold onto a small number of their fortresses, but the encroaching gentry forced the bohemians to retreat to a second-line defense.

The West Village bohemians got the city government to build artist housing, Westbeth, near the all-but-abandoned industrial section of the neighborhood; for this reason, clearance was made easier because relocation costs were less than in a densely populated area—but it was no longer a Bohemia. Soon, sprightly little grocery stores, charging top dollar and offering gourmet food, and upscale dry cleaners lined Greenwich Street. Facing exorbitant rents, many who were not able to relocate within the area, packed their bags, and moved east of Third Avenue or south of Houston Street as far as Chambers Street, which, by the 1970s, was experiencing its own deindustrialization.

From the early 1950s to about 1980, New York's Lower East Side, including the section north of Houston Street renamed by real estate brokers the East Village after its quasi-bohemian character, was the refuge of choice for those feeling homeless in the vast wasteland of suburbs that surrounded New York City, and who also colonized it, especially Queens and Staten Island, and for the thousands of Midwesterners fleeing from what they perceived to be the living death of the dwelling places of subjects of Grant Wood's *American Gothic*. As was their wont, they did their best to fix up their rent-controlled apartments in tenements, refurbished old buildings, including decrepit schoolhouses, as theaters, studios, and galleries, created cafes and coffee houses, and transformed working-class bars such as McSorley's into mixed watering holes.

Then, as C. Carr pointed out, having attracted media attention, like the Village of the 1920s and the 1940s, its character gradually changed. Aided by sharp real estate developers, East Village became joined to Greenwich Village by the hip. Although the housing stock remains much more shabby than its westerly twin, its social composition has gradually become similar. There remains a much-reduced Eastern European enclave in some of the choice streets between Third Avenue and Avenue A because the Poles and Ukrainians were smart enough to buy the houses that were once working-class slums, and the older Bohemia remains, in spots. The barrio lives but no longer thrives in Alphabet City as the conversions make their relentless way and the old Puerto Rican neighborhood is rapidly fading.

Now we should not confuse the idea of bohemia with the equally evocative notion of the avant-garde. Not all those who lived in the neighborhoods where the poor rubbed shoulders with artists and writers were avant-gardists and perhaps most in the avant-gardes of New York and San Francisco—the leading Bohemias after World War II—were not bohemians. The bohemians are marked by their refusal of the trappings of the straight world: jobs, careers, and new things. The avant-garde may or may not share this disdain, but in any case it is mainly concerned with artifacts, political or aesthetic. For instance, while in the late sixties I occasionally attended the great avant-garde jazz musician Ornette Coleman's Bowery concerts, held in a loft that sat next to a series of flophouses and not far from a soup kitchen managed by a Christian religious sect, many rebellious artists of similar originality played in top forties and anthology jazz bands, most of which performed in mainstream venues long past their cutting-edge years. Coleman chose to perform at the heart of Bohemia, but many artists work in more conventional middle-class environments. Other jazz musicians found jobs that were far from their real artistic sensibility. By 1960, jazz itself had been marginalized geographically and culturally as well—some say by rock 'n roll—so that a musician who had not been picked up by the major media or succeeded in attracting a cult following either squirreled around in the basement clubs of New York, Los Angeles, or San Francisco and barely kept body together in pursuit of his independent soul, got gigs with bands operated by one of the remaining Big Names, or practiced music as an avocation—or not at all.

A battalion of composers in the classical avant-garde found their way into the music conservatories, mostly those of universities and colleges. Elliot Carter and Milton Babbitt, among others, not only produced the American variant of Schoenberg's serial rows but trained two generations of composers to follow them. The works of these musicians have always appealed to small audiences, mostly fellow musicians, and in time, their music was pretty much confined to the academy. In fact, their hegemony over the contemporary classical music scene produced a countermovement of minimalism and romantic tonality that currently rules the roost—but in no way is sympathetic to the modernist musical avant-garde.

The Bohemias were located in slum neighborhoods for one simple reason: cheap rent. Cheap rent meant that the artist or would-be artist could survive on part-time and temporary paid work or, if they sold their paintings, articles, stories, poems or, if musicians, got occasional performance dates, could live, even if not in comfort, let alone splendor. Sometimes they formed living communes without using that ideological name. As often as not, the rent was shared among an indeterminate number of tenants who cohabited in one of the many railroad flats that littered the Lower East Side or, if they craved space, moved into the mini-barrio of the western streets of South Brooklyn or slowly drifted into the abandoned factories of Long Island City and Williamsburg, where they were promptly trailed by the media and the real estate vultures.

In 1969, I took a fourth-floor walkup apartment at 26 Saint Marks Place from a friend who moved in with her lover. Located a few steps west of Second Avenue, the building had once housed traditional two- or three-bedroom apartments but had recently been converted into studio and one-bedroom digs suitable for single people or couples without children. Across the street was a rowdy rock music club, The Dom, and because of the crowds and the noise I tried hard to stay away on weekends, if I wanted to sleep. Even on weekdays, the streets were cluttered with locals and visitors. I frequently took my meals in the several Polish and Ukrainian restaurants on Second Avenue and Avenue A (especially Voselka and the Second Avenue delicatessen), bought my next morning's paper at Gem Spa on the corner at twelve midnight and read it while sipping an egg cream. Around the corner on Second Avenue, Bill Graham had opened Filmore East where, of an evening, Herbert Marcuse, then perhaps the most prominent radical intellectual in the country, was scheduled to give a talk to an overflowing house. No sooner had he opened his mouth when a group of protesters, The Up against the Wall Motherfuckers led by his stepson, Tom Neumann, disrupted the meeting for its traditional character, for Marcuse's bourgeois lifestyle, for the fact that Marcuse had married Tom's mother and was rumored to have had an affair with her when Franz, Tom's father, was still alive, and for the hell of it. This group placed itself in implacable opposition to the prevailing culture and expressed its disgust of hypocritical liberals in the most direct ways possible. It had rejected the application for membership of Abbie Hoffman (of 9 St. Marks Place) because he did not meet their high radical standard. After all, Abbie consorted with liberal types like lawyers and politicians, not to mention their perception that he pandered to the media. Abbie was furious at his rejection and wrote a passionate defense of his radical credentials in the *Voice*. The Motherfuckers never had more than a few members, but they made a lot of noise and managed to influence hundreds of radicals who *wished* they could muster the nerve to express their feelings directly and in public venues like the Motherfuckers did.

Perhaps the most important press medium of the East Village Bohemia was *The East Village Other*, which, in it short existence during the mid-sixties, managed to make the *Voice* appear rather staid. It excoriated the gentrifiers, was culturally hip, and tried hard to reconcile Bohemia with the Puerto Rican and black barrios. Also in the area were two other publications: *The Guardian*, a national newsweekly of distinctly Old Left origins on East Fourth Street but which had become perhaps the main paper of the New Left, although not of the counterculture; and *The Rat,* a local sheet which tried to combine a counter-cultural esprit with revolutionary politics. Both papers failed to survive scorch-ing splits over social issues, chiefly feminism. Women seized power at *The Rat* but couldn't make it work when the conspirators split over ideological issues. *The Guardian* apparently survived its internal dissension but lost Old Left financial support and folded a decade later.

Bohemianism has fallen on hard times. Most have found that the margins on which they once made it have shrunk to a very thin line and only a small num-ber have held out in the freelance. Although there are still remnants in the old East Village and Lower East Side haunts and there is some bohemian life in Williamsburg, the fight to capture control over time has shifted from geograph-ic living spaces to the workplace. Seeing that they were often forced to choose between eating and paying the rent, some went to law school or graduate school, took editorial or publicity jobs with publishers or nonprofit organiza-tions, or became editors and art directors of labor newspapers, corporate newsletters, or speechwriters for CEOs and other top officers of leading corpo-rations. Most who managed to earn Ph.D. degrees have academic jobs, but not always full time. Although some enjoy tenured professorial positions, many have ended up as "lifer" adjuncts, eking out a bare living as part-time instruc-tors in English composition or introductory social science. Many became com-puter experts and started small businesses as consultants to beleaguered users, often their fellow writers, academics who couldn't handle the frozen screen and frequent text losses, or worked as information systems specialists for universi-ties, public agencies, and private corporations.

The vast majority of artists and writers who became teachers or book, ad, and magazine designers are still groping for a way to fight the exploitation inher-ent in casual labor; some resist taking on the cultural trappings that usually accompany the workplace. Some don't have much choice; from spatial margins they have entered the margins of the institutions that want to hire them, but only as casual labor. If teachers, they are often hired as adjuncts, full- or part-time substitutes in schools of all sorts, and frequently work without benefits. If artists, photographers, and writers, they are almost certainly freelancers but can-not make a living. Most will eventually seek full-time employment or regular part-time work.

Many bohemians find themselves confronted with labor issues but of a spe-cial type. They enter the workplace armed with the experience of having once enjoyed a measure of freedom and with the conceit that their credentials entitle them to some job autonomy. Instead, they find the law offices, corporate suites, and nonprofit agencies such as hospitals and schools have become knowledge factories that break your head rather than your back, and even if the pay is halfway decent, everyday life is a nightmare. For example, for social workers and physicians, managed care constrains their ability to make decisions concerning patient needs; the overriding rule is to find the fastest way to get rid of patients and to care for them in the cheapest way possible. Teachers in city K-12 schools face unparalleled speedup; the conditions of work in public and most private colleges and universities are not much better.

They often join unions and participate in organizing campaigns. The film-maker Tami Gold, now a full-time teacher, is an activist in her union chapter at Hunter College. Literary scholar Barbara Bowen, a former union organizer and now Queens College English professor, is president of the faculty and staff union at CUNY. Psychologists are joining the Service Employees International Union and there is a fairly sizeable National Writers Union local in New York City, most of whom are freelancers. They have concentrated their efforts on Internet copyright issues and on fighting book and magazine contracts that force them to surrender their intellectual property as a price for getting printed or gaining access to paid Internet writing. This is the optimistic scenario. Many who occupy professional and technical jobs have not yet found their voice, but when intellectuals and artists fight for salary increases and health and pension benefits, the next step is to fight for time. It's not the same as the old Village(s), but it's the same fight.

In a world dominated by the bottom line, the New York Intellectuals no less than the Beats and the countercultural sixties bohemians are largely history. We still make the grievous error of calling academics intellectuals, for most of them have become technicians of knowledge. They work in colleges and universities as salaried purveyors of received wisdom and only occasionally manage to make the classroom into a place of genuine exploration and creativity. Whether exaggerated or not, the New York Intellectuals had at least adversarial pretensions, but the word and concept *Bohemia* has disappeared from the language along with those who legitimately filled its shoes. Bohemia lives in the South Bronx where some young Latino artists have reclaimed old buildings and created new performance spaces. There are pockets of bohemian activity in Jersey City, Newark, Brooklyn, and Queens. There can be little doubt that its protagonists are pioneers of an outer-borough rebellion against the job machine, but they also are playing their historic role as the agents of urban gentrification—but not until the likely rear-guard turf battle has been spent. Like Paris in the nineteenth century, the appearance of Bohemia almost always functions as a wake-up call to capital to clean up its act and figure out how to take advantage of the free services that accrue from their putative adversaries.

If there is any hope for a bohemian revival, its future lies in the Bronx and the farthest corners of Brooklyn. What would prevent these communities from following in the steps of their forbearers? The settlers would not be oblivious to the surroundings into which they have landed. They would be obliged to join with their mostly working-class neighbors in fighting the gentrification that inevitably follows in the wake of their urban redevelopment activities. Like the protagonist of *Last Exit to Brooklyn,* whose tragic fate is sealed by the gulf that separates class and sexual issues, and the working-class *Angie* who dreams of life beyond Bay Ridge, the new bohemians must try to reach out beyond their own specific cultural formation. Even then, the chance of survival would be slim. For just as Baraka has ended up in Newark and his generation of black and white bohemians is dispersed, so succeeding generations have had the same fate. Now the fight for time is squarely in the sites of that dispersal: the pseudoartistic, pseudoeducational, and technical workplaces.

II

EDUCATION AND DEMOCRACY

4

THINKING BEYOND
"SCHOOL FAILURE"

FREIRE'S LEGACY

Not long ago I visited a small, alternative public high school in New York and attended classes on racial discrimination and corporate influence in contemporary higher education. The school is one of the twenty or so small, mostly teacher-run high schools the sclerotic New York City Board of Education is obliged to recognize and to fund in the 1990s despite its better judgment. The board and its chancellor distrust any schools they don't control and for this reason do not leave the alternative schools to their own devices. In a system in which big is invariably viewed as better, they are called to account for every aspect of their operation: costs per student, number of enrolled students, their performance on standard tests, curriculum, and licensure of teachers and administrators. Like most others, this school was established by teachers rather than administrators, and for this reason, their ability to survive has remained in doubt for all the years of its existence.

They benefit from public perception that many large, board-administered high schools have failed by almost any measure: academic performance, graduation rates, college admissions, and of course, the volume of dropouts. Most importantly, the large secondary school behemoths fail to ignite students' passion for learning, let alone fail to demonstrate their competence by conventional testing criteria. In the typical 3,000- to 4,000-student New York City public high school, kids say "nothing is going on" except what can be provided by the occasional, unusually dedicated teacher who manages to overcome her role as a cop (keeping order is the highest priority in many of these schools) and a few energetic and entrepreneurial educators who have deigned to operate small programs to keep the most highly motivated from leaving the school.

The chancellor and his minions lose no opportunity to rail against these fragile experiments as cost-ineffective and irrelevant, but so far the administration has been unable to sink them because they are backed by parents and education activists and initially gained leverage on the system by raising outside foundation money to defray many start-up costs. The one I visited is among the more successful. Like many of its cohorts, it began as a small outpost within a larger school to "contain" some of the more discontented students and many who would drop out unless otherwise motivated. The central administration tacitly recognizes the alternative program as a convenient way to appease an increasingly restive public and to address some of the discipline problems in many of the large factory-like institutions.

With some 150 students, many of them Latino but also a substantial number of "whites"(some of whom have dropped out of the city's handful of "elite" high schools) and blacks, the five-year-old experiment has graduated some students and helped others to pass the battery of tests devised by the state to winnow the school population. These small victories resulted in its being declared a free-standing institution with its own principal. In line with the general drift, this school is organized around a "theme" although the curriculum does not suggest much specialization.

From the kids' vantage point, "Alternative High" is a magical place. Unlike many of the bigger schools that are more day prisons than educational sites, students are not hassled by guards and assistant principals; even more importantly, teachers and administrators respect and care for and about them. For many students, this is a last-chance saloon: fuck this one up and forget about a diploma let alone college. Don't make it and it's back to the streets and maybe jail. Classes are about half the size of regular high schools, the teachers are mostly young, and several went to Ivy League schools. All work hard to engage kids in dialogue on the subject matter. The party "line" of the school is antiracist and antisexist. Possessing a modest degree of autonomy, teachers use materials such as newspapers, magazines, and books as much as possible rather than texts drawn from the board-prescribed reading lists. Under its "urban" program, students go out into the city to find out about neighborhood conditions, other schools, and about economic issues such as joblessness. The math and science teachers are trying to integrate their subject matters and to make them concept- rather than procedure-oriented. Faculty in all of the disciplines struggle to find the handles to simultaneously prepare students for the Regents Examinations, a required endgame whose results have enormous bearing on whether the school will continue to exist and on what the teachers view as genuine education.

Among the teachers, the name Paulo Freire is iconographic alongside the luminaries of the women's and black freedom movements; many staff members have actually read his *Pedagogy of the Oppressed* or, in a general way, know something of what it contains. The actual practice of most teachers, although relentlessly dialogic (I observed no sustained classroom lectures that followed a prescribed "lesson plan"), remained at considerable distance from Freire's own thought, however. At best, following the dictum of the medical profession, the school has achieved to "first, do no harm." This is no small achievement in a system that routinely inflicts incredible damage on almost all kids, and not just on working-class kids from racial, sexual, or gendered strata. Alternative High's students displayed veritable exhilaration at being there. They felt safe. I suspect that the school's greatest accomplishment has been to establish relations of trust among the slender corps of administrators, teachers, and students. What is truly innovative about the school is its fealty to one of Freire's prerequisites: respect for kids and what they already know. As to education, however, it has a long way to go. In fact, in concert with many liberal and radical educators, some teachers have interpreted liberal education to chiefly mean instilling humanistic values in a nonrepressive way. The school seems to be a massive exercise geared towards values clarification.

1

These are dark times for educational innovation and its protagonists. In schools and universities, "reactionaries" (as Paulo Freire calls them) have all but overwhelmed the "progressives." Their agenda to construe the very concept of education as training dominates schooling in public universities and is steadily gaining ground in private institutions as well. To suggest otherwise is to commit an unholy violation of the new common sense that the highest mission and overriding purpose of schooling is to prepare students, at different levels, to take their places in the corporate order. The banking or transmission theory of school knowledge that Freire identified more than thirty years ago as the culprit standing in the way of critical consciousness has returned with a vengeance. Once widely scorned by educators from diverse educational philosophies as a flagrant violation of the democratic educational mission, this new common sense has been thrust to the fore of nearly all official pedagogy. According to this view, students are "objects" into which teachers pour prescribed knowledge, primarily mathematics and rote science. Where once liberal, let alone radical, educators insisted that education be at the core of an activity of self-exploration through which the student attempted to discover her own subjectivity through intellectual and affective encounters, now nearly all learning space is occupied by an elaborate testing apparatus to measure the student's "progress" in ingesting externally imposed curricula. Even more insidiously, this new "education" provides a sorting device to reproduce the inequalities inherent in the capitalist market system. In effect, the image of the learner (when not viewed as a bundle of uncontrollable animal urges) has reverted to Locke's infamous tabula rasa. In turn, the teacher becomes the instrument of approved intellectual and moral culture, charged with the task of expunging destructive impulses and fueling the empty mental tank. The student must be permitted no autonomy lest the evil spirits which lurk in everyday life regain lost ground.

These perspectives have reached across the ideological spectrum. In various degrees, academics and school authorities have embraced the new mantra that the student and radical movements of the 1960s and 1970s internationally forced educational reforms (such as open classrooms, student-generated curricula, black, women's, and ethnic studies programs) and introduced into the canon of many human sciences the works of Marx and the Marxists, Derrida, Foucault, Deleuze, and French feminists as intellectual terrorists—to the detriment of modern students (or so the new mantra states). Especially after the fall of the Berlin Wall, some discovered their own liberalism and others kept drifting rightward. In the United States, a range of erstwhile leftists—even those who had perpetrated what philosopher Sidney Hook once described as elements of academic "anarchy"—began to accept chairs and grant money from leading conservative institutions such as the Olin Foundation, to enjoy the company of the enemies of critical learning. For many, the radicalism of the 1960s and 1970s turned out to be a horror show of "political correctness," a menace to the integrity of the academic enterprise, the highest value of which was dispassionate, disinterested scientific investigation. The radicals became "ideologues" because they took sides; the others were "scholars" because their side was the liberal academy with its panoply of discipline-based departments, professional associations, and literatures. For them, what America and the world needed was schooling that obliged students to keep their collective noses to the grindstone in order to imbibe the best that had been thought and said. The highest curricular value was the dissemination of the great traditions of what they called "Western Civilization."

For example, the reactionaries have recently begun to eliminate "recess" in elementary schools, the small opportunity kids still enjoy to play during the school day. For the mavens of authoritarian education, such frivolous pursuits must be replaced by the industrial model that had been reserved for secondary school in former periods. In this age of the subsumption of the human spirit

under the imperatives of alienated work without end, society has lost its tolerance for even kid pleasures; school authorities have, sometimes enthusiastically,
subordinated themselves to business by imaging schools in the modalities of the
factory or the large corporate office. Even where the values of business civilization are not (yet) openly trumpeted by administrators, tolerance for changes
suggested by the new social movements has worn thin.

In this environment, *Pedagogy of Freedom*—Paulo Freire's last book—is a
utopian text. Its utopianism consists in the wild and seemingly anachronistic
idea that, among other things, education is "that specifically human act of intervening in the world. When I speak of intervention," Freire says,

> I refer both to the aspiration for radical changes in the field of economics, human
> relations, the right to employment, to land, to education, to health and also, on
> the other hand, to the reactionary position whose aim is to immobilize history
> and maintain an unjust socio-economic and cultural order."[1]

As he utters these words, I can imagine Freire almost hearing an interlocutor's sigh, "Yeah, yeah, yeah, we've heard all that before, but what makes you
think any change is possible in the era of unfettered global capitalism when the
forces of progressive reason have yielded even the territory of the imagination to
its adversaries?" Or what amounts to the same thing: "Poor people cannot afford
idle dreams, professor. Get real. What kids need is job readiness." In fact, he
acknowledged that many have succumbed to fatalism, pessimism, and to the
program of neoliberalism—the doctrine according to which we have no choice
but to adapt both our hopes and our abilities to the new global market. In short,
this book contains no dewy-eyed ingenuous optimism. Freire simply stated what
genuine education consisted of and defined the role of the teacher and learner in
the process. He renounced the prevailing pretense of the teacher's "neutrality"
or "impartiality." Indeed, he argued that few teachers could sustain this claim in
a time when schooling was undergoing unprecedented regimentation.

What, then, is the basis of hope for genuine education, as Freire defined it,
when the corporate CEO is a culture hero, when technoscientific training has
been elevated to the pedagogic norm, when the remnants of the once vast army
of educational liberals have retreated to the sacred texts? How can anyone fail
to realize that the language of radical change, let alone the chance of its realization, toppled with the Berlin Wall a decade ago and now belongs with other
relics of that bygone era? Freire answered that he has an "obstinate fascination
with everything that has to do with men and women." For him, it was never a
question of demonstrating that education was likely, only that it was possible.
Freire aligned himself with those who still dreamed and kept alive hope for a

world without exploitation, inequality, and cultural enslavement. Unlike neoliberals and some leftists, his conviction is not borne out by some "scientific" assessment of the current situation. Instead, Freire's belief in the emancipation of "men and women" was rooted in an "existential" commitment to an ethical ideal rather than to historical inevitability. In our period of crass opportunism and crushed aspirations, his book is a beacon for those with whom he is affiliated: "the wretched of the earth, the excluded." Unlike those who, sixty years earlier, despaired for a better world at the moment of fascism's rise and could offer only the "Great Refusal," a negative prescription to resist the totalitarian machine, Freire found affirmation in the achievements of countless teachers and students who defied the new authoritarian machine to conquer illiteracy, to assert their "critical curiosity," to intervene. Careful to distinguish educational activity from revolutionary transformation, he nevertheless defended it as a significant break from the status quo and a necessary step on the road to a different future than that proposed by the reactionaries. Freire seems to suggest that a radical futurity depends upon the work of radical educators today.

Since the English translation thirty years ago of *Pedagogy of the Oppressed*, Freire's work has suffered the misreadings of well-meaning educators who have interpreted his work as a "brilliant methodology," a kind of manual for teachers who would bring out the best in their otherwise indifferent students. Such characterizations are undoubtedly fed by the common identification of pedagogy merely with compassionate teaching: what is taught is unproblematic; the only issue is how to teach on the basis of caring. The authority of the teacher as a certified possessor of legitimate knowledge is always fundamentally already established and the student's position as a consumer of knowledge is equally unquestioned. Many read Freire's dialogic pedagogy as a tool for student motivation and cannot recognize that, for him, dialogue has a content whose goal is social as much as individual change. In Freire's educational philosophy, the first principle is that the conventional distinction between teacher as expert and learner as an empty biophysiological shell is questioned. Education takes place when there are two learners who occupy somewhat different spaces in an ongoing dialogue. Both participants bring knowledge to the relationship and one of the objects of the pedagogic process is to explore what each knows, and what they can teach each other. A second object is to foster reflection on the self as actor in the world in consequence of knowing.

Against the prevailing wisdom, Freire rejected the idea of teacher as transmitter of received knowledge. He also spurned the degraded idea that the teacher is chiefly a "facilitator" of commonsense wisdom and of values clarification. Alternatively, he argued for the teacher as an intellectual who, like the student, is engaged preeminently in producing knowledge. In order to create new knowledge, the teacher and the student come to the learning situation as possessors of past knowledge, albeit of different sorts. The student arrives with his life experience and his previous schooling in hand. An important moment in the learning situation is when the student critically evaluates what she knows and not only for the purpose of overcoming this knowledge. Consistent with the Hegelianism inherent in his own practice, Freire wanted to preserve as well as transform what the student knew, and to make it available in the process of knowledge production. Reflection is an occasion for the student's intervention in examining and changing life.

The teacher brings to the relationship several different "contents." As opposed to some of his most fervent supporters, Freire did not hesitate to put his own intellectual sources on the table: in the first place, Marx, who grasped the historicity of all social and economic systems and declared that the producers, including the producers of knowledge, were capable of making their own history. (In *Pedagogy of Freedom,* Freire carefully distanced himself from the "end of history" crowd, placing them in the neoliberal camp.) Then, with the radicals within psychology who, like Erich Fromm, explored the burning question of why people fear the freedom that comes with knowing/acting in the world, Freire identified what may be termed the internalized authority of the master as the source of the reproduction of oppression and an obstacle to the formation of the "subject."

Freire did not reify the bearers of progressive ideologies. To the insight that people are often invested in their own oppression and resist change because, in addition to taking on the worldview of the master, they recoil at taking risk, he added that the practice of some who would assist in the project of human emancipation belied their intentions. It is not only the Right that proposes to bring predigested enlightenment to the masses from on high. Although, in the present book, his critique of authoritarian leftism is not explicit—he aimed most of his fire at those within Brazil and elsewhere who, in cynical despair, have turned from the radical project—his disdain for change *from above,* regardless from what end of the political spectrum, is crystal clear. Freire insisted on the ineluctable connection between democracy from below—radical democracy—and human liberation. No doubt this worldview will come as a surprise to many who have only consulted his early work that is still influenced by political and intellectual vanguardism. Since Freire's later position is that radical futurity is indeterminate and he has taken into account the pitfalls of the actual experience of revolutionary regimes, including some with which he collaborated, there is no question of working from a series of received truths.

Between his early and late writings, the third source—the phenomenological and existential philosophy of writers like Jean-Paul Sartre—remains as perhaps the most controversial. Controversial to those who seek to root hope in the dialectic of history, who would, despite all, refuse Freire's problematization of specific historical agents. Perhaps his shift from certainty to indeterminacy may be ascribed to the circumstances of his own political experience, to the failures as much as the successes of his own work, and to his observations of others' attempts to change the world by applying formulaic Marxism to concrete conditions. In this and his more recent writings, Freire's commitments are rooted neither in the inevitability of historical transformation nor in the leadership of revolutionary vanguards. Although Freire reminds us the teacher is an actor on the social and political stage, the educator's task is to encourage human agency not mould it in the manner of Pygmalion. What propels his unceasing efforts to marshal the spirit of "rebelliousness" is ethical rather than scientific conviction, the belief that, having taken sides, the teacher is obliged to struggle with only hope of realizing his own ideals.

He remains a humanist in two ways. His discourse is anthropocentric despite recent ecological and paleobiological evidence that the link between some mammals and humans is closer at virtually all developmental levels than was previously believed. For Freire, humans alone have critical capacities, a judgment which is certainly arguable. That Freire chose to assert this faith should be seen in the context of the battles he waged against those who would deny to education its critical function. His is a humanist ethic insofar as class societies retard the development of the capacities of people to take control of their own destinies. Holding that education is a form of "ideology," Freire believes the teacher takes sides between those who have appropriated the wealth, the land, and the knowledge of the social and cultural system and the dispossessed. Freire judged current social and political arrangements by the criterion of whether they had taken steps to ameliorate (much less reverse) the long tradition of authoritarian societies to exclude substantial portions of their populations from participation in economic, social, and cultural life and whether they further or retard humanity's project of self-fulfillment. Finding that in his native Brazil neoliberalism has done little to change the conditions of life for ordinary people, he joined the opposition Workers Party and became its first secretary of education when it took power in the city of São Paulo in 1991.

Pedagogy of Freedom is, in part, a reflection on this experience. Even though there is little in the way of a memoir of his two years as a government official, Freire tacitly admits the huge frustration of trying to undertake school reform within a system that, in large measure, is deprived and, in turn, deprives students of the most elementary tools of education: adequate funds with which to ensure a full school day, materials, and safe facilities; a commitment to kids as "subjects"; and teachers who are aware that theirs is a political as well as intellectual project. That in the face of bitter disappointments Freire sees fit to reiterate the principle of hope that underlies his life's work is altogether remarkable. There is also a powerfully prescriptive side to this text. Even more than in its predecessors, Freire has delineated what a pedagogy of freedom entails.

Although written from Brazil in the late 1990s when the early promise of renewal after the passing of the military dictatorship has been betrayed by, among others, some of the very intellectuals who hastened its demise, *Pedagogy of Freedom* is more than an inspiring testament by an old warrior. It is nothing less than an invocation to those who seek an alternative to repressive education to renew the struggle for emancipatory education. First, it calls for a "rigorous ethical formation" in the teacher's determination to combat "racial, sexual and class discrimination."[2] Second, it advocates the concept that education is open-ended "scientific formation" since people are conditioned but not determined by their circumstances. What does Freire mean by science in this regard? Surely not the humdrum formulaic techniques characteristic of most of our school pedagogies. Freire calls for the learner's "critical reflection" on the social, economic, and cultural conditions within which education occurs; learning begins with taking the self as the first—but not the last—object of knowledge. Education does not stop with dialogue. The teacher is obliged to engage in "exposition and explanation" of those economic and social conditions that bear on the educational process and to expose students to many of the sacred texts without which education degenerates into opinion. For Freire, the self is a social concept, one that entails the whole world.

Finally, since the teacher is a learner as well, he is not a figure independent of the social process. Teachers are chronically underpaid, subject to onerous working and living conditions, and, I would add, often poorly educated. Part of Freire's ethical idea is the absolute necessity of teachers' self-defense of their own dignity, a struggle that includes their "right" to academic freedom, to have "autonomy" in the construction of the curriculum and of the pedagogic process. In this respect he invokes two separate rationales. Dedicated to the unity of theory and practice, the teacher can hardly make credible the link between education and action if she, herself, is not so engaged. Teachers cannot be effective when they remain in the thrall of an exploitative school system that robs them of their own voices.

2

These principles, enunciated on the heels of Freire's more recent urban frame of reference and contrasted with his earlier focus on rural communities, especially in Brazil and Africa, should make his ideas more resonant to educators and activists in more advanced industrial societies. São Paulo, a city of more than twelve million inhabitants, exhibits the full range of social, cultural, and economic conditions of any of the world's large cities: Mexico City, New York, London, Los Angeles, or Atlanta. It is a place of wealth, basic industry, and grinding poverty born of the rural crisis and chronic unemployment. Like elsewhere, its middle class is embattled under the weight of multiple uncertainties wrought by globalization and political turmoil. Freire's special concern has not diminished for the "ragpickers" and the "wretched" who live in *favellas,* those vast stretches of impoverished communities composed of the unemployed and underemployed, living in conditions of makeshift tin and cardboard dwellings in São Paulo and many other major cities of Latin America, yet he takes pains to speak of his pedagogy as "universal." In this respect, we may take *Pedagogy of Freedom* as the basis of what Nietzsche calls "new principles of evaluation," where the term "evaluation" indicates not a fixed set of criteria from which to make superficial measurements of social policies but a series of concepts by which to forge a new educational process.

Among these is the open, full-throated declaration that the idea of the educator as a disinterested purveyor of "objective" knowledge, the incontrovertible "facts" which form the foundation of dominant values, is itself a form of ideological discourse. If Freire does not go so far as to declare that there are no "facts" for which power is the underlying legitimation or that every statement about the world is an interpretation, he does criticize the doctrine according to which the "givens" of the taken-for-granted world must be viewed as the immutable starting points of learning and its companion, the privileged position of "methodology" for learning. How to square such principles with his oft-repeated dedication to "scientific" formation? Freire's notion of science is difficult for Anglo-American readers because it seems to grate against conventional conceptions of science's social "neutrality" and value freedom.

Freire stands firmly in the tradition for which the definition of science is critical and not positivistic. Educational formation becomes "scientific" when the learner grasps the link between theory and practice through a process whose assumption is that the individual is, in every respect, "unfinished." The accomplishment of critical consciousness consists, in the first place, in the learner's capacity to situate herself in her own historicity, for example, to grasp the class, race, and sexual aspects of education and social formation and to understand the complexity of the relations that have produced this situation. This entails a critical examination of received wisdom, not as a storehouse of eternal truths but as itself situated in its own historicity. Implicit in this process is the concept that each of us embodies universality but that universality does not necessarily dominate us. Thus, the active knower, not the mind as a repository of "information," is the end of education.

The widespread acquiescence by students and their families to the rigors of technoscientific training may be explained by the artificial imposition of a new scarcity regime in the global capitalist system. As good jobs disappear and are replaced by temporary, contingent, and part-time work, competition among prospective workers intensifies. The school responds by making testing the object of teaching and, in the bargain, robs teachers of their intellectual autonomy, not to say intellectual function. As education is suppressed and replaced by training, students learn that critical consciousness is dangerous to the end of technoscientific formation because it may jeopardize their chance for a job, let alone a career. Critical educators may be admired but dismissed as propagandists; fearing marginalization, some teachers may try to reconcile their views with those of neoliberalism by arguing that Freire's "method" might produce more creative employees for entrepreneurial corporations, or might lift some poor and working-class students from inexorable subordination to individual social mobility. After all, even the most conservative cultures require self-justification by picking out a few subalterns to promote as emblems of the system's flexibility.

But Freire's admirers should remember that in 1964 the military regime sent him into exile for his ideas, and that he was forced to roam the world for the next twenty-five years before it was possible to return home. The authoritarians in Western societies and the new liberal democracies of Latin America may or may not resort to exile or imprisonment to silence critical educators. The will to power almost inevitably requires that subversive ideas such as these be silenced or so mutated that only the husk is recognized as legitimate. Even in ostensibly democratic societies, those who would bring dialogic and critical practices into classrooms risk marginalization.

Under these circumstances, critical educators have no alternative but to organize through unions, study groups, institutes, schools, and other sites to actively propagate these new principles of educational evaluation. Needless to say, in this conservative era, the task is daunting. One of the most important uncompleted tasks before those who would preserve Freire's legacy is to elaborate an educational philosophy and strategy for economically developed societies and for an increasingly economically and culturally interdependent world. Perhaps the most significant intervention would be in the raging educational debates of our time. In the current climate, liberal educators are hopelessly outgunned—intellectually as well as politically and financially. They have retreated from their humanistic positions, conceding the need for vocationalization of the lion's share of the school curriculum in working-class communities. Even educators in elite schools are constrained to hold the line against corporate incursions. In major private universities, there is little resistance to the inducements of conservative, corporate foundations who have offered chairs in virtually every field if the institution will accept or consider the foundation's nominee seriously. None has evaluated the effect on the nature and scope of scientific inquiry of proliferating agreements between researchers and biotechnology and information corporations to focus research on applications that lead directly to product development. Nor are the celebrants of the Human Genome Project, the largest U.S. government-supported science program, visibly fazed by the enormous implications of the program: vast possibilities for surveillance of ordinary citizens; a virulent revival of eugenically oriented education as well as bioengineering programs, military applications, and so on.

Today, many defend the humanities and arts curricula as valuable adjuncts to business and occupationally oriented programs at the secondary as well as higher educational levels. They argue that the well-rounded accountant should know something about opera, that the financial counselor or broker needs to write a literate memo or report, that managers perform their jobs better if they understand human psychology. As humanities and social science majors continue to drop or stagnate at undergraduate institutions, the professoriat is under intense market pressure to justify its existence. Schools measure their hipness by the number of computers they can place in the classroom, whether they have a viable internship program with prospective employers, and in universities and colleges, value their "development" (grant-seeking) activities above all others in the academic "enterprise."

The critical educational project faces an uphill battle if it argues that "critical consciousness" as opposed to critical thinking as a "skill" should be the motive force of education and that its process as well as its outcome is a generation of interveners in the social and political life of this planet. Not only would this program encounter opposition from the reactionaries whose agenda is, more and more, to subsume schools to corporate requirements but also from liberals and progressives who cling to the neutrality of education just as scientists insist on their inculpability regarding the uses of their discoveries and inventions. Critical education must expose the new alliance of many in the liberal intelligentsia with the dominant culture without fixing moral blame. Although Freire calls on teachers and others to take sides on ethical precepts, I have detected not a sentence of guilt-mongering or accusation against intellectuals who have responded to the ideological and political assaults against education by bending their principles to the program of the Right. In *Pedagogy of Freedom*, he implies an explanation for this capitulation. Their political spirit has been degraded by their inability to offer resistance and alternatives, to act on their own behalf when working conditions deteriorate and salaries are under attack. Freire points to collective solutions as well as individual responsibility for intervening. His critique is political and not moral.

While a bold critique of the Right is urgent, a critical educational movement would be obliged to undertake a dialogue with the teachers in places like Alternative High as well as progressives in educational programs in communities, labor unions, and mainstream schools. While their hearts are pure and motivation impeccable, many in the alternative school movement have settled for providing a safe haven for troubled students and in the bargain have, often unwittingly, adopted anti-intellectualism as armor against those who would destroy even this basic gain. Teachers in mainstream schools feel embattled and are grateful to insert a bit of critical learning within the confines of the classroom. Trade union educators, especially in the United States, have narrowed their horizon to encompass the bare bones of union contract administration and a little legislative and political education. But "consciensization," Freire's perennial phrase for critical self-consciousness, requires the teacher be able to undertake "exposition and explanation" as elements of the dialogue. In order to facilitate the critical faculties and the intellectual development, the teacher must offer theoretical perspectives as well as a loving environment for student self-expression without conveying the message that these are "party line" standpoints and texts are chosen only to buttress them. As every good teacher knows, if students perceive that the teacher is pro-student there are few limits to possible manipulation. At Alternative High, students were well aware of the party line and it was a regular butt of their bitterly ironic humor.

This makes it necessary for the teacher to take the role of the "other" to present the most reasonable and articulate version of opposing views, to assign persuasive conservative texts, and to treat those texts seriously by means of exposition as well as refutation. In this process, the teacher is aware that well-wrought hegemonic ideas may persuade better than her own counterhegemonies. The risk of critical education is that if schools are constructed as genuine public spheres, outcomes are not guaranteed.

That Freire's last testament should focus on the question of freedom may, at first glance, confuse some readers. Isn't "freedom" the favorite slogan of the antiradicals? What, indeed does freedom mean and with respect to education? On the plane of politics, Freire clearly took his stand with those who would create the social and economic arrangements that, while dedicated to more equality, go beyond the urgent task of eliminating poverty, hunger, and disease. The good life is not merely having a job, enough to eat, and decent shelter. Authoritarians have, from time to time, been able to deliver this much, at least for limited periods. Freire holds that a humanized society requires cultural freedom, the ability of the individual to choose values and

rules of conduct that violate conventional social norms, and in political and
civil society, the full participation of all of its inhabitants in every aspect of
public life. People cannot raise themselves to bid for power unless their
curiosity has been aroused to ask the hard questions, "why" as well as
"what." For Freire, "the foundation stone of the whole [educational] process
is human curiosity. This is what makes me question, know, act, ask again, recognize." A learner who has reached this point is ready to demand the power
that, after all, is the object of any pedagogy of freedom.

5

VIOLENCE AND THE MYTH
OF DEMOCRACY

In this essay I adopt the commonsense conception of violence in which someone has been physically assaulted by another or, in international relations,
armies and whole populations are subject to weapons of destruction. Now, I do
not deny the limited utility of ideas such as "symbolic violence" when applied
to education, for instance,[1] or the idea that communication may be fraught with
linguistic violence that hurts feelings, bears on self-esteem, and so forth. I am
aware that, in the course of describing relations between men and women, violence has become a descriptive and an explanatory tool for feminists and that
many writers do not employ the word metaphorically.

But I am not inclined to accept the tendency, all too pervasive in the academy,
to broaden the use of the term "violence" so widely that it loses its specificity. To
equate invective, linguistic manipulation and the like with physical acts aimed at
intimidation and which may threaten life itself misses the point of the rise of violence in this century and loses the grave consequences of its deployment.
Moreover, when applied to communicative action its use conceals more than it
reveals. For example, it is perfectly true that the power of schooling on kids
occurs on more than the level of discipline. The curriculum is an unwanted
imposition, but this insight hardly amounts to "violence." At some point the student who sticks with the curriculum must buy in and succeed in its terms. How
else could it be? And there is no question that many of the routines associated

with marriage and other gender and sexual relations hide the coercion visited by the structure on women. But how to distinguish acts of physical force from those that function at the institutional and psychological levels? There is, of course, such a thing as psychological warfare, economic warfare, and so forth. The stronger surely holds the advantage over the weaker combatant. But, even though the subtext of many instances of these forms of struggle is the possibility that the loser may be subject to force, the moments of involuntary detention, torture, and the prospect of death are qualitatively different from "symbolic" violence and its consequences. Let us grant at the outset that there is a continuum rather than a categorical break between language and force. But it is important to maintain the difference. So, although I shall have occasion below to refer to the more nuanced usages of violence, it is by way of illustration of the process by which insult may become physically imposed terror.

Spring 1999 was a bloody one in Kosovo, Yugoslavia, and Littleton, Colorado, among other sites where violence was the decisive method to solve political and social conflicts. Violence is not all that unites these incidents. Like most events in modern war they shared a tendency to rope in noncombatants who happened to be in the way of guns and bombs. Senseless? Maybe so. But there might good reasons for these bad outcomes which, however unjustified on moral grounds, often make good strategy. Having set up Yugoslav President Slobodon Milosevic as a reliable supplicant of the U.S.-dominated International Monetary Fund (IMF), and unconscionably dawdled during his ethnic cleansing program in Bosnia, the Clinton administration and its European allies, belatedly found reasons to turn on him. When, responding to mounting protests and guerrilla activity, Yugoslav troops entered Kosovo and drove nearly a million people from their homes, the Clinton administration wasted little time bombing military and civilian targets in Belgrade and other Yugoslav cities as well as in Kosovo. The relatively swift military response to the Kosovan crisis contrasted sharply with Allied hesitation during the earlier conflict when NATO remained paralyzed for months as Yugoslav bombs rained on Sarajevo and Serbian militia allied to the Yugoslav government killed and maimed thousands and forced many more to flee their homes.

For the purposes of this essay I want to reserve discussion of whether the wars against Yugoslavia and Iraq were "justified" on human rights criteria. I do not accept the idea advanced by many critics that since the U.S. actions were selective they should inevitably be shunned. "What about Rwanda and other African cases of genocide? After promising to support the Kurds why didn't the United States stop Turkey's victimization of its Kurdish minority?" Although I take the point that United States policy is more concerned with conflicts in

Europe than those in the South or the East, the logic of such thinking is that unless one is an equal opportunity human rights intervenor, no intervention that might save some lives is legitimate. Nor is the view promulgated by some nurtured in the Vietnam War era that *any* United States military action is to be condemned before the fact as evidence that as an imperialist power any American intervention must necessarily be an extension of a policy of aggrandizement. While it can be shown that U.S. intervention in Kosovo was surely not free of political motivations, only naïve moralists could plausibly demand as a condition of support that war aims be pure. On such criteria U.S. participation in the war against fascism could be, and was, condemned by those who were not pacifists. For the moment it is enough to note that unless one renounces the use of force to resolve conflicts between sovereign states under any conditions, the criteria for determining the difference between just and unjust war stand between approbation and condemnation.

Let us acknowledge that the issues are complicated. In the Yugoslav case, was the U.S. claim to have defended human rights undermined by the scope and the effects of the bombings? Or can it be argued that when the majority of the Serbian population knowingly supports acts such as ethnic cleansing the concept of "civilian" loses its traditional meaning? Note well the uneven parallel between arguments about murderous American raids on German cities such as Dresden during World War II, the nuclear bombing of Hiroshima and Nagasaki, and the recent Belgrade bombings. Although by no means equivalent in their destructive outcomes, they are held together by the common thread: punishing civilian populations as if they were complicit in the war aims of their leaders.

Should the whole people have been held responsible for the calumnies of its leaders? Fifty-five years after the fact, the debate about the degree of responsibility of the German people for the Holocaust still rages. And, even if this distinction is untenable, can it be shown that the consequences of these apparently brutal bombings shortened their respective wars, as Paul Fussell has recently claimed, and ultimately saved more lives than were lost?[2] The U.S. government's program of beating the enemy into submission by uprooting and terrorizing the civilian population, as well as disabling its military capability, is continuous from Dresden to the two Japanese cities, from the wanton bombing and arson committed by U.S. forces in Southeast Asia to Baghdad and Belgrade.

The policy may be viewed as an instance of a de facto rule of modern technological war: Once the major war aim is the enemy's unconditional surrender, it is strategically criminal not to deploy every conventional weapon of mass destruction at "our" disposal where, after Hiroshima, "conventional" means any instrument of mass destruction but chemical and nuclear weapons. For it does appear that, Fussell's and Harry Truman's argument notwithstanding, the political costs of using these weapons have become prohibitive. As a result modern warfare has trod a very thin line. Many conventional weapons have become so powerful that their use over a relatively short period of time can all but destroy in a matter of weeks the economic and military infrastructure of a country the size of Pennsylvania and, according to some experts, cause as much destruction as medium-sized nuclear weapons. In this regard, the willingness of some nuclear powers such as the United States to ban nuclear weapons may not be viewed with as much relief as might be the case if technologically sophisticated conventional arms were not nearly as deadly.

The saliency of my discourse on war to local acts of violence becomes apparent when we inquire into the question of the use of violence to resolve apparently local conflicts between groups. It may be objected that relations between nations are different from those between political groups such as Kosovan and Serbian nationalists within the scope of single nation-state. Yet, as we have seen, the concept of national sovereignty has come under substantial revision since the Vietnam war when perhaps a majority of the American people questioned the justice of American engagement in what was perceived as a civil war. Under the newly established rules of engagement it is possible for an external power to intervene in the internal affairs of a nation-state if it can persuasively claim egregious human rights violations by one or both sides. What seems remarkable is that the notion of a "civil war" about which the rest of the world may remain indifferent has, since the collapse of the Soviet Union, lost its traditional sway. Until the 1990s the Great Powers confined their support for one or another side to military matériel, money, and political power on the international stage.

But many would argue that personal relations are of a different logical type from political relations in both their international and intranational contexts. Indeed the distinction underlies the bourgeois-liberal insistence on the separation of the private and public. Theorists like Hannah Arendt have warned about the threat to freedom posed by the increasing tendency of liberal-democratic states, let alone those of the totalitarian variety, to intrude into the private sphere.[3] Of course she does not deny that private life is increasingly subject to public scrutiny and state regulation, and she reminds us that in advanced industrial societies the space for freedom is ever narrower. Even if it is true that, despite the rightward turn in American politics after 1968, on questions of political speech American courts have made at least a ninety-degree turn to protect the First Amendment since the 1950s, no national administration except for the Nixon presidency has done more to set the clock back on civil liberties than that of Bill Clinton's.

Since there is no serious political opposition in the United States, political repression has been displaced to wider police surveillance and control of the poor, numerous incidents of brutality and criminal frameups against members of racial minorities, and to the war against crime. The sweeping deployment of electronic devices by private and police authorities to monitor individuals and groups deemed dangerous, not only to public safety and occasionally to national security but also to the industrial secrets of corporations, is notorious and quite public. In the name of fighting the drug wars, it has undertaken semisecret military action in Latin America, pouring billions into the military capability of reactionary governments if they agree to fight the communist guerrillas as well as the drug lords. At home the Clinton administration has sought wider powers to restrict personal freedom in the name of fighting crime and violence. In the course of a critique of Hillary Clinton's liberalism, Wendy Kaminer argues:

> Consider Clinton's tacit support for the repressive juvenile justice bill proposed by the Senate. . . . It was the vehicle for a few modest restrictions on guns and ammunition sales, passed with enthusiastic Administration support by Al Gore's dramatic tie-breaking vote. When Clinton joined her husband (and most Senate Democrats) in celebrating new initiatives to protect kids from guns, she was in effect urging passage of a law that encourages states to prosecute 14 year olds as adults, loosens restrictions on housing juveniles with adult offenders, relieves states of the obligation to address racial disparities in juvenile justice systems, federalizes more juvenile crime and imposes harsh mandatory sentences on children.[4]

Add to these the Clinton administration's antidrug policies: federalizing and enforcing longer mandatory sentences for growers and dealers; authorizing the Bureau of Alcohol, Tobacco, and Firearms to burn marijuana crops in California and arrest growers (a step now emulated by state authorities in Florida), and supporting legislation to add 100,000 police to the cities to fight crime, much of it drug-related, the result of which is a booming prison-industrial complex, itself aided by federal funds.

From wife beating to child abuse, in ambiguous as well as precise understandings of these terms, state institutions have assumed broad jurisdiction over family life. For example children may be taken from parents if the police and investigating social service agencies suspect wrong-doing even before hearings before a judge are held. Often in collaboration with private religious and social service organizations which assume the mantle of sex police, many state authorities have seized on archaic state laws and local ordinances to regulate sexual behavior among adults as much as children. Although contested by civil libertarians and gay activists, severe antisodomy laws are still employed in some states to justify arrest and imprisonment of adults engaged in consensual sex. And consensual sex between an adult and a minor subjects its adult participant in all states to stiff legal penalties.

With respect to inheritance, health benefits, and child adoption, in most states unmarried partners typically do not enjoy the same rights as those who are married, and gay partners, when not subject to criminal sanctions, are not recognized for the purposes of any civil action. Needless to say, neither the Clinton administration nor the Democratic minority in Congress has proposed legislation to remedy discriminatory local laws against unmarried partners of whatever sexual preference. Moreover, the clear prejudice of the courts is to restrict custody rights of single women parents if their former husband remarries or claims custody on the ground that he earns more money than the mother and can provide the child with more opportunities.

The war at home in 1999 was exemplified by the shootings at Columbine High School in Littleton, Colorado, Atlanta, Georgia, and elsewhere which, alongside the Kosovan conflagration were catapulted to the front pages and the top of TV screens. These events, which involved mass shootings by middle-class white kids of other middle-class white kids, shocked the media and the public because of the challenge they posed to the conventional wisdom about who uses violence. In this narrative, violence as a method of resolving differences is reserved for the most part, if not exclusively, to those who are economically and culturally deprived or, in its more anthropological expression, to those caught in the "culture of poverty."[5]

Some social scientists acknowledge that, in precincts of the economically and culturally impoverished, lawlessness is a product, even an entailment, of powerlessness and social disorganization. The poor simply have little purchase on the game of peaceful conflict resolution and for this reason have little motive to observe its rules. Looking a little deeper, it turns out since, as Jay McLeod reports for black male youth, "there ain't no makin' it" [in white middle-class society], some stuck at the bottom make up their own rules.[6] In this game violence is an acceptable tool of conflict resolution as it is for warriors of the nation-state. Moreover, to refuse to play the game on these terms may subject the individual to the group's ethic of retributive justice—once viewed as an anomaly in a caring society, but now elevated to a state policy principle. So it does not matter whether an individual agrees with the rule of force or not. As long as she stays in the discursive or geographic community, she is as obliged to observe its rules as a driver is to stop at a red light. Since for most members who are subject to the power group that rules the streets or the school, there is no option of voice or participation, the only recourse to consent or, in the vernacular, "loyalty," is to exit.

Our common understanding is that the regime of the rule of violence does not apply to middle-class communities except in extreme individual cases of severe mental imbalance such as serial killers, wanton pedophiles, angry lovers, and unusual family disputes. The main narrative of how the middle class deals with conflicts is by means of rules and procedures and the presuppositions upon which they are based. The basis is a contract: In exchange for renouncing force as a means of resolving differences individuals and groups submit to the rule of "law" which assures justice and restricts the arbitrary exercise of authority. Individuals and groups are assumed to have different interests, but not so different that they cannot find common ground upon which to resolve differences. The tacit agreement is to achieve compromise if possible and justice if necessary, which must be voluntarily observed by the disputants. When the power to impose justice is vested in administrative authorities it works if, and only if, the disputants recognize this authority as legitimate. Following Hobbes's advice they have renounced their power to take direct action or even negotiate directly with their adversary because they have faith in the state and its institutions to administer justice.[7]

Albert O. Hirschman argues that people in social, political, or economic organizations have three options to express their consent or dissent: They confer *loyalty* upon those in power and, on this choice, suspend disbelief in the leadership's decisions either on conviction or on a system of rewards of which they are beneficiaries; they may exercise *voice* in criticism of, and propose alternatives to, the existing leadership but, even when defeated, elect to remain within the system; or they may *exit*, in which case they have determined that they have no place in the system and renounce their right to participate. Plainly the selection of the exit option is by far the riskiest choice. In the absence of alternatives that allow for what Arendt calls "irregular" behavior, opting out of the system may result in isolation and even greater powerlessness than would eventuate if the individual or group exercised their voice(s). Yet, without the ability to exit, the consequent structural limits on individual freedom may result in the stagnation and decline of a community or society.[8]

For even when rarely used, under some circumstances, exit may be the only way to retain opposition. If individuals are deprived of the exit option, those in power can and do force people out of the community under terms that benefit the system, not the individual. Such was the case in Nazi Germany: Communists, gays, Gypsies, and Jews were denied the choice to leave, except when escorted by the Nazis to the camps. No less genocidal, the Rwanda example differs insofar as the method of extermination lacked subterfuge. The victims were shot on the spot. In the light of what seems to be an unlimited effort by established powers to indiscriminately bring ever-widening types of conduct within the purview of the definition of "crime" thereby erasing the necessary distinction between crime and irregularity, it is no wonder that, absent the possibility of being heard within the system, many in all walks of life, not only those at the bottom, opt out or suffer the closure of options.

The unstated feature of liberal (middle-class) justice and the basis of consent is that the aggrieved possesses "rights" or voice. Those who participate are assured that some form of institutional justice exists to air or to mediate their individual complaints. In its ideal form the participant enjoys democratic rights, at least to choose representatives and at most to participate directly in decision making. However, even as in most workplaces and in schools where these institutional forms are not routinely available to the person as a matter of right, she is more likely confer loyalty when some procedures are available to adjudicate her grievances. The manager or the school authority may hear the dispute and make a decision, but based on her personal sense of justice because no explicit rules have been disseminated against which to evaluate her decision. Whether the individual wins or loses in this game, he must come away feeling that he has had his day in court and that he understands the rationale underlying the resolution.

Thus, for example, if a child misbehaves in class by talking to his friend while the teacher is talking and is sent to the assistant principal's office, he may wax resentful about the punishment but knows the reason for it. Presumably, if he disagrees with the punishment he may complain to the assistant principal who, ideally, will carefully consider his argument(s). Even if the teacher is upheld in her action, as is likely to be the case, the student is secure in the knowledge that he has, at least, been heard. From the point of view of authority the ultimate solution is, of course, that even if he does not internalize restraint when others, especially the teacher, is speaking the child is able to exercise self-control. This is a sign he respects the rule that he must raise his hand to gain the right to participate in class. The student knows that under no circumstance may he disrupt its proceedings. Since the middle-class student recognizes the authority of the teacher he will obey the rules that govern classroom decorum.

Extend this simple and well-known example to relations among peers. Suppose a schoolmate hurls an epithet in the halls of the school such as "hey, faggot," which is not interpreted as a playful jibe uttered by a friend but as a verbal assault with malicious intent of sometime in the future committing violence against the "irregular." The rules of nonviolent response prescribe that the person who is the object of the insult confront the offender with his wrongful outburst, expressing his own feelings of hurt and degradation that the remark has provoked. The possibility of a nonviolent resolution presupposes that both share the same set of values that whatever one's evaluation, sexual preference is a private matter. Therefore accusing another of a deviant, that is, nonsanctioned sexual orientation is wrong or the orientation is not deviant and should be treated as "normal." In which case, although accurate, the accusation is unwarrant-ed in its pejorative connotation, and there is reason to expect that the person whose utterance was intended as the verbal equivalent of a "slap in the face" will relent in the wake of the confrontation with the victim. If the liberal-democratic assumption that everyone in the discursive community has "voice" holds, the victim may ask for an apology or at least the opportunity to engage in fruitful discussion. He should expect his taunter to express remorse. Failing productive dialogue, under the rules the offended has no right to strike back either verbal-ly or physically but is obliged either to "turn the other cheek," in the expecta-tion that his interlocutor will eventually see the light, or if sufficiently distraught (it might be the latest in a long series of similar incidents) to report the incident to proper authorities in the hope of gaining redress.

What's wrong with this scenario? In film and television, as much as "real life," traditional liberal models of justice and of mediation are experiencing a major crisis, not only among the poor where, it can be argued, the models are never really applied, but respect for the contract has also eroded substantially in the working class and professional and technical fractions of the middle classes. While a "few" scattered instances of unexpected violence may not describe the activity of a whole generation of middle-class youth, there is reason to insist that coherent models of nonviolent social conduct are losing their moral suasion; rather, they are increasingly projected by school and other societal authorities as a cultural ideal rather than as a practical model. In the criminal justice sys-tem's growing disregard for human rights, such as those manifested in the police abuse of Abner Louima and Amadou Diallo, as much as the new pen-chant of the nation to engage in "total" war, organs of established power are pro-viding models that cannot be reconciled with the prescribed rules of middle-class justice. Consequently, why shouldn't we expect kids to invent rules of combat that correspond more to what they observe in the theater of history than to models of liberal rationality?

After being ignored by the school and vilified by their peers for being "weird" and "faggots" the kids who committed the heinous crime at Littleton had, in fact, chosen the exit option; they separated themselves from the mainstream but remained caught in the system's tentacles. The school still had legal authority over them. As academically ambitious students they were obliged to attend class-es where they interacted with fellow students who had, in effect, forced their exit but maintained psychological pressure, reminding them that as "weirdos" they were rank outsiders and were held in utter contempt. As Jessie Klein and Lynn Chancer argue,[9] they may be victims of the masculinist prejudices of their classmates. The mass shootings were not the actions of badly socialized individ-uals. On the contrary, some were academically successful. Their fatal aggression against fellow students may be interpreted as both a rebellion against ostracism perpetrated by homophobic male teenagers and as an attempt to offer proof of their own masculinity. Exemplified by war, crime, and horror movies where with few exceptions women are victims, the prevailing images of masculinity are inextricably linked to violence. But Littleton may be read as an instance of how difficult is the life of marginality in a society that demands loyalty even in the wake of its refusal to provide space for irregular voices but, simultaneously, denies the option of exit, except in suicide.

We may seek a clue to the agony of the contemporary teen condition by briefly examining one of the more ubiquitous of current film genres, the teen film. Once consigned to a fairly restricted niche whose narratives were chiefly romantic and often combined with the musical and romantic-comedy genres, the teen romantic film has taken a back seat to horror and crime genres. The last decade of teen films, which in the 1990s commands a huge audience and market share in the industry, may be grouped under three distinct variants: the black, male gang movies, coded in terms of the "hood," a double entendre of neighborhood and hoodlum; the middle-class horror film; and comedies, but no longer of the conventional romantic type. The new teen comedy persists in exploring relationships between the sexes, but often exhibits graphic sexual exploration ingeniously packaged to avoid the "R" rating.

The gang film is a narrative of hopelessness and almost invariably depicts the inexorable devolution of black youth towards crime and mayhem. This genre rarely concerns the so-called underclass or the culture of poverty. In these films we can see a powerful metacommentary on the inapplicability of middle-class rules of the game to "ghetto" youth. But their neighborhoods are inhabited, not by welfare cheats or lowlifes, but by people who work, live in families, and are homeowners. The older generation of black parents stands in for the conventional morality of the working middle class, but young people almost invariably refuse to imbibe their parents' ethics of hard work, church going, and other family values. There are different rules on the streets. The kids simply do not believe they can achieve their parents' level of middle-class comfort through hard work and frugality. The upward mobility that might be available through attending to the school curriculum is ignored except by rejection. The prevailing rule here is group loyalty; voice within the community is always contested and the option of exit extremely improbable. In this genre violence rules as the ultimate arbiter of all relations between people, between the individual and society and its institutions.

In its ideal/typical form exemplified by the late 1970s and 1980s *Halloween* series, violence is portrayed in psychoanalytic strokes as the work of the death wish in comfortable suburban middle-class surroundings. *Scream* is representative of films about middle-class teen life in the 1990s. Kids of relatively homogeneous social class families attend the same (suburban) high school and hold a huge party in the large luxurious home of one of the crowd. Two boys, both of them well integrated into the society of the kids, plan and execute veritable serial killings of their friends. They have confused motives: jealousy, fascination with violence, and sheer hubris. At the bottom they exhibit an appalling nihilism that seems to be the main caution of these films. When a respect for the sanctity of human life is lacking, base instincts are bound to take over. Born and raised in the same comfortable suburban environment as the boys who murdered their classmates in Littleton and Georgia or raped a retarded girl in Glen Ridge, New Jersey, earlier in the 1990s, we are left at the end without genuine understanding of why the rules no longer apply save the invocation to remain loyal to conventional morality in all of its connotations.

At first glance the third genre seems far more innocent. The rush of these films into theaters may be viewed as a repudiation of recent attempts by the sex police to block and reverse the growing acceptance among wide layers of society that teen sexuality may be expressed openly. In *American Pie* the only male adult character of consequence, a boy's father, is guilty of only one sin: trying to counsel his son on the ABCs of sex. His glaring ineptitude provides one of the more humorous moments in the film. Needless to say, the father recognizes it is too late to advocate teen abstinence but perhaps not to offer a cautionary tale of restraint. We may understand the middle-class teen romance film as perhaps the most serious attempt in the wake of the reconciliation of most middle-class parents to the prospect that their children are fated to be sexually active before marriage—or even not to get married—to redeem the convention that sex is meaningless without love or similar feelings of empathy.

In contrast to the teen horror and the black hood genres, in the current teen comedy genre things fall apart only temporarily, but in concert with the comedy genre they have happy endings. Recall that the earlier teen musicals of the 1950s and 1960s were content to suggest the latency of sexuality, but their characters, played by Sandra Dee and Frankie Avalon, remained chaste. On the surface the new variant of teen comedies may be seen as more sexually explicit versions of "coming of age" narratives that, despite their apparent amorality, are heavily laden with anti-nihilistic moral lessons. In many of these films, the boys are obsessed with their own overripe virginity and seem to spend most of their time and energy in the pursuit of getting laid. Much of the plot is devoted to the process by which, in their own confusion and gross fumbling, it is left to the girls to seduce them. But not all of the young women are concerned to convince them there is more to relationships than the physical acts of sex.

In *American Pie* (1999), since the woman is taken as instrumental object, not as a partner lacking a concept of sex as a reciprocal act, nihilistic sex is a stand-in for male violence and social insensitivity. In *American Pie*, violence is systematically displaced to sports, innocuous verbal abuse, fairly brutal scenes of male sexual anxiety coded as slapstick, and by what may be described as "grossed-out" humor. Violence appears in the guise of embarrassment rather than inducing us to recoil in horror. It has to do with the graphic display of various bodily functions discharged under bizarre circumstances such as defecation (an extreme case of dysentery caused by a friend's surreptitious administration of a laxative), masturbation (with an apple pie), and premature ejaculation in the midst of foreplay with an eager female partner. Another crucial difference from the early forms of this genre is the decisive break with the stereotype that while men respond to their gonads all women are driven by love and caring. In a tacit acknowledgment of the sexual revolution among women in this film two of the women, one the parent of the boy's friend, are interested in sex, period.

Films like *American Pie* break ostentatiously with the rule of concealment that marks the older teen comedies, just as the tendency of many American films to leave less to the sexual imagination have violated the old invocation to leave sex to viewer inference. But I do not interpret these shifts as signs that films are encouraging violence or even explicit sexual behavior among teens. Instead the new modalities may be read as signs that, despite the best efforts of the sex police in and out of government to censor films, sexuality itself can scarcely be denied. But there is reason to see these films in relation to the spiritual and physical violence that surrounds us. And they may also be comprehended in terms of the growing despair, shared by many teens, that our key institutions of loyalty and of voice are decrepit while teens see no alternative in trying to make them work. As Donna Gaines showed in her study of North Jersey suburban youth, *Teenage Wasteland*, for many there is no exit except self-destruction.

Recognizing the danger inherent in the rash of teen and preteen violence that seems to be sweeping suburban as well as urban schools and neighborhoods, there is today a national movement known as *mediation*. The adult leaders of this movement understand that the exercise of the arbitrary authority of adults in and out of state institutions, such as schools and the criminal justice system, cannot hope to stem the epidemic of guns and other lethal weapons that now are in the hands of many young men and boys. Consequently they have embarked on a preventive program that begins in elementary school to teach kids how to resolve conflicts without the use of force. Instead of relying on adult authority, the program, usually led by a teacher, "trains" a select group of kids to become peer mediators. The training is tacitly oriented toward establishing unconventional institutional mechanisms for justice—in effect, trying to provide space for the voice option rather than relying on established adult power, abstract loyalty to the school and its promise of success, or risking the social costs of exit.

Mediators do not enjoy sovereignty in resolving differences between kids and between kids and the school; they work on a track parallel to institutional power, and for this reason their efforts are frequently undermined by the authority of the principal and his administration. In rare instances where the authorities are fairly benign and willing to surrender some their prerogatives, the procedures of mediation may work to resolve some disputes. But the program is frequently disarmed by politicians, more comfortable with supply-side repression than with education, imposing policies that restrict access to guns; placing restrictive labels about violent and explicit sexual content on films, television, and records; and sermonizing among parents to inculcate guilt.[10]

School officials, religious leaders, and the media have targeted parents to act as a home guard. They recruit parents to assist their children in homework assignments and admonish them to participate in censoring what their children watch on television and what records they listen to. But since the school as the main site of socialization has, in the wake of the turmoil, remained embedded in the traditions of bureaucratic authority, these interventions are largely ineffective in convincing kids to confer loyalty upon the system. Needless to say, the main effect is to keep parents anxious and busy. Most kids know these censorious programs are a sham; teens often outmaneuver "R" rated movies and record store restrictions by buying forged ID documents. When they perform well in class, they are often driven by fear, not learning. And what they do in their free time is mostly hidden from adults. The society of kids is often cruel and unyielding to outsiders and intolerant of otherness, whatever its forms, but it is not a place where adults can easily enter. And it has ever been thus. Emotional separation from parental and school authority is the condition for the formation of the adult self, and secrecy is a powerful weapon of youth. What is different today is the near-hysterical environment that drives authorities to try to intrude and, failing moral suasion, to put in place practices of legal retribution ranging from wholesale school expulsions to imprisonment.

The symbols of violence appear in urban high schools in the personae of armed and unarmed guards at the entrances and exits, assistant principals and assigned teachers patrolling the hallways, and a regime of school discipline which increasingly imitates the criminal justice system. The official story is that these shackles have been placed upon the schools to restrain a significant minority of kids who are disruptive of teachers and of those students who wish to learn, and who may even be dangerous to the safety of members of the school "community." Certainly schools have always contained (in the double sense) a significant number of students who see little or no sense in being there. State

laws forbid school-leaving before students are sixteen because child-labor legislation bars minors from holding industrial and many service jobs. So some students who might respond to good occupational and alternative academic programs are offered neither, choose to cut most of their classes, and when they
attend, express their displeasure with acts of disruption, as defined by school
authorities. Failing to engage them in mastering the curriculum and resisting
developing an alternative to it, the schools blame the students for their disaffec-
tion, and many students are marginalized and blamed again for their school failure. Equipped with psychological categories to label marginal kids "hyperkinet-
ic," "disruptive," intellectually challenged—or worse, psychotic—school authorities see little alternative to meting out punishments that fit the crime of what
may, for many students, be a case of undisguised boredom.

We know that many children, including teenagers, get bored easily. Even
"high achievers" light matches, take drugs, or become unruly when they have
"nothing to do." Since school pedagogy is often stilted and, in any case, is oriented to the student who, highly motivated to succeed in conventional academic terms, will tolerate whatever the teacher dishes out, marginalization and punishment may result in a more angry and ultimately violent response from the
intolerant.

Why did the governments of the United States and of Europe remain silent when,
after the breakup of Yugoslavia, Milosevic, in 1989, canceled Kosovan political
autonomy, annexed the region directly into the new Serb-dominated Republic,
and gave no support to the internal Serbian opposition? Recall the snail-like reaction of the United States and European powers to Milosevic's attempt to create a
greater Yugoslavia by colonizing Bosnia, mercilessly bombing Sarejevo and
undertaking a systematic program of ethnic cleansing. The NATO powers were
not concerned about Kosovan political autonomy; from their point of view this
had been an internal affair. It was only when Milosevic attempted to loosen his
regime's ties to the International Monetary Fund (IMF), which held a virtual
mortgage on the Yugoslav economy, and took steps to solidify Serbian control
over a rebellious Kosovo, that the U.S. government was prompted to intervene
and European planes joined the campaign. But Milosevic's attempt to break from
his debt obligations and NATO's embarrassment of allowing his government to
occupy Kosovo with troops and militia, which promptly began a continuation of
the program of ethnic cleansing, had, after the Bosnian scandal, become unacceptable. Within weeks after suffering losses estimated at 60 percent of the country's industrial and commercial resources, thousands of civilian as well as military
casualties, and growing popular unrest, the Yugoslav government agreed to withdraw its troops and submit to allied occupation of the province.

From the perspective of the fabled "Vietnam Syndrome"—that American public opinion will not tolerate significant losses and injuries to its servicemen and women, at least for the conduct of "little" wars—it was a felicitous illustration of U.S. military strategy first unleashed during World War II but perfected in the Gulf War. Without sustaining appreciable American casualties, the United States has adopted the doctrine of victory through the brutal use of overwhelming airpower to clobber the enemy into submission. The operative word here is "brutal," for the U.S. government justified bombing nonmilitary industrial plants and inflicting heavy civilian casualties on the grounds of the veritable genocidal policy of the Yugoslav government in Kosovo.

Taking the high ground to legitimate military and economic warfare, the U.S. government has, in the postcommunist era, routinely insisted that human rights trump national sovereignty. On the other hand, the scope of the bombings to include civilian and nonmilitary industrial targets, for example to destroy a cigarette factory as a strategic target aimed at the civilian population which depends as much on cigarettes as it does on food, was among the few instances of the more or less overt tie between our increasingly "eye for an eye" domestic criminal justice policies and international military policy. The Gulf and Kosovan wars provide convincing evidence that visiting terror against civilian populations in order to invert public indignation against their own governments, rather than the putative aggressor, is becoming an acceptable aspect of warfare.

Ours is an era when loyalty is the value that overrides the other options. We know that Saddam Hussein had made Iraq a reliable outpost of the West before the Kuwait invasion. And had Milosevic, who managed to win the confidence of the IMF long enough to considerably amplify the huge $22 billion loan inherited from the Tito era, maintained some kind of payment schedule instead of trying to get out from under its thrall, it is conceivable that he could have weathered criticism of his internal policies and made permanent the American government's hesitation to disturb the status quo. The problem is that the price of IMF support is that recipients fully embrace austerity policies which entail dismantling the elaborate social welfare systems that sustained communist and socialist power, privatizing state enterprises, and opening wide the door to foreign investment on terms that many would not expect from more stable capitalist countries. The leaders were willing, but it turned out that these demands were politically risky. In Yugoslavia, a population that was long cynical of bureaucratic, authoritarian socialism had nonetheless become accustomed to one of its entailments, a measure of economic security. In consequence, the IMF philosophy of detaching citizens from their economic rights, even as it was indifferent to their civil rights, became controversial, especially after the Russian debacle of relentless privatization and free-market economic suicide. Fearful that submission might bring social disorder, the Iraqi and Serbian leaderships quelled the emerging opposition by means of aggressive nationalism, a step that temporarily consolidated their power but earned both regimes severe military reprisals and exclusion from the international economic and political system.

Loyalty broke down in Yugoslavia and Littleton; when there are no means with which to express difference, whether by speaking out within the system without severe reprisals or by exiting from it, the likely outcome is rebellion against established power and authority, or implosion. Even when they cannot express themselves, those who choose to rebel usually have a program of creative destruction and rebuilding the system on a different foundation. We may hope for explosions to topple the regimes in Baghdad and in Belgrade. But the kids cannot hope to inherit the system they oppose. Their best chance lies with the remnant of progressive reformers who have enough vision to see that the educational system cannot expect to win the loyalty of youth unless it concedes some power. Lacking this improbable outcome we may expect more instances where youth turn on the system and attempt to blow it, and themselves, up. Those who act to implode the system have lost hope; redemption is sought in bringing down themselves as well as the edifice that has oppressed them. And in recent years we have witnessed what kids will do when avenues of escape or reform are closed. If the school system wishes to save its own ability to command the loyalty of its teenage members, it could try to initiate reforms that amplify the opportunities for participation—even for dissent—without penalty of expulsion or worse, forms of detention. But there is less than a glimmer of expectation that either the Yugoslav authorities or those who run our high schools possess the imagination and generosity needed to save their institutional orders.

6

HIGHER EDUCATION AS A PUBLIC GOOD

1

Higher education has become a major public issue for the first time since the late 1960s, when student demonstrations and occupations forced open admissions in many public colleges and universities. There are three questions that define the debate: the commitment of legislative and executive authorities to maintaining public higher education at a level of funding adequate enough to enable institutions to offer a high-quality education to students; who should be admitted and who should be excluded from higher education (the so-called access debate); and finally, especially in recent years, the question of curriculum. These three questions are neither simple nor simplistic. Regarding the access debate, should higher education be a "right" like elementary and secondary schooling? Or should it be, like its European counterparts, a privilege reserved for those who have a requisite level of academic achievement? In this debate, one hears such comments as "After all, not everyone should be in college; what about the millions who work in factories or offices?" Curriculum has been thrust closer to center stage. The chief bone of contention is whether the once-presumed liberal arts should be available to every college student; indeed, should every student, regardless of the discipline, be required to imbibe at least a sampling of literature, philosophy, history, and the social sciences? Or as some have argued—and many institutions have agreed—should students in technical and professional areas like computer science, engineering, and even natural science largely be exempt from such encumbrances? This argument applies to both high-level technical universities, such as Carnegie Mellon, Rensselaer Polytechnic Institute, and Case, and to the large number of community colleges whose "mission" is now almost exclusively confined to preparing trained workers for the corporations with whom they have developed close relationships.

Higher education has become prominent on the political screen as the widespread perception that earning a bachelor's degree is the absolute precondition for obtaining a better niche in the occupational structure. But as postsecondary credentials have become a necessary qualification for nearly every technical (let alone professional) job, higher education costs—both tuition and living expenses—have skyrocketed. At the same time, more students and their families are seeking places in private colleges and universities and, with the exception of a handful of elite public research universities, interpret failure to secure admission to leading private schools as a major personal and economic defeat. The bare truth is that in the last decade of neoliberal economic and social ideologies, public postsecondary schools have taken a severe beating in the commonweal. In the current environment, budget cuts and downsizing are prescribed by policymakers as the zeitgeist has shifted to the view that only the marketplace represents quality and anything connected to public goods that does not submit itself to the business environment is a secondhand article.

The effect of this persistent and merciless attack on public higher education has been to demoralize faculty, and prompt conservative-dominated legislatures to impose a regime of permanent austerity that, with the exception of a handful of public research universities (notably those of the University of California and of the Big Ten), has resulted in sharpening the distinction between the two research tiers of the academic system on the one hand and the "third tier" of public teaching institutions, both senior and community colleges, on the other. Former Berkeley Chancellor Clark Kerr's notorious proposal, first announced in 1958 and inscribed in the California state systems in the early 1960s, that the research tiers be fiercely defended from the horde by establishing a clear cleavage between those institutions that produce knowledge and those that transmit, has succeeded beyond his and his critics' wildest expectations. Today, this mantra has been advanced by the proposition that only certain teaching institutions and some private four-year colleges are "excellent" enough to qualify for the transmission task.

The Kerr plan was no mere speculation; it contained a detailed program to ensure the separation. Research university faculty members were to teach one or two courses a semester and even be able to purchase their teaching time with research grants. In contrast, the third-tier universities and colleges obliged faculty to teach three or four courses, and community colleges as much as five. The reward systems in the two tiers would be different insofar as publication would play a distinctly subordinate role in the third tier. At the same time, Kerr envisioned substantial salary differentials. The only means for moving upward in the new academic system would be through research, writing, and of course, administration.

Yet creating tiers of higher education hit a snag in the 1960s. Two distinct movements for university reform gained momentum. The first was the insistent demands by black, Latino, and working-class students for access to the institutions as a sign of equality as well as equality of opportunity; the second was the profound dissatisfaction by mostly white, middle-class students in elite universities with the growing trend toward focusing on technical/scientific knowledge production in what Kerr called the "multiversity." At Berkeley and elsewhere, they came together in the early 1960s in a mass student movement in which these two quite different thrusts were merged in the struggle against the emergence of the corporate university. The success of the demand for extending higher education access to virtually any high school graduate depended, in part, on the authority of the civil rights movement that undergirded student protest and on the crisis of legitimacy of the national government in the wake of its unpopular Vietnam War policies. It was made feasible, as well, by the relative buoyancy of the war-suffused United States' economy, which enabled federal and state governments to supply the funds needed to expand the public university system.

Students made their protest on questions of curriculum and, for a time, forced faculty and university administrations to give some ground. Although the Berkeley Free Speech Movement was detonated by the policy of the technocratic Kerr administration barring "outside" political groups from the campus, its apogee was in the achievement of significant curricular reforms. In the UC system, Berkeley, San Diego, and Irvine students wanted the right to select their own courses and choose instructors to teach them. In some places, they demanded and won exemption from course requirements and from large introductory classes and protested the authoritarian pedagogical styles of some professors, which prompted the most obdurate among them to resign and go elsewhere. These struggles, which dominated many campuses until the emergence of the antiwar movement in the late 1960s, succeeded in changing higher education's culture for the next twenty years. Beginning with Harvard University's reimposition of the core curriculum in 1979 and the ebbing of the student movement, faculty and administration slowly regained the upper hand in the next two decades.

With the triumph of market principles in higher education, in which everything from student enrollments, curriculum, and tuition costs was determined by the sales effort, the job market, the ebbing of the black freedom movement, and mass antiwar movement, the astounding expansion of public colleges and universities came to screeching halt. Suddenly, in this most advanced of advanced industrial societies, corporate and government economists announced a "fiscal crisis" in public goods, including higher education. The "public" (read business, professional, and corporate farm interests) was simply unwilling to pay the bill for education, health, and other elements of the social wage. They suggested that the way out of the crisis was that user taxes be imposed on public goods; students and their families should be required to substantially pay for public higher education. If enrollees in the private schools were willing to pay large tuition fees, why not those in public universities?

Conservatives in and out of higher education had never accepted open admissions policies. By their lights, the democratization of access to public colleges—and to the elite and private schools as well—degraded the value of the degree. Changes in public higher education in the late 1960s were brought about by the entrance into colleges and universities of perhaps a million additional blacks, Latinos, and other racial minorities who, absent the civil rights movement, would never have reached their gates; there was considerable pressure on the Ivy League colleges and other private schools to undertake policies which, in effect, modified their traditions of cronyism, nepotism, and their meritocratic bias. Contrary to popular myth, neither the public nor the private sector was indiscriminate in its admissions policies; open admissions never meant that students with low grade-point averages and lower scores on the SAT and other standardized tests gained entrance to public senior colleges, let alone the private elite colleges and universities. Although these schools often provided remediation services to students, especially to those who failed the math sections of the SAT or did not take enough math to qualify, admission policies remained selective. In most states, open admissions had been confined to community colleges and some third-tier senior colleges.

Abetted by the media, which seem to swallow almost any attack on public higher education emanating from conservative education think tanks like the Hudson and Manhattan Institutes, the educational Right has mounted what may be the most concerted and coordinated attack against public goods in this century. With the possible exception of the widespread belief that charter schools and vouchers are needed to radically issue a wake-up call to public elementary and secondary education, in recent educational history, policy is more than ever driven by the conservative ideology of hierarchy and privatization.

2

The rise of mass public higher education in America was a result of several influences, chiefly those that resulted from the problems associated with the post–World War II era. Perhaps the most important piece of social engineering after the war was the Servicemen's Readjustment Act of 1944, popularly known as the GI Bill of Rights. At the urging of President Franklin D. Roosevelt, who feared mass unemployment in the postwar period, Congress passed a bill providing returning veterans with income support for a one-year period and funds to enter educational programs, including higher education. Between 1945 and 1952, a million veterans entered mostly private colleges and universities armed with the price of tuition and modest living expenses. All manner of institutions, including the Ivy Leagues and other elite schools, gladly accepted these veterans and the government money that accompanied them.

Public higher education has a long history. Founded in 1847 by Townsend Harris, the City College of New York was intended to provide an opportunity for "talented" young people of modest means to gain the benefits of a college education on a tuition-free basis. The municipal college movement spread slowly and was never really embraced by a large number of communities, but its example inspired parallel efforts at the state level. After the founding of City College, the most substantial event in the emergence of public higher education was the Morrell Act of 1862. Large tracts of federal land were supplied to states that were willing to found universities for the purpose of providing their people with general education in all areas of learning but chiefly scientific and technical research and assistance to agriculture and industry.

Within a half century, many Midwestern states and several in the Northeast and in the South established "land grant" colleges. Despite the intention of the Morrell Act, many of them remained glorified teachers colleges, but some, like the Universities of Michigan, Wisconsin, Illinois, and Indiana, took on characteristics identified with the modern research university. Together with the University of California at Berkeley and Cornell University, they—along with Harvard, MIT, and Princeton among the private schools—constituted the basis for the development of the modern research university, which came into its own with the government's rearmament program on the eve of World War II.

After World War II, the state universities and public municipal colleges also benefited from the largesse of the federal government. In fact, under the imperatives of the Korean War, which drafted more than a million men and women, the GI bill was extended. The Cold War provided a substantial boost to the research programs of public state universities. Having exploded a nuclear device by 1949, the Soviet Union accelerated its military nuclear and space programs which, among other windfalls, prompted the U.S. government to support higher education in a concerted attempt to stem the "Sputnik effect," the alleged Soviet superiority in space exploration and its perceived nuclear parity. By the late 1950s, the federal government had committed itself to long-term support for postsecondary schooling, especially to students seeking careers in natural science and technology, but also supported the humanities and social sciences. States were pouring substantial funds into higher education as well, and by 1960 the public sector was larger than the private sector; a decade later, it accounted for more than 70 percent of student enrollment.

After more than sixty years of public colleges and universities gradually supplanting private schools as the dominant sector of higher education, we are now witnessing the return of tradition. The private sector of postsecondary education is growing faster than the public and, perhaps more to the point, is widely perceived as superior. If the measure of quality is, for all practical purposes, equivalent to a school's ability to exclude students because of the institution's marketability, then the elite private schools have gained substantially on similarly placed public institutions. To be sure, some public systems such as the Big Ten and the University of California schools are still highly competitive, but private institutions such as Brown, Harvard, and Yale, for example, reject more than four of every five applicants; many others, such as the "little" Ivies, have similar records of exclusion.

The economic reasons for this state of affairs are not difficult to discern: faced with deregulation and the threat of globalization, Congress and state legislatures hurried to court the favor of business interests and deprogressivize taxes, made it difficult to raise public funds for public education by raising the standard by which such bills would be passed, and removed authority for new taxes to the voters. In California, Massachusetts, and many other states, the referenda (whose origin was in the Progressive Era's skeptical response to "bought" politicians of those years) were used to provoke what Richard Elman called "The Poorhouse State." In California, the Northeast, and the Southwest, for example, annual budget cuts, either in monetary or real terms, have been imposed by many state legislatures. The consequent systematic replacement of full-time professors with adjuncts, teaching assistants, and temporary professors in teaching the undergraduate curricula is rife. The slide in salaries for full-timers causes many of those with some lateral mobility to move on to private institutions. We witness the drying-up of funds for construction and maintenance of aging physical plant.

But money tells only part of the story. Private colleges and universities mounted a huge public relations effort to persuade those parents and prospective students with resources to pay that the advantages they offer are worth the price of exorbitant tuition, especially in comparison with the costs of public education. They are brazenly attempting to capture disaffected students from public education and shed no tears when their appeal results in huge debt for families that can ill afford the price of private tuition. Needless to say, getting a good education is only part of the consideration. Above all, the private schools, especially the elite ones, offer prestige—which leads to effective job placement in the corporate world, valuable contacts among peers for future jobs, and a more comfortable student life exemplified in better facilities such as dorms, sports, and recreation centers.

Beyond these trumpeted advantages is the systematic attack against public higher education emanating from right-wing think tanks and conservatives whose views find a receptive ear in the media. For example, the New York media gave enormous and favorable publicity to a recent report on City University of New York (CUNY) by a mayoral commission headed by former Yale President Benno Schmidt, and among whose members were conservatives of all stripes as well as employees of the mayor's. The commission found the two hundred thousand students at CUNY "adrift" and in need of reform. It recommended major changes, among them further administrative centralization to ensure that the reform program would be effective. The report covered the erosion of faculty governance, since the faculty was judged a leading obstacle to changes anticipated by the report, and recommended provisions to undermine the faculty's professional autonomy; it also recommended "mission differentiation," a code term for creating several new tiers in the system to ensure that the top tier was protected against the community colleges, and took a hard look at tenure with a view to abolishing or severely restricting it. Currently the leader of the Edison Project, a for-profit corporation that organizes and consults with public schools around the country in search of privatization, Schmidt included Heather McDonald (a fellow of the Manhattan Institute, a conservative think tank) and an array of similarly oriented members on his commission. Shortly after issuing the CUNY report, which has become a blueprint for the new administration that took office at the end of 1999, Schmidt became vice-chair of CUNY's Board of Trustees.

The prospective transformation of CUNY from a beacon of open admissions for the city's minority and working-class population to a genuine competitor in the elite game that has swept through higher education would be a step into the pre-1960s when New York City's four colleges were held to a higher standard than nearly all of the area's higher education institutions. To gain entrance to tuition-free schools, students were required to earn grade-point averages (GPAs) of eighty-five or higher from a secondary school system that was second to none in the entire country. In fact, the four original city colleges and Baruch, the system's business college, still require high GPAs as well as passing grades on each of three "placement" (that is, admission) tests. The difference in the intervening forty years is that these grades are held in the majority by blacks, Latinos, and Asians and for this reason are considered by CUNY's detractors to be "inflated."

Curiously, the charge of grade inflation, which has been made and tacitly acknowledged by several Ivy League schools, has failed to diminish their prestige. What accounts for a school such as Princeton, which recently abolished the grade of A-plus, is that it rejects many more applicants than it accepts and has a sumptuous endowment; accordingly, Princeton retains its elite standing. Similarly, in an article on the alleged revival of Columbia University, *New York Times* reporter Karen Aronson pointed out that one of the major indicators that the school enjoys a revived reputation is that it admitted only 13.7 percent of applicants last year, a figure which placed it second only to Brown, whose rejection rate is 87 percent. In none of the recent reports of the booming private college industry has the question of educational quality figured in the evaluation of their successes. The measure of quality seems to rely heavily on whether school admission is considered a valuable commodity to prospective students; in other words, is it a product that can command high tuition and many applicants?

In fact, as a grim 1999 report from the University of Chicago attests, according to the university administration, this paragon of the vaunted Great Books curriculum was having trouble in its recruitment campaign precisely because, in the face of the zeitgeist pointing in the opposite direction, it retained too much academic rigor. Consequently, the board and the administration announced a new emphasis away from its classical educational focus and towards a more lenient academic program and added sports facilities and stronger placement services. Appalled members of the faculty and student body protested the shift, after which the university's president announced his resignation to take up teaching duties, but the board has neither retracted its program nor expressed any intention of modifying it. Despite its prestige, many on the faculty have discovered that even in matters of curriculum, the heart of faculty sovereignty, their powers are limited.

In the sciences, technologies, and graduate professional education, the two dozen or so leading public research universities are holding their own in this competition. Despite budget constraints imposed by state legislatures eager to reduce taxes for their business and upper-middle-class constituents, many have retained their ability to raise substantial research grants. For example, UC-Irvine and UC-San Diego are major recipients of grants for bioengineering from agencies such as the National Institutes of Health and the Centers for Disease Control; Cornell, Berkeley, and Illinois are leading research institutions in physics; and Penn State and Pittsburgh are among the most important of the technical science research institutions. Where the legislature has cut back on operating funds, the proceeds from research activity often manage to keep many programs in the humanities and arts alive.

The most severe problem institutions in public higher education are those in the tier below the two categories of research universities. Apart from the departments and schools of teacher education that, while not prospering in this age of academic austerity, have substantial social utility (even by conservative lights), many universities and community colleges are scrambling to find a "mission" sufficiently attractive to convince skeptical legislators that they have an economically viable role. The new mantra of higher education is that by training technically competent labor, but also by providing income to a large number of blue-collar, clerical, and professional workers, postsecondary schooling makes significant contributions to local and regional economies. Consequently, schools are making agreements with private corporations to provide curricula and teaching staff for dedicated skills training. Even when specific deals do not drive the curriculum, vocationalization does. As students get the message that a higher education credential is necessary for survival in this global economy, many feel they do not have the luxury to indulge their artistic, critical, or literary interests and must instead keep their collective noses to the technical grindstone. As a result, many social sciences departments are relegated to the status of providers of "breadth" requirements or are encouraged or forced to adopt vocational majors in order prevent being closed down, and when majors have declined steeply, English departments are often little more than composition mills.

For the time being, there is no imminent threat of school closings in most state systems. However, university and college administrations in the third (nonresearch) tier are admonished by regents and state commissions of higher education to find ways to close budget shortfalls by raising tuition, making alliances with corporations or otherwise turning their predominantly liberal arts institutions into vocational schools, or adding more research capacity to their faculty and facilities. A history professor acquaintance tells me that once a broad general education school with a few scientific and technical programs, the third-tier Illinois public university in which he teaches now consists largely of business and technical majors. Similar trends are evident in New York, New Jersey, Colorado, and California. The separation of their "flagship" schools and their largely undergraduate and masters-level institutions is widening. For the latter, the message is clear: sink or swim. Needless to say, few administrators in public higher education are willing to risk the severe penalties of smaller enrollments and diminished income by retaining their liberal arts focus. The brute fact is that undergraduate humanities majors are few; only in fields like economics (because of its predominant business ties), political science (because it is understood as a good pre-law major), and sociology (because of the still lively interest in the social services as a profession) has there been some growth in student interest.

Even some private school students exhibit anxiety about the future and are demanding better placement services and sticking more closely to fields that have direct occupational outcomes rather than using their undergraduate schooling as a time of exploration and creative uncertainty. Some elite schools, public as well as private, remain beacons for English and other language majors; some, like Pittsburgh, have attractive undergraduate philosophy and history programs. But major state schools, such as the four SUNY research universities, Rutgers, and many in the UC system, report a decline in undergraduate majors in history, philosophy, and literatures. While most of these are in no imminent danger of becoming composition factories for technical majors even as they retain their highly rated Ph.D. programs, the so-called economic boom has failed to produce a new era of relaxation. Students remain enervated because, I suspect, they know what the media has ignored: there is a lot of work but few jobs—if by jobs we mean work that is accompanied by the amenities of security, benefits, and a career ladder that enables them to gain income and authority along with their experience. Moreover, they know from their own parents' experience that corporate downsizing has affected middle management and professionals as well as blue-collar workers.

The economic and social environment of the late 1990s is inimical to the development of a system of public higher education in which the goals are defined beyond the utilitarian uses of credentials and acquisition of job skills. Far from being citadels of education, many public colleges and universities are constituted as labor exchanges and not as public spaces where adults of all ages can take noncredit-bearing courses in world affairs, as well as craft and art forms such as pottery, or participate in forums and conferences of all sorts. As for one of the historic aims of public higher education, the development of citizens able to participate in key decisions affecting the polity, this role has been consigned to one of the "distribution" requirements of the first two years of a baccalaureate degree. The hard fact is that continuing and citizenship education are now conceived by administrators as a moneymaking activity and are most effective in private institutions. Threadbare, many public schools are bereft of these programs or offer only a limited range of skills-oriented courses.

3

With their victory in reimposing a core curriculum in most colleges and universities, education leaders in higher education are in the throes of a second stage of curriculum "reform" which has provoked considerable debate: is education for whom and for what? The dispute over the curriculum takes many forms. Feminist, black, Asian, and Latino educators responded to the imposition of core curricula that resuscitated the traditional literary canon as a site of privileged learning by insisting on the inclusion of global, postcolonial, and otherwise marginalized literatures and philosophy. But the so-called multicultural or diversity curriculum only peripherally addresses the central problem that afflicts public universities. The command from executive authorities in and out of the institution is that public schools justify their existence by proving value to the larger society, in most cases read "business interests." In turn, educational leaders such as presidents and provosts are inclined to seek a "mission" that simultaneously translates as vocationalization, which entails leasing or selling huge portions of its curriculum and its research products directly to companies.

As a result, the public research universities are dusting off one of Kerr's most important suggestions: undergraduates as well as graduate students should be recruited to participate in the research activities of the professoriat, especially in the sciences. Like sports, research now demands a considerable time commitment from the practitioner. In some places, notably UC universities such as San Diego and Irvine, schools are reducing the obligation of science and technology majors to the humanities and social sciences so they can more accurately mimic the practices of the great private technical universities. This, of course, raises the question of whether the public universities as public goods should maintain their obligation to educate students to citizenship as well as in job skills.

As a professor in UC-Irvine's school of social sciences, I can recall legislative hearings in the 1970s conducted by the chair of the higher education committee of the California State Assembly. The chair and other committee members were concerned that faculty members were avoiding undergraduate teaching in the service of their research and that the state universities were slighting programs aimed at educating for citizenship. The university administration appeared to bow to the legislators' stern warning that if they did not alter the situation, their budgets would feel heat. Unfortunately, as with all attempts by legislatures to micromanage education, it did not take long for the administration and the faculty to regain lost ground. Today, most UC campuses are monuments to technoscience, and with few exceptions at the undergraduate level, the humanities and social sciences are gradually being relegated to the status of ornaments and service departments.

In the third tier, the forms of privatization and vocationalization are far more explicit. For example, the New York telephone company Bell Atlantic developed relationships with public community and senior colleges throughout the state on condition that the schools agreed to enroll and train students for specific occupations needed by the company. While in most cases no money changes hands, the school benefits by additional enrollment and because it shows the legislature and other politicians that it is playing a role in increasing worker productivity and enhancing economic growth, and for these reasons should be rewarded with funds. In addition to a degree, the employees learn occupational skills that often lead to upgrading, and the company transfers the costs of training it would have to do anyway to the public. Ironically, the Communications Workers of America, the collective bargaining representative, takes credit for the program by including the right of certain high seniority members to an "education" in the contract—read here as upgrading opportunities without themselves assuming the cost of tuition.

The question at issue is whether schools should forge direct corporate partnerships and, in effect, sell their teaching staff—let alone hand over the curriculum to vocational ends. Needless to say, in the occupational programs I have examined, the liberal arts, especially English and history, play a service role; at Nassau Community College in Long Island, students are required to take a course in labor history, and their English requirement is confined to composition. Otherwise, the remainder of the two-year curriculum is devoted to technical subjects of direct applicability to the telephone industry. Third-tier public colleges and universities are under direct pressure to reduce their humanities and social sciences offerings to introductory and service courses in the technical and scientific curriculum. In effect, the prospective English or sociology majors face a huge obstacle to obtain a degree in their chosen discipline because there are often not enough electives to fulfill the major. As a result, we can observe the rush to mergers of social sciences departments in many third-tier public schools.

Sociology, anthropology, and political science departments are consolidating. At Cameron State University in Lawton, Oklahoma, the two philosophers on campus are now in the social sciences department, which includes the traditional disciplines, and teach courses such as business ethics. In order to maintain viability, the department has majors in occupational specializations such as the large major in social welfare, a vocational sequence designed to train counselors and low-level professionals in the criminal justice system—a thriving industry in the state. Absent a social and political theorist, these required courses are taught by a criminologist. With almost five hundred majors, the eleven full-time members of the department each teach more than 120 students in four course-loads a semester, in addition to academic and professional advisement of bachelor's and master's students. Many courses are taught by adjuncts. Since the university has many business majors, a favorite of dozens of third-tier schools, the humanities and social sciences departments are crucial for fulfilling the shriveling "breadth" requirements.

Economic pressures as much as the ideological assaults on the liberal arts account for the change in the curriculum that is in process in public higher education. Students and their families feel more acutely the urgency of getting a leg up in the race for survival. The relative luxury of the liberal arts might be reserved for the few who are liberated from paid work during their college years. The consequence is that the human sciences are squeezed from the bottom as well as the top as students demand "relevance" in the curriculum and lose their thirst for reflection.

It may safely be declared that only in the larger cities, and then not uniformly, have faculty and students successfully defended the liberal arts. At CUNY, a decade of determined faculty resistance has slowed, but not reversed, the trend. As the new century dawned, CUNY administration was preparing its version of distance learning, one of the more blatant efforts to end the traditional reliance on classroom learning in favor of a model that focuses on the use of technology to produce more standard packages of predigested knowledge. In addition, it is an answer to the fiscal crisis suffered by many public schools because the style of learning reduces the number and proportion of full-time faculty to adjuncts, transforms brick-and-mortar locations into cyberspace so that building and maintenance costs are reduced, and through standardization eliminates the mediation of a critical intellectual to interpret transmitted knowledge. The latter saving does not refer as much to cost as to the centralization of political and social control.

The bare fact is that neither the discourse nor the practices of critical learning are abroad in public higher education except as the rear-guard protests of a much-exhausted faculty and a fragment of the largely demobilized student body. Blindsided by the sixties, many educators went along with student demands for ending requirements and ended up with the marketplace in which demand-driven criteria determined curricular choices. In other words, neoliberalism entered the academy through the backdoor of student protest. For progressive educators, the task remains to demand a rigorous core of knowledge as a requisite of any postsecondary credential. Today, such a demand is a radical act. To capitulate to the "market" (which, arguably, wants something else because in a panic about an uncertain future, students and their parents really do not believe in the palaver of the "boom economy") is to surrender the idea of higher education as a public good. Educators would acknowledge that these institutions largely paid for by the working and middle classes should not promote critical thinking, should not explore the meaning of citizenship in the new neoliberal era, and should abhor the project of democratic appropriation of both Western and subaltern (marginal) traditions through attitudes of bold skepticism.

Perhaps it is too early to propose that public higher education be thoroughly decommodified and shorn of its corporate characteristics and that all tuition
costs be paid by a tax system that must be reprogressivized. Perhaps the battle
cry that at least in the first two years only science, philosophy, literature, and history (understood in the context of social theory) be taught and learned and that
specializations be confined to the last two years, are so controversial, even
among critics of current trends, that they remain too countercultural. Yet if
higher education is to become a public good in the double meaning of the
term—as a decommodified resource for the people and as an ethically legitimate
institution that does not submit to the business imperative—then beyond access
we would have to promote a national debate about what is to be taught—and
what is to be learned—if citizenship and critical thought are to remain, even at
the level of intention, at the heart of the higher learning.

7

EDUCATION FOR CITZENSHIP

GRAMSCI'S "COMMON SCHOOL" TODAY

The celebrated *Quaderni* (prison notebooks) by Antonio Gramsci were published under the auspices of the Italian Communist Party more than a decade after the author's death in 1937. Later translated by the Italian American trade unionist and political activist Carl Marzani, pieces of the notebooks appeared in the late 1950s (in the wake of the Twentieth Congress of the Soviet Communist Party) as *The Open Marxism of Antonio Gramsci.*[1] Marzani introduced this hitherto obscure Italian Marxist thinker to an English-speaking audience; the work was generally regarded as a "revisionist" document by both the orthodox Leninists and by Gramsci's admirers. Gramsci's works seemed to vindicate the anti-Stalinist tenor of Khrushchev's main report to the Congress but, more to the point, suggested a departure from the prevailing Marxist-Leninist orthodoxy that had reigned for forty years.

Perhaps most salient of Gramsci's points was his reconceptualization of civil society. In the *Philosophy of Right,* Hegel had made the radical move to argue that, in the capitalist epoch, every question resolved itself to the cash nexus rather than constituting a sphere of free discussion among equals. Consequently, civil society was coterminous with market relations. To the extent Marx presupposed Hegel's distinction between state and civil society, now transmogrified into the binary categories of infrastructure and superstructure, the Marxist tradition tended to ignore the significance of the public sphere, including such institutions as media, voluntary organizations, educational institutions, and so forth. Gramsci's insistence that since all capitalist societies, even the fascist dictatorships, tend to rule by consent rather than primarily by force, the key to the rule of capital was to be found in its ability to achieve hegemony over "civil society," conceived as the sphere of public life that was neither, strictly speaking, of the economy nor of the state. On the contrary, it was precisely the degree to which classes in modern society established their power over "common sense" and thus appeared independent from the coercion of economic and state relations that their rule was made possible.

Marzani's slim volume of some of Gramsci's writings made little impact in the wake of the breakup of the American and British Communist Parties, but Gramsci's concepts of revolutionary politics were in sync with many in the New Left who sought an alternative Marxist tradition to that of Stalinism and even Trotskyism, which they viewed as authoritarian. Despite its fragmentary character, the most widely read of these is the second English-language selection published in 1971 under the title *Selections from the Prison Notebooks of Antonio Gramsci*.[2] Much longer and better annotated than the Marzani version, until recently it stood alone as a definitive scholarly rendition. Edited with a long introduction and copious notes by Quintin Hoare, it managed to provide most of Gramsci's central ideas by thematically dividing and synthesizing what were otherwise pithy notes, often provocative but sometimes banal. Despite Hoare's New Left credentials, the volume appeared under the imprint of the U.K. and U.S. Communist Party publishing houses and remains to this day the central source of the "popular" reception of Gramsci's thought. A companion volume extracted the large number of entries on culture; there now exist *Further Selections*, selections from the *Prison Notebooks* on culture, two volumes of the earlier political writings, the prison letters, and two volumes of a projected six-volume edition of the entire *Quaderni*. The essays that mark Gramsci's most sustained contributions to philosophy, to political, social, and cultural theory, and to the strategy and tactics of revolutionary struggle are contained in *Selections from the Prison Notebooks*.

Despite the diverse topics which occupied Gramsci's interest during his eleven-year internment (he was trained as a "traditional," that is, humanistic intellectual) and the obscurity of many of his references to contemporary Italian writers, most of whom are long forgotten, activists as much as scholars still find much to fascinate. Indeed, despite the virtual disappearance of official communism after the collapse of the Soviet Union, the commentaries continue, including the present one, on almost every aspect of his writings. What can the work of a general secretary of the Italian Communist Party whose major work was done during the fascist era say to us at a time when the political problematic to which

Gramsci addressed himself seems surpassed, a condition which perhaps was not evident in the immediate postwar years when the *Quaderni* were published? It is not only that the Soviet Union and its minions have disappeared from the world stage or that the Communist Parties of Eastern as much as Western Europe have degenerated into pale imitations of the Social Democratic formations they once despised. Or that what is left of official communism—Cuba, China, and North Korea—are social formations that, to say the least, have proven incapable of sustaining autarchic economies, even as their political systems are, to one degree or another, Stalinist throwbacks, an asymmetry not likely to last.

Equally to the point, a strong argument can be made for the historicity of many of Gramsci's formulations, especially his distinction between the war of position and the war of maneuver, where the latter signifies the strategy and tactics of revolutionary struggle. Although socialist revolution may not be permanently foreclosed, the prospects for such an event seem dim, at least for the coming decades. What remains are the elaborations of the war of position—the long march through institutions, in civil society, and in struggles for intermediate power within the capitalist state, where my term *intermediate* signifies an extension of popular power from the institutions of civil society to the state, but still a capitalist state.

There is much in Gramsci's writings that mark him as a significant scholar. Let us stipulate at the outset that just as Marx was among the greatest Hegelian commentators, Gramsci must be ranked as a major writer on Machiavelli. His "Notes on Italian History," especially his remarks on the so-called Southern Question, is a landmark in our collective understanding of why politics, even of an international variety, must always take national and regional specificities into account.[3] Moreover, his contributions to the development of historical materialism, configured as a critique of Nicolai Bukharin's attempt at a Popular Manual as well as in other comments on the significance of culture and language in the formation and reproduction of the nation-state (found chiefly in his "Problems of Marxism" in *Selections from the Prison Notebooks*) are among the most powerful statements of the nondogmatic Marxism, which later transmuted into what Perry Anderson called "Western" Marxism. These are contributions that richly deserve the scholarly attention the *Notebooks* continue to receive, even after the end of official communism.

There is, of course, a lively debate on Gramsci's ideas about education. I believe his remarks on education and the implicit educational issues addressed in many other places remain among the most salient for us. In the United States, the conversation has been mainly conducted among educational theorists and researchers who, given that they are largely ensconced in universities and work, at best, within a reformist environment, tend to focus on schools. Indeed,

Gramsci's views on the "common school" could be easily inserted into the contemporary curriculum debate. He insisted that the common school should privilege "formative" rather than vocational/technical education on grounds that are familiar today.

> The tendency today [in the public or common schools] is to abolish every type of schooling that is "disinterested" (not serving immediate interests) or "formative"—keeping at most only a small-scale version to serve a tiny elite of ladies and gentlemen who do not have to worry about assuring themselves of a future career. Instead there is a steady growth of specialized vocational schools, in which the pupil's destiny and future activity are determined in advance. A rational solution to the crisis ought to adopt the following lines. First, a common basic education, imparting a general, humanistic, formative culture; this would strike the right balance between development of the capacity for working manually (technically, industrially) and the development of capacities required for intellectual work.[4]

Gramsci's discussion is directed not only to the existing educational system but to what an educational system must provide under conditions where the key institutions of the economy and civil society are under popular control. Gramsci remarked that contemporary "deliberative bodies" distinguished their work into two "organic" spheres: the first were the essential decisions they must make; the second were the "technical-cultural" activities that precede decision making and are undertaken by "experts." His reference to "deliberative bodies" signified what popular or workers' councils would have to consider in establishing common schools. Far from denigrating technical education, he called for a balance so that those at the top levels of political leadership would possess familiarity with problems of production. Although the new society would inevitably require experts and he did not foresee the possibility of abolishing the capitalist division of labor anytime soon, Gramsci insisted that "destiny" not be established at the outset of a child's schooling by what we would now term "tracking" and that schools would play a role in enabling manual and technical workers to engage in the intellectual work required of members of deliberative bodies that direct the system. In short, his position on the common school embodied his theory of democratic politics and his social philosophy in which popular participation as well as representatives constituted the twin elements of any future democracy. His educational ideas were directed not so much at improving schools for the sake of reform but for the sake of making possible a new kind of social rule in every institution of the state and civil society.

Gramsci devoted considerable attention to education, among other institutions because, even in the wake of fascism, schools are primary sites for achieving mass consent for social rule. The great Gramscian, Louis Althusser, argues that among the state's *ideological* apparatuses, as opposed to the *repressive* apparatuses (law, courts, police, army, prisons), educational institutions are the most important. The school is the state institution par excellence that prepares children and youth for their appropriate economic and political niches within the prevailing order. It acts as a sorting machine, forming and reproducing the classes of society according to what Bourdieu terms degrees of attainment of cultural capital. They transmit the dominant culture, habits of mind, and perhaps most important of all, inculcate to a large portion of the society's population the knowledge and values that are deemed appropriate for citizenship in a given social formation. But technical and manual workers are not only formed by specialized curricula. A plethora of commentators—notably Paul Willis—have added that school "failure" is a crucial marker of working-class formation at the level of everyday life. Manual or low-level service workers are formed by their refusal (coded as failure) of the standard curriculum, which constitutes the basis for the accumulation of cultural capital.

Gramsci-inspired writers on schools in advanced capitalist societies have, with some notable exceptions, taken education to mean schooling. Although many writers have engaged in a sharp critique of the role and function of schooling in terms of what Henry Giroux and I have called "reproductive" theory, there is considerable reluctance to reveal the inner tensions of schools—that is, the degree to which movements within schools have attempted to offer both resistance and alternatives to the dominant program of technicalization and the systematic devaluation of formative education. Indeed, there is considerable evidence that many contemporary Gramscians recoil, on populist or libertarian grounds, at Gramsci's call for a curriculum which brings forward some of the features of the "old school of grammatic study of Latin and Greek together with the study of their respective literatures and political histories." Gramsci extols the old school, admittedly reserved for a tiny elite, as a guide for a new common educational program.

> Individual facts were not learnt for immediate practical or professional end. The end seemed disinterested, because the real interest was the interior development of personality, the formation of character by means of the absorption and assimilation of the whole cultural past of modern European civilization. Pupils did not learn Latin and Greek in order to speak them, to become waiters, interpreters or commercial letter-writers. They learnt in order to know at first hand the civilization of Greece and of Rome, a civilization that was a necessary precondition of our modern civilization; in other words, they learnt them in order to be themselves and know themselves consciously.[5]

Gramsci defends the old common school for its ability to impart habits of

> diligence, precision, poise (even physical poise), ability to concentrate on specific subjects, which cannot be acquired without the mechanical repetition of disciplined and methodical act. If one wants to produce great scholars, one still has to start at this point and apply pressure throughout the educational system in order to succeed in creating those thousands or hundreds or even dozens of scholars of the highest quality which are necessary to every civilization.[6]

Clearly, if the criteria of contemporary relevance, of practical scientific and technical knowledge, and of specialization guide the educational system, these scholars are not likely to be produced and the consequences for civilization would be deleterious. To form scholars, he argued, one must master more than one language and civilization, to engage in the "analysis of distincts," Croce's amendment of the dialectic to signify difference without contradiction. The student becomes an intellectual—no less than a scholar—by "plunging" into knowledge and life, by being subjected to the discipline of learning.

The old school was intended for the education of the ruling class. Its restriction to the upper reaches of society was intended not only to train succeeding generations of elites but to subject the subalterns to technical and vocational niches, a "destiny" which deprived them of the means by which any democracy may emerge. For Gramsci, democracy "by definition" meant that the distinction between the ruler and ruled narrowed, that "citizenship" beyond consent to participation be widely instituted. Yet apart from providing in his prescription for school reform a common curriculum of early, disinterested education, he hesitated to draw the logical conclusion of his own analysis: the mass intellectual education of the subalterns. To use his terminology, he remained skeptical of schooling that aimed at the transformation of the masses from spontaneous philosophers to philosophically as well as technically educated social actors.

Gramsci despaired of translating old elite schooling to a mass educational system, chiefly because workers and peasants lacked the time and the cultural preconditions for study. Until the establishment of a new social order, his recommended strategy was to put education in the service of the formation of an intellectual elite, where the concept of elite is transformed from its class-specific location in the traditional rulers to social groups in whose interest the formation of a new, egalitarian social order may come into being—the historical bloc of discontented social groups led by the working class. Short of an extensive program of formative schooling conducted by the revolutionary party itself, a task that may be necessary under conditions of the surrender of the public schools to occupational priorities, the struggle for reform of the common school curriculum in the direction of formative education was a necessary precondition for producing this elite.

Gramsci's concept of education is, however, only secondarily directed to schooling. The key is the formation of an "intellectual moral bloc" capable of contesting the prevailing common sense and providing in its stead, more or less systematically, a "scientific" understanding of the social world and of politics that can be widely disseminated in the institutions and other social spaces of civil society. Here, the concept "science" signified not the common usage of industrial societies in which the object of knowledge is nature or a naturalized social world and the methods of knowing are experimental and mathematical, which strictly excludes intuition and speculation. Gramsci invoked a more traditional idea of science—the preindustrial, according to which science meant only the effort to achieve systematic knowledge in which philosophy as much as the traditional natural and social sciences were legitimate modes of knowledge acquisition.

Under the gaze of the censors, the term Gramsci employed to designate social science was "the philosophy of praxis." For nearly all commentators, it stood in for Marxism and, indeed, his texts provide some confirmation for this view. But there is a sense in which the philosophy of praxis may be understood as the unity of theory and practice. Unlike Leninist orthodoxy where theory is conceived in "the service" of practice, its "handmaid" or as a "guide," Gramsci understood their unity as two sides of the same totality; there was no structure of dominance. As his essays "The Study of Philosophy" and the compendium of comments from the *Notebooks* grouped under the title "Problems of Marxism" make clear, Gramsci's historical materialism and philosophy are directed principally and highly polemically against "mechanical materialism"— the dominant ideology of the Third Stalinist International—especially ideas of historical inevitability with which Bukharin had, under pressure from Stalin, no doubt, identified himself, as did many in the leadership of the Italian Communist Party. The philosophy of praxis is the core paradigm, if you will, from which the intellectual moral bloc needs to be formed to assist the masses to overcome the simple reductionism of bourgeois or the Catholic Church's common sense, both of which are content to leave them at a "low level" of understanding. The point of the bloc is "to make politically possible the progress of the mass and not only small intellectual groups."[7]

> The active man-in-the-mass has a practical activity, but has no clear theoretical consciousness of his practical activity, which nonetheless involves understanding the world in so far as it transforms it. His theoretical consciousness can indeed be

historically in opposition to his activity. One might almost say that he has two theoretical consciousnesses (or one contradictory consciousness): one which is
implicit in his activity and which in reality unites him with his fellow-workers in
the practical transformation of the real world; and one, superficially explicit or
verbal, which he has inherited from the past and uncritically absorbed. It holds
together a specific social group, it influences moral conduct and the direction of
will . . . but often powerfully enough to produce a situation in which the contradictory state of consciousness does not permit of any action, any decision or any
choice, and produces a condition of moral and political passivity. Critical understanding of self takes place therefore through struggle of political "hegemonies"
and of opposing directions, first in the ethical field and a higher level of one's own
conception of reality. Consciousness of being part of a particular hegemonic force
(that is to say political consciousness) is the first stage toward a further progressive self-consciousness in which theory and practice will finally be one.[8]

It is evident that the crucial educational issue is how to address the political
hegemonies, how to bring the practical and theoretical consciousness of the
most "advanced" political actors together, in short, beyond the "masses" to
overcome the power of common sense among those who are charged with political leadership within the great social movements. For Gramsci, the intellectuals
are not to be conceived as the technicians of power but its sinews. No class in
modern society, he argued, could organize itself for power—for the war of
maneuver, that is, the revolutionary activity—without the participation of intellectuals whose ultimate task was to embody the unity of theory and organization. It was they who contested in the institutions of civil society, the trade
unions, as well as the universities.

Which brings us to the central question of how to achieve scientific understanding in ever-wider groups of the underlying population. In *The Modern
Prince,* Gramsci offers a particularly clear formulation of the task.[9] He spoke of
the need for "intellectual and moral reform" and suggested that the key to it is
the development of a "national-popular collective" which replaced the "divini-
ty and the categorical imperative" by linking moral with economic reform, all at
the cultural level.

Perhaps Gramsci's major innovation was to have recalled Machiavelli's insistence on the science of politics as an autonomous discourse and the idea that
politics is the main science. Thus the struggle for a new scientific understanding as a new common sense always entails taking the point of view of "the man
of action" rather than that of the scholar or, in current fashion, the nomadic
intellectual.

III

CULTURE, IDENTITY, AND DEMOCRACY

THE DOUBLE BIND OF RACE

Some ten years ago, I was invited by the Afro-American Studies program at Yale to give a talk about Richard Wright's political writings. I argued, among other things, that a coherent and reasonable—admirable, even—vision animated Wright's writings from early to late. I was unprepared for the storm of controversy that followed.

My focus was on Wright's 1954 political travelogue, *Black Power*, subtitled *A Record of Reactions in a Land of Pathos*.[1] Written seven years after his permanent departure from the United States, the book seemed distant in topic and tone from the writings on black America that had propelled Wright to fame. *Black Power* is a controversial study of Nkrumah's Ghana (then "Gold Coast"), exploring the conflict between modernization and tradition that faced all developing countries on the verge of independence. At a time when the decolonizing societies of Asia and Africa were often dazzled by the lure of tradition, Wright entered the debate on the side of modernity, urging Nkrumah to refuse the tribalist temptation as well as the prevailing anti-Western ideology of the period and to pursue a program of relentless political, economic, and *cultural* modernization.

Wright was fully aware that the success of such a campaign would depend on the capital and expertise of the colonial powers, and the risks that would entail. But, while admitting a limited role for indigenous traditions, he outlined a clear-eyed course for emerging African nations that incorporated the benefits of modernity: democracy, industrialization, and personal freedom. My interest in talking about the later Wright was to show that his refusal of cultural nationalism was nonetheless a vision of black liberation, and that his cosmopolitanism represented a genuine alternative to what I perceived as a tendency in the 1970s and 1980s of black intellectuals and sympathetic whites to embrace one or another variant of ethnocentricity. I suggested that Wright's cosmopolitanism represented an eclipsed tradition in black intellectual culture.

My listeners included some of the leading scholars in the field, and they were not particularly sympathetic to the idea of resuscitating this notorious side of Wright's corpus. For them, Wright's political writings had no place in the emerging canon of African American literature, if only because he had, more or less explicitly, renounced that designation for what he considered its misguided nationalist connotations. His unapologetic restatement of the virtues of the Enlightenment, including the much-criticized humanisms of both liberalism and Marxism, was an embarrassment. The Wright of the political writings was swimming against a current for which modernity itself was in question.

After my lecture, the late Charles Davis suggested that, although he appreciated my account of the political writings, Wright's work was not only seriously flawed, it was little short of blasphemy. Others wondered why I had bothered to bring these discredited views to their attention. In an environment in which the black "tradition" was being constructed along the lines of an ethnically based vernacular and folk culture—a turn dictated by the quest for a usable past— Wright's later writings were nothing less than an affront to the projects of Afrocentricity and African Americanness itself. Arnold Rampersad, the editor of the New American Library's definitive edition of Wright's works, agreed: his version of the Wright canon closes in 1953, with the novel *The Outsiders*, leaving the political writings out of the Library of America altogether.

Even before his death in 1960, Richard Wright was best known for *Native Son* (published in 1940, and the first Book-of-the-Month Club selection by a black writer) and for *Black Boy* (1945), his stunning autobiographical essay. Both were heralded at the time of their publication as among the most important narratives of black American life. With the establishment of black studies departments in American universities, these works, along with his short stories and newly discovered writings from his early years (including *American Hunger*, the second, unpublished half of the original manuscript for *Black Boy*) have been given a central place in the African American canon.

Despite the evident Marxism of Wright's writings from this period, texts like *Twelve Million Black Voices* (1941) have retained a certain academic élan. That book, an account of the social, economic, and psychological complexities of black life in the wake of the Great Migration, has been praised for telling the story of blacks outside the respectable, middle-class bounds of the Talented Tenth. Michel Fabre, one of Wright's biographers, has argued that *Twelve Million Black Voices* made an important contribution to sundering racial stereotypes by depicting the diversity of blacks and their communities.

But Wright's self-imposed exile to Paris in 1947 struck his contemporaries as a kind of apostasy. As Paul Gilroy notes in the Wright chapter of his remarkable book, *The Black Atlantic*, "The consensus stipulates as far as his art was concerned the move to Europe was disastrous."[2]

> This argument takes several forms. . . . It dismisses Wright's entitlement to hold a view of modernity at all and has grave implications for how we place his work in debates about black modernism(s). It is claimed that after moving to France Wright's work was corrupted by his dabbling in philosophical modes of thought entirely alien to his African-American history and vernacular style. Secondly, it is argued that the interest in psychiatry and psychoanalysis which had, in any case, preceded his transatlantic move got out of control in the European milieu. Third, it is suggested that, once resident in Europe, Wright was simply too remote from the vital folk sources which made his early work so uniquely powerful.

Wright's "Paris" novels—*The Long Dream, Savage Holiday*, and especially *The Outsider*—revealed the powerful influence of Jean-Paul Sartre and French existentialism on his writing. The Paris books were neither commercially nor critically successful in the United States (*Savage Holiday*, a paperback original, went unreviewed), in part because these works broke with the naturalist conventions of black fiction that Wright himself had helped establish. After *Native Son*, black writing was supposed to reveal the degradation of black everyday life through uncompromising narratives that reveal the depth and scope of black oppression in White America.

Savage Holiday, in fact, breaks an unwritten rule: not only does it not concern itself with poverty and the withering realities of black life, it doesn't have a single black character. Informed by Wright's increasing attraction to existential themes, it's a story of *white* oppression in White America. Its protagonist is a midlevel insurance executive, age forty-three, who is dismissed after twenty-five years of faithful service. Like all of Wright's fiction, early and late, *Savage Holiday* concerns the crisis of social and psychological identity in the face of capitalist modernity. Remarkably, it anticipates the fate of many middle managers in the corporate merger and acquisition fever of the early 1990s. By invoking a white "victim" of the corporate culture that nurtured him, revealing the precarious position of even relatively privileged inhabitants of the mainstream, the creator of Bigger Thomas raised universal issues of identity and belonging.

What does a person do when he or she is no longer integrated by a culture? What remains of the self when the corporate self—our contemporary experience of community, however degraded—evaporates? That these are questions for everyone—we are increasingly interpellated by our jobs—violates the still-prevalent notion that *only* the color line prevents African Americans from enjoying the fruits of modernity understood not simply as economic well-being, but as a sense of being at home in the world.

Wright's abiding concern remained, of course, the fate of blacks on an international scale. In *The Black Atlantic* Gilroy takes Wright's permanent expatriation from the United States as a sign, not of betrayal, but of a broadening of his commitment to black freedom. As Wright wrote in his journals, "I took my subject matter with me in the baggage of my memory when I left America." His nonfiction of this period, especially *White Man, Listen!*,[3] *The Color Curtain*,[4] and *Black Power*, are serious, albeit unorthodox, attempts to come to grips with the question raised at the opening of Gilroy's book: The "transverse dynamics of racial politics . . . [and] the broader questions of ethnic identity" linked to the project of "striving to be both European and black." (And, one might add, American.) In Gilroy's thoughtful attempt to address the complex questions of modernity, race, and ethnic identity, Wright appears (with W. E. B. Du Bois) as the most courageous pan-African intellectual of the last half of this century.

Wright's legacy, fully resumed by Gilroy in *The Black Atlantic*, is to acknowledge the contradictory ambitions of the quest for an autonomous black identity in the face of inescapable modernity. Gilroy constructs a new and alternative narrative of the past five centuries of black politics and culture, heavily indebted to Wright's (and Du Bois's) insistence that the black diaspora is globally indivisible, and on the implicit call for a community of black expressive cultures. As we have seen, he reiterates Wright's forthright defense of modernity as a desirable (or at least, inescapable) aspect of black identity.

To begin with, the title itself signals two departures from the mainstream of African American cultural studies. Gilroy uses the term *black* to make clear his rejection of ethnocentric perspectives represented by terms such as *African American*, *black British*, and *Afro-Caribbean*, as well as nationalist accounts that would deny the discrete existence of the African diaspora; for him, "black" is a transverse signifier that subordinates nationality to a more or less common history. The word evokes the scattering of already differentiated and diverse African peoples via their enslavement, from the sixteenth through nineteenth centuries. Moreover, as the *diaspora* of the title implies, their dispersal to the Americas, the Caribbean, and Europe parallels the Jewish diaspora, both in its geographic breadth and in its economic and political, if not cultural, unity.

That there are differences of circumstance between blacks and Jews, differences of settlement and of degree of cultural assimilation and exclusion (and, therefore, "race" consciousness), Gilroy does not deny. But he insists that the analogy between the Jewish and black diaspora is more than a literary elegance: it describes two peoples systematically deprived of their homelands and, for this reason, condemned permanently to negotiate with "host" societies for whom they remain ineluctably "other." He writes:

> In the preparation of this book I have been repeatedly drawn to the work of Jewish thinkers [notably Walter Benjamin] in order to find both inspiration and resources with which to map the ambivalent experiences of blacks inside and outside modernity. I want to acknowledge these debts openly in the hope that in some small way the link they reveal might contribute to a better political relationship between Jews and blacks at some distant future point. Many writers have been struck by some of the correspondences between histories of these groups, but thinkers from both communities are not always prepared to admit them, let alone explore any possible connections in an uninhibited way.

By awarding pride of place in his own analysis to the concept of diaspora, Gilroy signifies his intention to be less inhibited. As Gilroy notes, pan-Africanism was significantly modeled on Zionism. Just as the Zionists adopted, after much consideration, the biblical designation of Palestine as the Jewish homeland, Marcus Garvey and Martin Delany sought, in various ways, to unite the dispersed people of Africa to a project of "return."

Gilroy's acknowledgment of the continuing influence of nationalism should not be confused either with cultural nationalism or with the integrationist dissolution of ethnic identity into patriotism within a single country. His own vision of black nationalism, indebted to Du Bois, is a kind of ethnic particularism without a country, a "nation" in permanent exile. His central argument is that while nationality plays a significant role in black and Jewish historical formation, the crucial event was that of *dispersal*. Following Du Bois, he claims that blacks throughout Europe and the Americas were forced into a position of "double consciousness." This dual awareness, of being black and a citizen of a white-majority liberal democratic nation, placed a heavy burden on programs of complete assimilation as well as those of pan-Africanism. Contrary to some neo-Marxist efforts (including Du Bois's own *Black Reconstruction*) to model blackness on the image of the nineteenth-century proletariat, "in, but not of, society," Gilroy suggests that the black Atlantic is culturally modern *and* possesses its own unique racialized identity within Western culture. In his chapter on Wright, Gilroy observes a crucial interaction, a conversation between Wright, already in exile in the French countryside, and the great Trinidadian critic and activist

C. L. R. James. Gesturing to a bookshelf full of Kierkegaard, Wright exclaimed, "Look here, . . . you see those books there? . . . Everything that he writes in those books I knew before I had them." Gilroy cites James' gloss on the event: "What [Wright] was telling me was that he was a black man in the United States and that gave him an insight into what today is the universal opinion and attitude of the *modern* perspective" (emphasis added).

One of Gilroy's striking contributions to the theory of black identity is his profound exploration of the interiority of black consciousness. Following Raymond Williams's injunction that critical theory find the ways in which cultural expressions plumb "structures of feeling," Gilroy references black music as often as more traditional forms of "high" culture like the novel and the essay. In *The Black Atlantic* the juxtapositions between the treatise and the song are always apposite. The chapter on Toni Morrison, for example, sports twin epigraphs: one a famous quote from the "Theses on the Philosophy of History" of Frankfurt School fellow traveler Walter Benjamin, the other a sensitive reflection—"Slavery was a terrible thing, but when black people in America finally got out from under that crushing system, they were stronger. . . . I admire that kind of strength. People who have it take a stand and put their blood and soul into what they believe"—from Michael Jackson, the King of Pop. To open his complex chapter on Du Bois, whose characteristic statement was the scholarly tract, the memoir, the manifesto, Gilroy finds that "in the space and time that separate Robert Johnson's 'Hellhound on My Trail' and the Wailers' exhortation to 'Keep on Moving,' and the more recent Soul II Soul piece with the same name, the expressive cultures of the black Atlantic world have been dominated by a special mood of restlessness."

These songs, according to Gilroy, reverse the usual designation of homelessness or exile as a "curse." Diasporic dispersal becomes an affirmation, a repossession of a condition usually exclusively associated with subordination. This "restless sensibility" comes to characterize Gilroy's vision of the black Atlantic, a corrective, one infers, to "rooted" particularisms like Jesse Jackson's "African American" or even Albert Murray's "Omni-American." Gilroy acutely observes that "the appeal to and for roots became an urgent issue when diaspora blacks sought to construct a political agenda in which the ideal of rootedness was identified as a prerequisite for the forms of cultural integrity that would guarantee the nationhood and statehood to which they aspired." This historicizing method displaces the conventional ethnicism of writers who take the search for roots as a transhistorical feature of self and group affirmation. Gilroy instead understands it as a response to the *specificity* of black dispersal under determinate historical conditions. In this respect he names racism as an agent in configuring black political identity as a *national* project.

It's at this point, however, that Gilroy's transatlantic vision runs aground. Missing from his text is any extended treatment of the differentiated economic and cultural position of blacks within Western nations. He observes that black double consciousness is modernity's secret sharer: "Racial subordination is integral to the processes of development and social and economic progress known as modernization." This, of course, has been the contention of such eminent scholars as Orlando Patterson, Eric Williams, C. L. R. James, and Du Bois himself. Recall Williams's claim, drawn from the extensive Caribbean experience, that slavery was the bedrock of the entire structure of social and political domination characteristic of Western capitalist societies. Patterson has argued that slavery remains an intrinsic feature of Western culture, and it is more than symbolic; contrary to the conventional wisdom, capitalism has never wholly dispensed with slavery. Racial subordination, and its impoverishment of the majority of U.S., Latin American, and Caribbean blacks, remains one of the conditions of accumulation.

If these analyses are correct, one may not take racism as an aberrant or anomalous feature of modernity. Nor is racism entirely subject to legal remedy. Rather, the position of blacks in both economically developed and underdeveloped societies suggests that racial formation is at one relatively autonomous from class formation and a crucial aspect of it—and that, as Gilroy recognizes, is the dirty secret of modernity. All the more interesting, then, that *The Black Atlantic* does not fully address the legacy of slavery and its political and economic consequences. Gilroy cites James's magisterial *Black Jacobins* and refers briefly to *Black Reconstruction*, but he mostly avoids consideration of the later Du Bois and the massive Caribbean contributions to the modernity debates.

Gilroy's predicament is itself completely modern, and again points toward an affinity with the thinkers of the Frankfurt School. For if capitalism, slavery, and modernity are irrevocably linked, then one might well question the very ideals of the Enlightenment—democracy, industrialization, and personal freedom—extolled by Wright in the 1950s. This is precisely the problematic that generated Max Horkheimer and Theodor Adorno's *Dialectic of Enlightenment*, a critical interrogation of what we might call the "double consciousness" of the Enlightenment.

Written during World War II, the book attempted to grapple with the implications of the rise of National Socialism in Germany, one of the most revered of Western cultures. German fascism seemed to give the lie to the very idea of the West, revealing the interpenetration of civilization and barbarism. The core of Adorno and Horkheimer's argument was the age-old project of mastery over nature, which had promised human liberation, had also made possible the wholesale destruction of human life. Rather than serving human ends, the machinery of progress signaled the end of humanity.

Modernity and its cognates—freedom, democracy, progress—depend, in part, on the externalization of their own inner contradictions. For the Enlightenment of the eighteenth century it was science, that magnificent warrior against religious superstition, which, in showing us how to strip nature of its mystery, had wreaked havoc on ecological systems the world over. Even as the Germans led the world in science and the arts, they also perfected the "technology" that would enable the Nazis to run the Jewish death camps with a supremely efficient bureaucracy. The New World, with its individualism, industrialization, and explicit rhetoric of human rights, was no less dependent on the otherness of black slaves and mass industrial workers, of Mexicans and other Latinos, and of various foreign enemies—first the Germans, in two world wars, and then the "gooks" of Japan, Korea, and Vietnam. In *Black Reconstruction*, twelve years before the publication of *Dialectic of Enlightenment*, Du Bois had argued that the black *worker*, laboring under slave and then near-slave conditions in factories and industrialized farms, provided the basis for American modernity—the surplus labor needed for capital accumulation and the development of manufacturing, as well as the leisure necessary to the creation of culture.

One may interpret these contemporary critiques of modernity as expressing the contradictions of progressive reason. The political construction and economic exploitation of otherness appears be to be an unresolved, and perhaps unresolvable, aspect of modernity. While *Dialectic of Enlightenment* suggests the weight of this contradiction—that Enlightenment and barbarism are coterminous, but that Enlightenment remains our only hope—it was unable to provide a satisfactory answer to the riddle of the modern. Adorno never did find a way to project that hope beyond a series of indeterminate negations. In one of his last works, *Negative Dialectics*, he declared the inevitability of *difference*, a signal that Hegelian reconciliation was utopian, in the bad sense.

It's here, perhaps, that Walter Benjamin's cautious invocation of agency, a product of his study of Jewish mysticism and Cabalistic thought, can be understood as the hope of the hopeless. Benjamin's idiosyncratic melding of Marx's insight that "men make their own history" and the Jewish command to redeem the unfinished tasks of the past by creating a new world was dismissed by Adorno as an unacceptable concession to tradition. Yet Benjamin stood for a critical modernism, critical because it was acutely aware of modernity's potential for inhumanity. Where Adorno lamented that "after Auschwitz, all poetry is garbage," Benjamin (and after him Marcuse) suggested that despite all the atrocities that had been committed in the name of progress, we cannot help but make history (if not universal history) by engaging in local struggles to make life better.

In *The Black Atlantic* Gilroy makes a new application of Benjamin's claim that "there is no document of civilization which is not at the same time a document of barbarism." But in his totalizing conception of a black diaspora consciousness, Gilroy is less attentive to the way that the fact of New World slavery localized black struggles for freedom and happiness as *national* projects.

Gilroy's avoidance of the historical problem posed by slavery in the Atlantic world might also explain something about the weakness of his analyses of specific, nationalized experiences of double consciousness—the unique trajectories of "integrationist" projects in the Caribbean (where Creolistes strive to be both Martinican and black) and the United States. The aspiration to American citizenship is a red thread that runs through the history of the black freedom movement in the twentieth century; despite a steep decline in the past twenty years, it may not yet have reached its historical limit. Although varieties of black nationalism from Martin Delany and Alexander Crummell, to Marcus Garvey and Louis Farrakhan, have had considerable influence over the black "masses," political and economic integration, if not cultural assimilation, remains the endpoint of struggles for civil rights in this country. While the "the black Atlantic" may describe a more comprehensive reality than "African American," it's difficult to rally behind its as-yet amorphous banner.

For most of this century, movements for civil rights have been strongly Americanist in orientation. The career of W. E. B. Du Bois, and Gilroy's interpretation of it, is instructive here. Gilroy makes Du Bois the leading black Atlantic figure by having him shed his American "roots."

> Du Bois' analysis of modernity also expressed his turn away from the United
> States. That country ceased to be the locus of his political aspirations once it
> became clear that the commitments to private rectitude and public reason for
> which he had argued so powerfully would not be sufficient to precipitate the com-
> prehensive reforms demanded by black suffering in the North as well as the South.

In light of Du Bois's restless journey—from a middle-class New England childhood to Harvard, on to Europe, back to America to teach in black colleges in the South and thence to Ghana—this is a highly selective claim. *The Souls of Black Folk* was published in 1903. A few years later Du Bois spearheaded the Niagara movement, which was shortly thereafter institutionalized as the National Association for the Advancement of Colored People, still the leading civil rights organization in the country.

To be sure, Du Bois became less inclined to rely exclusively on domestic reform. After decades of dedication to altering the legal and economic conditions of American blacks (a project that led him to support Woodrow Wilson and American entrance into World War I), he joined with George Padmore and others in the incipient pan-African movement. But he returned in *Black Reconstruction* (1935) to a consideration of the fate of the black worker in the postbellum South, and, in a shift from his socialist sentiments, joined the Communist Party, of which he remained a member until his death, in Nkrumah's Ghana, in 1963. The interpenetration of these consciousnesses— black, American, pan-Africanist, Communist—was complex, and Du Bois's "turn away from America" was never as definitive as Gilroy would have it.

Struggles for "civil rights" have always been about more than the assertion of narrowly political rights; in marching on Washington, blacks have always been expressing a determination to tie their economic fortunes with those of other Americans. "Washington" became a metaphor for the power that could deliver blacks from social, political, and *economic* servitude. The crucial event was the New Deal. Roosevelt's activist state was committed to redistributive policies aimed at alleviating poverty, as well as job creation. The Democrats, once viewed as the party of the lynch mob, segregation, and the plantation aristocracy, were now in a position to appeal to blacks, some of whom were already entering the new industrial unions on the promise that they would break from the old Jim Crow policies of the American Federation of Labor.

Wright's *Twelve Million Black Voices* was, in part, a popular front document of the times. Gilroy reads it convincingly as an early example of the conflict between Wright's interests in psychoanalysis and Marxism. But the book fairly bristles with the accusation that blacks may be excluded from the economic prosperity already on the horizon. As the historian Harvard Sitkoff has shown, it was a moment in which the objections of Southern Democrats were causing Roosevelt to hold back on pursuing social and economic equality for blacks.

Under these conditions, it was A. Philip Randolph, the black leader of the Brotherhood of Sleeping Car Porters (AFL), who emerged as the most powerful exemplar of double consciousness: as a thinker and organizer he was deeply and practically committed to black people *and* their place in the American project. With war clouds looming, he threatened a potentially embarrassing mass march to force Roosevelt to open the gates of war industries to blacks—a threat sufficiently credible for Roosevelt to issue an executive order barring employers who would do business with the federal government from discriminating against blacks.

As a Socialist and war opponent, Randolph couldn't have cared less about Roosevelt's political dilemma. But, perhaps unwittingly, he provoked the Democrats into a qualitatively new alliance with blacks, one that had the long-term effect of encouraging the development of a mass civil rights movement whose fundamental aim was integration. Indeed, in the quarter century after Randolph's bold initiative, black nationalism fell on hard times. Many blacks and whites believed in the possibility that blacks could one day evolve into just another ethnic group.

Talk about modernity. No oppressed people in human history has more thoroughly embraced the leading features of modernity than American blacks. In the 1960s the most militant and radical contingent of the Black Power movement declared voter registration its supreme aspiration. With the murder of Martin Luther King Jr., the nation lost the quintessential figure of American modernity; nobody was more loyal to the American Dream. Even after, many blacks responded by even more fervently dedicating themselves to the integrationist principles for which he gave his life. They entered electoral politics with new energy, won a wide array of public offices, and, by the 1980s, when many white blue-collar workers deserted to the suburbs and to the Republicans, they had become the bedrock of the Democratic Party.

Ironically, the fires of black nationalism would flare again in the midst of the most rapid economic gains since Reconstruction. A new internationlism excited the collective imagination of young blacks. After the 1967 war, there was new enthusiasm for the Palestinian struggle, and a few years later American blacks reached out to South Africa. As the struggle against apartheid gained momentum in the 1980s, American blacks initiated and led an astonishingly effective boycott against American companies doing business with South Africa.

For an articulate minority, the assassinations of Martin and Malcolm, the urban riots of the 1960s, and the success of race-tinged "Southern strategies" in national presidential politics since 1968 confirmed the bankruptcy of the integrationist ideology of the bulk of black leaders. While Jesse Jackson's Rainbow Coalition injected some life into the old liberal faith, his rejection by a newly minted "centrist" Democratic Party provided further evidence that a broad-based civil rights movement was now history.

This, then, may be the ultimate meaning of Farrakhanism. The success of the Million Man March may well prove that the integrationist hegemony has finally been broken. Surely, the failure of Jackson or the NAACP to call for a different kind of march reveals the bankruptcy of the old liberal alliance to galvanize the black masses, even in the face of the most sustained assault on their living standards and basic human rights since the Great Depression. Without making a single demand on a political power structure that had announced open season on the welfare state, the march gathered *as if* it could still deliver.

In the end, Gilroy's brilliant, flawed book leaves the unhappy double consciousness intact. Karl Marx once criticized Hegel's dialectic of master and slave (one of the most famous sections of the *Phenomenology of Spirit*) in which the bondsman, through his struggle with the lord, attains reflexive *self-consciousness* but not liberation. Gilroy, too, has deferred a discourse of emancipation, one that supersedes ethnic particularity for some universal project. He is unable to find a way out of perhaps the most troubling contradiction of modernity: the two souls of nationality. His often brilliant readings seem to cancel the enormous impetus for reform bound up in nationalist projects. If nationally based liberal reform has failed the black Atlantic as well, alongside that other modernist ideology of liberation, communism, the path ahead awaits a new affirmative vision.

9

RACE RELATIONS IN THE TWENTY-FIRST CENTURY

1

The first moments of a recent documentary about the Students for a Democratic Society (SDS), *Rebels with a Cause,* recall one of the signal images of the 1960s civil rights struggle: police aiming torrents of water from fire hoses onto demonstrators in Birmingham, Alabama. According to its makers, the student New Left and the antiwar movement derived their principal inspiration from the struggle for black freedom.

In this phase of the movement, blacks and their allies sought three rights: integrated public schools; desegregation of public accommodations such as trains and buses, restrooms and water fountains, restaurants and, in much of the South, the right to walk down a street unmolested; and perhaps most importantly, voting rights. Nearly forty years later, the Birmingham confrontation reminds us not only of the violence of Southern resistance to these elementary components of black freedom but also how clear-cut these issues were. The simple justice embodied in these demands had lurked on the margins of American political life since the 1870s betrayal of black reconstruction by politicians and their masters, Northern industrialists. Not that proponents of black freedom were quiescent in the intervening years, but despite some victories and defeats, mainly in the fight against lynching and legal frame-ups, these demands remained controversial and largely sidelined. In 1940, Jim Crow was alive and well in the South and many other regions of America.

World War II and its aftermath changed all that. Under threat of a march on Washington by A. Phillip Randolph of the Sleeping Car Porters Union and other black leaders in 1941, President Roosevelt issued an executive order banning discrimination in defense industry hiring. When millions of black veterans returned from the war and found America had returned to business as usual even as the United States was embroiled in a cold war, claiming to be at the forefront of freedom and democracy, pressure mounted for a massive assault on discrimination and segregation. Shrewdly looking forward to an uphill reelection battle, President Harry Truman ordered the desegregation of the armed forces and the turbulent 1948 Democratic Convention passed the strongest civil rights plank of any party since the radical reconstruction laws of 1866. The Democratic Party consequently suffered the first of the defections of what became a long line of Southern political leaders when Strom Thurmond bolted and ran as the Dixecrat Party candidate for president. In the early 1950s, the NAACP mounted a series of legal cases against school segregation that culminated in the 1954 Supreme Court decision in *Brown v. Board of Education,* sustaining the plaintiffs' claim that the historic court doctrine of "separate but equal" was untenable. The Court agreed that school integration was the only way to guarantee equal education to black children. The next year, NAACP activist Rosa Parks refused to move to the back of a Montgomery, Alabama, bus, a disobedience that sparked a monumental boycott that finally ended in victory for the black community. In 1956, flanked by federal troops, James Meredith entered the University of Mississippi, and under similar circumstances, a black child, Autherine Lucy, broke the color bar in a Little Rock school.

As important as these breakthroughs were, they were regarded by some as only the first stage for what was considered to be the most important phase in the struggle, achieving black voting rights as a prelude to overturning white supremacist economic and political domination of the South. Many on both sides of the civil rights divide were convinced that the transformation of the South by ending black exclusion was the key to changing American politics. The struggle for voting rights proved as bloody as it was controversial because it threatened to reduce the Democratic Party to a permanent minority. In summer 1964, in the midst of a major effort by civil rights organizations to enroll thousands of new black voters, three field workers were murdered and many others were beaten, jailed, and in some cases forced to literally run for their lives. Fearing further losses in the less-than-solid South, the Kennedy administration had to be dragged kicking, if not screaming, to protect field workers of various civil rights groups. Indeed, beginning with the 1964 Republican presidential candidate Barry Goldwater and perfected to an art form by Richard Nixon, it may be argued that the key to Republican/conservative domination of national politics in the subsequent decades was the Right's infamous Southern Strategy. Driven by the exigencies of the Vietnam War as well as the wager that the Democrats could successfully cut their losses by winning the solid backing of millions of black and Latino voters, Lyndon Johnson's administration rapidly forced through Congress the Civil Rights and Voting Rights Acts. By 1965, a century of legally sanctioned black subordination apparently came to an end. The Democrats won black loyalty, which remains the irreducible condition of their ability to contend for national political power today.

Today, the predominant commentary on the state of race relations in the United States no longer focuses on discrimination but on the consequences of the economic and cultural chasm that separates black and white: white flight from the cities; the formation of a black middle class that, in pursuit of a better life, has tended to produce its own segregated suburban communities; and the persistence of black poverty. After more than three decades of "rights," the economic and cultural reality is that the separation between black and white has resurged with a vengeance. Housing segregation is perhaps more profound than in the pre–civil rights era; the tiering of the occupational structure still condemns a large percentage of blacks and Latinos to the bottom layer; and this combination has widened the educational gap that pro-integration advocates had hoped would be consigned to historical memory by now. In the wake of achievement of voting rights and antidiscrimination laws, some now worry more about whether blacks will maintain access to the elites of American society, especially in education and the economy. Others have discovered that, despite their confidence that legal rights are secure, the stigma of race remains the unmeltable condition of the black social and economic situation.

Even voting rights are in jeopardy. What are we to make of the spectacle of mob intimidation of election officials and the brazen theft of perhaps forty-five thousand black votes in Florida during the 2000 presidential election? Or the ideological and political mobilization of a conservative Supreme Court majority to halt the ballot recount of George W. Bush's razor-thin lead? Or the refusal of a single member of the United States Senate, fifty of whom are white Democrats, to join mainly black House members in requesting an investigation of the Florida voting events? Vincent Bugliosi has persuasively shown that Gore's lawyer did not use the best arguments to the Court.[1] And then there's the congressional battle over George W. Bush's nomination of John Ashcroft as attorney general, during which Ted Kennedy concluded that he could not muster the votes to sustain a filibuster and had to be content with joining forty-one of his colleagues in a largely symbolic protest vote against Ashcroft's confirmation.

Ashcroft's nomination was perhaps the Bush presidency's blatant reminder that the selection of Condoleezza Rice and Colin Powell to lead foreign policy positions should not be understood as having any relevance to the administration's stance on domestic racial politics. Contrary to progressives' expectation that the Democratic Party would constitute a genuine opposition to what has become a fairly strident right-wing government (as the events since November 7 have amply demonstrated), the Democrats seem to know their place.

These calumnies cast suspicion on the easy assumption that the civil rights struggle, even its legal aspect, largely ended in 1965. The deliberate denial of black suffrage in Florida was a statement by the Republican minority that it would not countenance the bold maneuver of the Gore campaign, in alliance with the AFL-CIO and the NAACP, to register and turn out tens of thousands of new black and non-Cuban Latino voters. As if to acknowledge his indiscretion, after it became clear that he "wuz robbed," Gore ordered his supporters not to take to the streets but, instead, contented himself with a weak and ultimately unsuccessful series of legal moves to undo the theft. Even if their hopes for victory always depended on blacks showing up at the polls in the battleground states, including Florida, Gore and the Democratic Party proved unwilling to fight fire with fire. In the end, the Right believes it has a royal right to political power because it is grounded in the power of big capital and in the legacy of racism; the Democrats believe, in their hearts, they are somehow illegitimate because of their dependence on blacks and organized labor.

Yet inspired by the notion that the United States is a nation of laws, some writers have interpreted the 1960s judicial and legislative gains to mean that the basis had been laid for full equality of opportunity for blacks, Latinos, and other oppressed groups. They cite affirmative action as evidence that blacks may be able to attain places in the commanding heights of corporate office, if not power—but they forget that Richard Nixon initiated affirmative action to derail efforts, inspired by the 1960s civil rights victories, to dramatically expand funding for education and other public goods. In the context of Nixon's abrogation of the Bretton Woods agreement, which destabilized world currencies and the restructuring the world's economy in the direction of massive third world investment and capital flight, affirmative action was the fig leaf covering the downsizing of the welfare state. As the political winds blew rightward, welfare "reform" became the mantra for his successors, from Jimmy Carter and Ronald Reagan through Bill Clinton. Needless to say, providing spaces for black students in a handful of elite colleges and universities was not, in itself, a bad idea. Affirmative action accompanied the Reagan tax cuts, ballooning military spending, and the gradual end of an income floor for the unemployed; severe spending cuts in housing, public health, and education demonstrated its purpose: to

expand the black professional and managerial class in the wake of deindustrialization, which left millions of industrial workers, many of them black and
Latino, stranded, and the hollowing out of the welfare state that, in contrast to
the gains of the 1960s, widened the gap between rich and poor.

If only the most naïve believed that racism would disappear in time, many
have misread William Julius Wilson's 1984 book, *The Declining Significance of
Race,* to argue that black inequality is not a sign of the persistence of institutional or structural racism, but is a remnant.[2] On the contrary, Wilson's claim is
that the persistence of black poverty may not be a sign of discrimination in the
old sense but an indication of the vulnerability of blacks to structural changes in
the economy. Race still frames the fate of many blacks, but there is also a crucial
class dimension to their social situation. Despite the acquisition by blacks of
comprehensive legal rights, deindustrialization of many large cities and black as
well as white middle-class flight has left working-class blacks in the lurch. Once,
many had well-paid union jobs in steel mills, auto plants, and other production
industries. Since the mid-1970s, most urban and rural areas where they live are
bereft of good jobs and local services. There are not enough jobs to go around
and those that are available are McJobs, service employment at or near the minimum wage; cities lack the tax base to provide citizens with decent education,
recreation, housing, and health facilities, and basic infrastructural needs such as
clean air and water. Lacking skills, many blacks are stuck in segregated ghettoes
without decent jobs, viable schools, hope, or options. To make things worse, the
neoliberal policies of both Democratic and Republican governments that dras-
tically slow public sector job growth have eliminated one of the main sources of
economic stability for blacks and Latinos. In fact, during his campaign, Al Gore
boasted that he was the architect of the Clinton administration's program of
streamlining the federal government through layoffs and attrition, an achievement that was undertaken to facilitate "paying down the debt." The private sector was expected to pick up the slack and it did. In many cases, laid-off public
employees joined unemployed industrial workers in low-paid construction,
nonunion factory jobs, or in retail trades.

The problems associated with race and class fail to detain some writers.
Having stipulated black economic progress without examining this claim in any
depth, their main concern is how to assure that blacks obtain places in the intellectual and managerial elites. As if to stress the urgency of this problem, they
adduce evidence showing that despite the broad application of affirmative
action, blacks have fallen back in educational attainment. For example, while
celebrating the civil rights movement's achievements, in his book about the
question of why black students still lag behind whites in educational attainment,
linguistics professor John W. McWhorter discounts the salience of racism.[3]

McWhorter allows that there remain some police brutality and discriminatory practices such as racial profiling, but believes these regrettable throwbacks are being eradicated. Accepting the federal government's definition of poverty ($20,000 a year or less for a household of four), McWhorter minimizes these problems by citing statistics showing that only 25 percent of America's black population lives in impoverished conditions in the inner cities, a decline from 40 percent in 1960. Of course, these federal standards have been severely criticized by liberal economists and activists for understating what people actually need to live in some of America's major cities.

Although $20,000 may constitute a realistic minimum standard in some rural areas and small towns (and even then there is considerable dispute about this figure), anyone living in New York, Chicago, Los Angeles, Philadelphia, Detroit, Oakland, Washington, or Atlanta (all cities with large black, Latino, and Asian populations) knows that this income is far below what people need to live. The United Way's regional survey of living standards found that households of *three* anywhere in New York City require at least $45,000 to meet minimum decent standards. While the amounts are less for other cities, in no case are they below $25,000 and most are higher. In many of these cities, two-bedroom apartments without utilities cannot be rented for less than $800 a month (add at least $100 for telephone, gas, and electricity), more than half the take-home pay of a household earning $25,000. In New York City, the rent is closer to $1,200, even in the far reaches of the Bronx and Brooklyn. Since median household income is about $35,000 a year for the whole population, many Americans—white as well as black—find themselves struggling to make it. Perhaps half of black households earn less than $40,000, the rock-bottom comfort level in most areas today.

None of this bothers McWhorter and other black centrists and conservatives. They know that when measured by grades and standardized tests, educational attainment among children of poor black families may fall short for reasons of poverty, insecurity, and broken homes. Why, they ask, do black students in the middle class perform consistently worse by every measure than comparable white students, even when, owing mainly to affirmative action, they gain admission to elite colleges and universities? Relying heavily on anecdotes drawn from his own teaching experience at UC-Berkeley, McWhorter advances the thesis that, across the class system, blacks are afflicted by three cultural barriers to higher educational attainment that are of their own making: victimology, according to which all blacks suffer from the racism that stands between them and success; separatism, a congenital suspicion of whites and of white norms, including high educational achievement; and, perhaps most salient of all, endemic anti-intellectualism among blacks, which regards those who study hard and care about learning as "nerds" and tends to hold them in contempt. To be "cool" is to slide by rather than doing well. The point of higher education is to obtain a credential that qualifies one for a good job, not to take academic learning seriously.

McWhorter is deeply embarrassed by the studied indifference of many of his black students (almost none of whom is economically disadvantaged) for intellectual pursuits and is equally disturbed by their low grades and inferior scores on tests. In the end, he attributes much of the problem to affirmative action—a "necessary first step"—but which he believes ultimately degrades blacks in the eyes of white society. McWhorter admits that he is troubled that he got tenure in four and a half years instead of the usual seven and that he was privileged in part because he was black. Like another "affirmative action baby" Stephen Carter, he is grateful for the boost but believes the door should be closed behind him because the policy has morally objectionable consequences, especially cynicism, the examples of which litter the pages of his book. Instead, he wants blacks "to spread their wings and compete" with others on an equal basis. Condemning the thesis of Richard Herrnstein and Charles Murray that affirmative action should be eliminated because blacks "are too dumb," at the same time he urges his readers to "combat anti-intellectualism" and victimology as cultural norms.

Before I discuss what I regard as the serious flaws in McWhorter's thesis, it is important to note that his feelings are by no means unique among a growing number of black as well as white pro–civil rights intellectuals. Having asserted that legislative and court victories effectively buried the "external" barriers to black advancement, these critics seek answers to the persistence of the racial educational disparity within the black community itself, particularly the "culture" of victimization, a culture that, however anachronistic from an objective standpoint, remains a powerful force. Unlike many black conservatives, McWhorter professes admiration for the icons of the civil rights struggle, especially Martin Luther King Jr. and Adam Clayton Powell Jr. He is not alone in possessing an uncritical assessment of the last half century as an era of black "progress." As a result, he discounts the idea that racism remains a structural barrier to blacks' further advances. Nor is there justification for the politics and culture of separatism; for McWhorter, blacks are shooting themselves in the foot because these values prevent them from overcoming the psychological and cultural legacy of slavery, the root cause of an anti-intellectualism that thwarts black students from performing well in an academic environment. This culture, he argues, is reproduced as well in the black family when parents refuse to take their children's failing or low grades as an occasion for scolding or punishment, and in the extreme peer pressure against the few kids who, as early as elementary school, are good scholars.

Academically bright black kids are ridiculed, called "nerd," and if the habit of scholarship persists, are charged with not being cool and loyal to the "race."

We have seen this pattern played out in a somewhat different mode among working-class white high school students. In his study, *Learning to Labor*, of male working-class students in an English comprehensive high school—the term that corresponds to our public schools—Paul Willis describes how the "lads" rebel against the curriculum and other forms of school authority and thereby prepare themselves for "working-class jobs" in a nearby car factory.[4] We can see in this and many other school experiences the same phenomena that McWhorter ascribes to racial culture. To study and achieve high enough grades to obtain a place in university is to betray the class and its traditions. One risks isolation from one's comrades for daring to be good. It is not merely anti-intellectualism that produces such behavior, it is a specific form of solidarity which violates the prevailing norm that the key to economic success for the individual working-class kid is educational attainment.

As a certified good student who, by his own account, suffered many of these indignities at the hands of classmates, this is beyond McWhorter's grasp. Since he sees no external barriers, anyone who refuses to succeed when he or she has been afforded the opportunity without really trying must be the prisoner of a retrograde culture. Since he defines anti-intellectualism in terms of comparative school performances in relation to whites, and there is no exploration of the concept of intellectual endeavor as such, he must avoid entering the territory of rampant American anti-intellectualism. It may come as a shock to some, but it can plausibly be claimed that we—whites, blacks, and everyone else—live in an anti-intellectual culture. Those who entertain ideas that have no apparent practical utility, enjoy reading books without being required by course assignment, play or listen to "classical" European or jazz music, or attend art museums on their own are sometimes labeled Mr. or Ms. Deadbrain. Moreover, as many have observed, the public intellectual—a person of ideas whose task is to hold a mirror to society and criticize it—is an endangered species in this country. McWhorter focuses absolutely no attention on the loss of intellectual life in this sense. His idea of intellectualism is entirely framed by conventional technical intelligence and by a sense of shame that blacks are coded as intellectually inferior. There is little justification of the life of the mind in *Losing the Race* except as a valuable career tool. McWhorter cares about educational attainment as a matter of racial pride and climbing the ladder. He cannot imagine that working-class and middle-class whites are routinely discouraged from spending their time in "useless" intellectual pursuits or that the disparity between black, Latino, Asian, and white school performances can be attributed to anything other than internal cultural deficits.

2

Scott Malcomson and Thomas Holt have cast different lights on race disparity in the post–civil rights era. Departing, but only implicitly from Tocqueville's delineation of the three races of American society—Indian, Black, and White—Malcomson, a freelance writer and journalist, offers a long, sometimes rambling history, fascinating autobiography, and social analysis of the career of race in America.[5] The main historical theme is that racial separatism is interwoven with virtually every aspect of American life from the sixteenth-century European explorations and conquest that led to the brutal massacres of Native Americans, slavery, and post-emancipation race relations. Malcomson's story is nothing less than a chronicle of the defeat of the ideal of one race and one nation. Black, Native American, and white remain throughout the centuries as races apart. Neither civil war, social movements, nor legislative change has succeeded in overcoming the fundamental pattern of white domination and the racializing of others. Nor has territorial and economic expansion allayed separatism and differential, racially burdened access to economic and political power.

Malcomson, the son of a white Protestant minister and civil rights activist, caps the book with a hundred-page memoir of his childhood and youth in the 1960s in Oakland, California. In these pages, the most original part of the book, Malcomson offers an affecting account of his own experience with race but also renders the history of three major twentieth-century Oakland celebrities, Jack London, William Knowland, and Bobby Seale and the Black Panthers. London was, of course, one of America' leading writers of the first two decades of the last century. He was famous not only for his adventure stories, which captured the imagination of millions of young adults and their parents as well, but also for his radical politics. He was a founder of the Intercollegiate Socialist Society, the student branch of a once-vibrant Socialist Party that, in California, regularly won local offices until World War I, and spawned the explosive political career of another writer, Upton Sinclair, who became the Democratic candidate for governor in 1934. Less well known was London's flaming racism, a sentiment shared by the archconservative *Tribune* publisher and later United States Senator, William Knowland. Deeply influenced by his parents' antiracist politics, Malcomson was enthralled by the movement and especially by the Panthers, whose ubiquitous presence in Oakland was unusual, even in their period of fame. But the pathos of his involvement is that his main reference group was neither black nor white: their separation was simply too painful for a young idealist to bear. Instead he hung out with a group of Asian students who, nevertheless, emulated black cultural mores. They did well in school but by this account nothing much except social life went on there. To satisfy his intellectual appetites, Malcomson sought refuge in extracurricular reading, an experience that I shared in my own high school days in the largely Jewish and Italian East Bronx of the 1940s and 1950s.

The point of the memoir is to provide a contemporary illustration of the red thread that runs through his book: the promise of a century and a half of struggle for black freedom, and especially of the end of racial separation and of racism that remains unfulfilled. Malcomson takes Oakland as a paradigmatic instance of a majority black population gaining political office but little power because the city's white economic elites simply refused to play, until civic disruption forced them (especially Knowland) to acknowledge that their power was threatened by the militancy of new political forces within the black community. With the waning of black power, like many other cities, Oakland reverted to its ghettoes, punctuated in the 1980s and 1990s by a wave of gentrification that threatened the fragile black neighborhoods and, in the wake of high rents, forced many to leave for cheaper quarters. As Malcomson returned home in the late 1990s after a few decades in New York, he found that the experiment of his late father and a local black preacher in interracial unity on behalf of community renewal had collapsed, leaving the clergyman with little hope but a firm conviction that since whites were unreliable allies, blacks had no alternative but to address the devastation of black neighborhoods alone.

Thomas Holt is a black University of Chicago social and cultural historian whose major work, *The Problem of Freedom,* is a brilliant multifaceted account of Jamaican race, labor, and politics in the nineteenth and early twentieth centuries.[6] The question he asks in his latest book-length essay is whether W. E. B. DuBois's comment that the color line is the problem of the twentieth century remains the main question for our century.[7] Holt addresses the issue from a global perspective on two axes: to place race in the context of both the national and global economies, and to adopt a "global" theoretical framework of analysis that situates race historically in terms of the transformations of production regimes from early to late capitalism. In bold but sharp strokes, the book outlines three stages based on the overarching concept of Fordism: pre-Fordism, Fordism and post-Fordism.

Fordism was more than a production system based on a continuously moving assembly line where workers performed repetitive tasks. The "ism" in the term signifies that mass production and mass consumption are locked in an ineluctable embrace: if the line makes possible mass production, ways must be found to provide for mass consumption. Fordism therefore entails the formation of a new consumer by means of raising wages but mainly by the vast expansion of the credit system. Now workers could buy cars, houses, and appliances, even send their kids to college on the principle of "buy now, pay later." This practical consideration led to a different conception of modernity. The advent of consumer society has changed the face of America and the rest of the capitalist world. Before Fordism, what Holt terms "pre-Fordism," the American economy was crucially dependent on slavery. Blacks were at the core of both the pre-Fordism and Fordism production regimes, whatever their egregious moral and ethical features. In the slave and post-Reconstruction eras, they planted and picked cotton and tobacco; during and after World War II, they were recruited into the vast network of industrial plants as unskilled and semiskilled labor. Indeed, they shared in the cornucopia of consumer society, owned late model cars and single-family homes, and in some instances, were able to send their kids to college. As Holt points out, exploitative as these relationships were, blacks occupied central places in American economic life.

The 1970s witnessed the restructure of world capitalism: the victories of the labor movement prompted capital to seek cheaper labor abroad, and cities like Detroit, Cleveland, New York, Oakland, and Chicago, where black workers constituted a significant proportion of the manufacturing labor force, were rapidly deindustrialized. In their place were not only retail establishments but a "new economy" consisting of computer-mediated industries such as hardware and software production, the "dot.coms," and financial services. The reindustrialization of the 1980s and 1990s occurred without the participation of blacks. In industries marked by the old technologies, hundreds of thousands of immigrants made garments, toys, and other consumer goods. Lacking capital, African Americans could not own the retail businesses in their own communities; these are largely owned by immigrants—Korean, Indian, Caribbean, and African merchants. Holt argues that American blacks are now largely excluded from the global economy; they occupy economic niches that are no longer at the center of production, positions that augur badly for the future of race in America. Even the growing black middle class located in the public sector since the 1980s is under severe attack. Moreover, he plainly rejects the judgment of "black progress" which leads to cultural explanations for the growing economic and social disparity between blacks and whites. Holt finds

> overwhelming contemporary evidence that racism permeates every institution, every pore of everyday life. Justice in our courts, earnings on our jobs, whether we have a job at all, the quality of our life, the means and timing of our death—all form the stacked deck every child born black must take up to play the game of life.[8]

Holt's essay ends with the faint hope that racial stigma and segregation may one day be overcome. For now, he insists, race remains—for all African Americans and not only those suffering the deprivations of ghetto life—the problem of the twenty-first century. But neither Malcomson nor Holt can find sources of resistance. In fact, Holt explicitly gives up on the labor movement—a prime mover within the Fordist regime. It has been severely weakened by post-Fordist globalization. Nor does he identify forces within the African American movements capable of leading a fight. Like other sharp critics of racism, such as Paul Gilroy, he finds that despair overwhelms hope.

Americans are always alert to the quick fix, so the concept that judicial and legislative prohibitions against discrimination are sufficient to erase the legacy of four centuries of social and economic oppression is deeply embedded in the American imagination. From this view follows the inevitable conclusion that if income and social disparities stubbornly refuse to go away, something must be wrong with the victim. Thus the tricky and misleading term "culture" as an explanation segues into proposals that blacks "pull up their socks" and reach for the main chance. Those who are passionate in their insistence that the elimination of the structurally induced racial divide will require a monumental struggle have hesitated before the gateway of class politics. For those like Holt and Malcomson who are less concerned with whether blacks enter corporate board rooms than with raising the bottom, there is little alternative to calling on the power of the labor movement to join the fray. It might be argued that organized labor, still dominated by a relatively conservative white leadership, has shown little inclination to mount a fierce defense of black interests. But as unions lose their traditional white blue-collar base, the labor movement is becoming more black and Latino, and certainly more female. As its constituency is transformed, there are signs that the top leadership is learning a few lessons. The AFL-CIO's 2000 call for a presidential pardon for undocumented immigrants was a move without historic precedent and its attempt to organize low-wage workers is a reversal of past practice. If race remains a central problem of the new century, the way forward is probably to reestablish the race/class alliance that fell on hard times in the 1960s and 1970s. Without it, black freedom is confined to a cry in the darkness.

10

BETWEEN NATIONALITY
AND CLASS

On the eve of the first anniversary of the astounding Million Man March, the journal *Black Renaissance* commemorated the event with a special section that, among other articles, contained a reporter's account and reflection on the significance of the march. Like many black intellectuals and liberals, author David Dent admitted his own skepticism; as he traveled from Hempstead, New York, on a bus filled with marchers, his doubts about participating in an event organized by Louis Farrakhan began to dissolve. Although the event was by no means a repeat of the great 1941 and 1963 marches, which focused on discrimination and political freedom, the talk on the bus concentrated on self-help, black economic development, and education.

> In many ways the March was a large-scale protraction of the tendency of African Americans in the nineties to create new cultural spaces where freedom and individuality can thrive independently of the baggage of race and racism. In this respect the March inadvertently created a new sense of redefining black maleness in popular and broad enough terms to reflect the reality and diversity of black America.[1]

The burden of Dent's report covered the bulk of the participants in the march: those who drove "Lexuses, Hondas, Mercedes, Tauruses" as well as those who rode buses and trains and were part of the growing black middle class and the better-paid workers. Dent's own term "African American" is an indicator that many in the community are eager to overcome the "otherness" that has plagued blacks for centuries. They want cultural affirmation in distinctly *American* terms, a validation that can be purchased only by enunciations such as self-help, individuality, and education. Indeed, the incredible response to Farrakhan's call for a convocation towards a new definition of black manhood may be understood as a movement from race to ethnicity among a considerable section of blacks. Its key words are "diversity" rather than "difference," "individuality" and not collective struggle, not "rights" but "self-help." The massive response to the march and especially to these key words indicated that many blacks were eager to adopt identities which marked them, for example, like Polish Americans or Jewish Americans rather than with the single terms "Latino," "black," "Haitian," and other diasporic significations.

Far from the confrontational style for which Farrakhan and the Black Muslims are famous, the march ratified the cardinal achievement of the black freedom movement in the twentieth century: it forced government and large corporations to provide jobs and, equally importantly, the opportunity for millions of blacks to achieve one of the crucial components of the American Dream—climbing out of poverty into (mainly) the salaried middle class. His voice dripping with irony, reggae singer Jimmy Cliff made fun of this possibility and even the desire that underlaid it, but there was no irony in the lovefest that marked the Million Man March. Even as conservative politicians, marching to the drumbeat of corporate demands for lower taxes and therefore budget cutting, adopted a slash-and-burn policy towards the public sector—a bastion of black achievement—and employers abolished many well-paid black factory jobs through technology and plant closings, the nineties were a time when the gap between the black poor and the black middle class approached canyon-like proportions. While annual incomes for the black poor have declined by 25 percent in the last decade, when measured by income criteria, the black middle class has grown in the same period from 12 percent of the black population to 15 percent. For most black women and men, the last decade has been an unmitigated disaster; for the ambitious and otherwise fortunate 15 percent, times have never been better. Such are the ambiguities of American life.

Ethnicity and American Culture

American ideology contains two principal elements: first, America is believed to confer equality of opportunity to each individual citizen even as it punishes many, such as immigrants of all descriptions who have not (yet) attained citizenship in the economic as well as political meaning of the status. The second is that, unlike other advanced industrial societies, America has no distinct classes or, in its more refined phrase, is an "open society." While some politicians and social scientists acknowledge the persistence of the color line in American life, the United States has no distinct class lines. A leading presidential contender even blurted during the 1996 campaign that the United States was classless. That conditions of birth do not determine the economic and social fate for many whites and some racial minorities is offered as proof that America is the great exception to the general rule that social class is destiny. In this paradigm of virtually unlimited opportunity, she who keeps her nose to the grindstone by working, especially to earn educational credentials, will eventually "make it" into the (salaried) middle class. In this narrative, the task of affording racial minorities and women the same chances to escape the working class as those enjoyed by white men defines a political goal that, since the Civil Rights Act of 1964, is well on the way to fulfillment.

In achieving social mobility, no institution plays a more important role than higher education. Since the emergence of the "new" middle class—salaried professional, technical, and managerial employees rather than self-employed entrepreneurs—colleges and universities provide the crucial rites of passage to the salariat more than any other institution in American society. But the centrality of postsecondary credentials for erecting the architectonic of mobility is not a force of nature. Although many advanced capitalist societies in Europe and Japan have significant systems of postsecondary education, the proportion of adult populations attending these institutions is far less than in the United States. Sixty-two percent of high school graduates enter college. With nearly fifteen million students, one of nine Americans under age sixty-five attends some sort of postsecondary school; half of them attend four-year colleges and universities and half are in community colleges. In contrast, European higher educational systems and those of Japan are far more restrictive: France, Germany, and the United Kingdom have fewer than a quarter of high school graduates in universities, and the extent of their total adult population in higher education is less than 5 percent. In 1995, the United States had more than 3,200 higher education schools, more than double the pre–World War II number, 70 percent of which were in the public sector. Europe and Japan have had a substantial growth but not nearly to the same extent as the United States.

A college or university degree does not guarantee a job, let alone a career, but it has become the premier sign that informs employers and other educational institutions that the candidate has endured a regime that on balance assures reliability. One may not acquire a set of job-ready skills in any educational institution except those, such as medicine and social work, whose curriculum includes on-the-job training as much as classroom instruction. The credential signifies the student's mobility aspiration, especially an ability to endure a long journey toward an indefinite conclusion, and a capacity to tolerate boredom. These, more than any specific content, are crucial job and educational skills. The "hidden" curriculum of schooling, including that of college, is that the student is willing to jump through hurdles without a definite employment outcome.

Since we have no antagonistic classes and competing political ideologies corresponding to a fundamental divide in society, the polity is said to act on the basis of consensus, which amounts to the statement that people make decisions on the basis of the generally agreed-upon national interest. Although Americans may differ with one another concerning economic and social policy and may form distinct political parties, on the whole they agree on the underlying free-market, capitalist framework of social arrangements. Among other things, this agreement presupposes the historic success of assimilation of immigrant groups to a common ground of values and beliefs. America is a land of immigrants and thus technically plural; in the felicitous phrase of the early twentieth-century Jewish poet and novelist Israel Zangwill, it is said to be a great "melting pot." Whatever one's background in the old country, the scions of immigrants are fully American in culture, politics, and religion by the second generation. According to this litany, individualism and consensus are so pervasive that whether the immigrant generation spoke German, Polish, or Greek, their children will speak English; folk culture may be displayed during holidays but is routinely ignored for the rest of the year; Granddad may have been a flaming socialist or anarchist, but, whatever their private sentiments, his grandchildren are persuaded that free-market capitalism and the American system of liberal democracy represent the best of all possible worlds.

Whether you are black or white, America is a deeply religious country whose people and morality are firmly planted in the Judeo-Christian tradition of the Ten Commandments and of One God. Others may practice their non-Western forms of worship, but these religions are considered to be leftovers of a bygone age. Although practitioners of Muslim or Buddhist faiths, for instance, may not convert to the dominant religions, they are usually obliged to observe the tenets of the dominant ideology in nearly every other respect—especially in business and education.

A corollary to the American consensus is the conception of public life as essentially white and male. The consensual society may, indeed, engage in the nefarious practice of exclusion, but such practices are contrary to its precept of integration and of equal opportunity. Even among those who discriminate on the basis of race or gender, many admit that law and custom must be changed to permit the excluded to enter into public life. Perhaps the most vivid example of this contradictory behavior is affirmative action. Acknowledging discrimination, institutions such as corporations and government agencies have put in place set-asides, quotas, and other programs to admit *some* minorities and women. The conditions for entrance are that one must accept a definite series of precondi-tions, the violation of which disqualifies the candidate from participation. Among them, none ranks higher than civility. American ideology disdains rancor and other indications of social division. Strikes, demonstrations, and other forms of "in-your-face" political protest violate the precept that in America we have orderly ways to resolve the temporary conflicts arising from (mostly) misunder-standings. Genuine conflicts are subject to democratic processes—such as legal remedies, legislation, and electoral resolutions—that preclude direct action.

Consensually, Americans believe blacks and women should be nominated and elected to public office and gain access to the leading professions—law, the professoriat, medicine, and the sciences, and that their interests and complaints should be granted a hearing in the corridors of power and under law. There is no question of recognizing the validity of counter or oppositional discursive practices and rules that not only differ from but contradict those of the domi-nant group. Thus, the debate about ebonics turns crucially on whether blacks accept Standard English as normative. Educational leaders and politicians have tolerance for the "other" as long as the other recognizes the practices of the dominant group as those to which all others must strive, regardless of the path they may take to achieve them. The task for society remains that of assimilating potential or actual dissent into a prescribed public sphere whose values remain unchanged, even as it makes room for new groups to join the American cele-bration in culture as well as politics and economics.

For example, jazz may be classified as America's "classical" music, a desig-nation that qualifies it to be performed at New York's Lincoln Center. This and other classical venues may display its virtues, which plants it firmly in the Western, high-cultural tradition. In this framework, Charlie Parker, Thelonius Monk, and John Coltrane are doing no more but no less than what we might expect of any twentieth-century composer, say, Stravinsky or Schoenberg. The novels of Richard Wright and Toni Morrison may be coded as "literature" and receive high awards, and some of the outpouring of women's fiction may be rec-ognized among the legitimate heirs to the traditional canon, but these works must be measured by the degree to which they correspond to that which is rec-ognized as high art. What has been coded as popular culture—rock 'n roll, hip-hop, heavy metal, alternative music, and all genres of television, except some of the products of public television—are distinctly low forms and have no place in the legitimate public sphere. In fact, they are subject in some circles to pro-scription if conventional morality deems them unfit for minors or even for adults. Finally, as art critic Senator Jesse Helms has remarked, every artist has the *right* to paint or write what he or she pleases—but the "American people" have no obligation to *fund* smut or radical ideas.

A New Concept of Ethnicity

What I want to call the "new" ethnicity arises on the ruins of nationhood. The term "Americanism" has been invoked to remind the millions of immigrants who have arrived on America's shores since 1880 that they may retain their cultural old-world identities but must shed their political and social allegiances of the past. Although such reminders retain their power among some, our collective sense of nationality is, to say the least, in crisis. Since the 1960s revealed the depth of difference in the America people, ethnicity is one of the names invoked to describe and explain what American ideology has denied: that difference may signify more than benign diversity and that it may signal conflict, especially when compared with the ideal of assimilation. Ethnicity has become ubiquitous in public conversation, but its boundaries have proven elusive to most investigators. W. Lloyd Warner's attempt in his 1949 book, *Social Class in America,* to introduce ethnicity, alongside class, as an important designation of individual and group identity as well as group and individual interest was largely ignored in the shadow of the Great Depression when the class divide was very hard to ignore.[2] Ethnicity reemerged in the wake of the postwar boom when Americans discovered both the possibilities of social and class mobility and its limitations. By the 1970s when, in pursuit of opportunity, an unprecedented half of high school graduates enrolled in the public institutions of postsecondary education, many found that—however necessary—a degree was not sufficient to achieve genuine social mobility—that is, the ability to move between classes and strata. Since in the conventional account there can be no structural job shortages, many began to ascribe their unexpected fate to the stigma of ethnic identity rather than to the end of economic expansion. Perceiving an alarming market glut for qualified labor, newly minted recipients of advanced degrees cast about for additional weapons to break open barriers to employment. For example, the difficulty a female Ph.D. in physics might experience getting a job may be ascribed to sexism as much as job shortages, or the fabled "glass ceiling" in corporations might prevent many women and minorities from rising to the middle or even to the top of managerial ranks. Some social scientists and civil rights activists grasped the significance of the degree hierarchy: we have equal opportunity, but some opportunity is more equal. Women and minorities sought to reach beyond the third-tier colleges and universities to gain admission to elite schools. In turn, ethnicity became a weapon of criticism of the prevailing state of affairs and was eagerly grasped by employers—public and private, as well as university and college administrators—as a new criterion for inclusion.

The *Oxford English Dictionary*'s definition of ethnicity, "a people or a nation," seems to have been transmuted in the literature.[3] Social scientists such as Nathan Glazer and Daniel Patrick Moynihan have identified ethnicity within almost any subculture. It stands between the nation and the individual as the embodiment of group identity but has no necessary implication that member-ship need have more than cultural consequences—that is, it has implications for explaining political and social behavior. Its emergence as a social category may be ascribed to the vicissitudes of assimilation under conditions where, differen-tially by national origin, a fair number of whites appeared to have transcended their collective conditions of birth but many blacks, Latinos, and women were left behind. In the 1960s, some white "ethnics" began to emulate their ancestors by forming job networks, and Italians and Poles discovered their civil rights had been abrogated by educational and employment discrimination and subse-quently formed associations to remedy their condition of deprivation.

Except for turn-of-the-century labor turmoil and the Great Depression of the 1930s, class discourse has never enjoyed much currency in America. During the long wave of U.S. economic expansion for Eastern and Southern Europeans—Jews and Christians alike—ethnicity as an occasion for economic, political, or cultural deprivation has been generally viewed as a temporary con-dition on the way to assimilation. The current reappearance of ethnicity may be explained by the shift by the labor movement away from class to interest group or associational discourse in the post–World War II era. After the war, organized labor abandoned its brief depression-period claim to identify labor's interests with the national or general interest and to its leadership of the entire working class. As labor retreated from its short-lived bid for cultural and political hege-mony, it left space for new discursive practices that could embody discontent. Responding invidiously to the apparent successes of the black freedom move-ment of the late 1960s, white ethnicity displaced the politics and culture of class during the 1970s when many groups of white industrial and service workers experienced a relative erosion of their living standards and social power. In major production industries, wage increases slowed and barely kept up with inflation; some nonunion production workers and service employees actually fell behind the inflation rate. On the whole, in the 1970s and 1980s, average real wages fell 20 percent, and the trend continued into the early 1990s in the wake of the 1987–1992 recession. At the same time, the appearance of ethnic dis-course among blacks and other racial minorities signaled the emergence of a new subaltern middle class for which "black" racial identity had become too confrontational with a social system within which it wanted to rise.

The 1950s were the years when trade unions seemed to shift from their depression-bred perspective of speaking for all working people to a return to the job-conscious, membership-based orientation of the older craft or business unionism against which industrial unions had rebelled. Industrial workers, once the epitome of an insurgent working class, were rapidly retreating from the public sphere to the quasi-corporatist security of the labor agreement. As plants moved from the center cities to the suburbs and as federally funded highway programs littered the geography, many war veterans were the beneficiaries of federal loan programs to assist them to move with the plant into one-family homes. To outward appearances, these workers—many of whom were highly paid—never looked back at the cities where black and Latino majorities were left to work in low-paid service industries and small factories—or, in growing numbers, were becoming permanently unemployed. Under these circumstances, to speak the vocabularies of class appeared anachronistic. From the perspective of consumer society, industrial workers—most of whom had few educational credentials—seemed to have joined the middle class. The workers in leading industrial corporations such as General Motors, General Electric, and Boeing, for example, were bringing home pay equivalent to or higher than that of most teachers, nurses, and social workers and equivalent to that of engineers and many professors. Race and gender appeared to have permanently displaced class as a negative signifier in political and economic terms.

Twenty years later, many of these workers were facing unemployment and underemployment due to technological displacement or as employers closed older industrial plants and moved to the American South or overseas. Unions, which had established the private welfare state through the union contract, negotiated away many of these benefits (such as fully paid health care and steadily rising paid holidays and paid vacations) in hopes of hanging on to workers' jobs. During the 1980s, according to Barry Bluestone and Bennett Harrison's calculations in *The Deindustrialization of America,* half of the best industrial jobs disappeared.[4] Many white workers rediscovered their ethnic ties and instead of turning toward the politics of class solidarity blamed blacks and women who, they perceived, were the real culprits causing their pain. During this period, once-militant industrial unions were conceding to employers the hard-won gains and, in their tribute to the rule of law, at almost every turn opposed rank-and-file resistance.

Accordingly, although the American ideology seems unshaken—most still believe they can "make it" if they really try—political scientists and sociologists claim people have increasingly discovered that their economic and political interests as well as their cultural sentiments may be expressed through the formation of ethnic blocs rather than through class affiliation. While in the first half of the twentieth-century ethnicity was regarded as a cultural identity that, nevertheless, did not disturb the progress of assimilation, by the 1960s it had become increasingly evident that ethnicity was the designation that expressed discontent as well as hope, and its emergence spurred a new debate.

Ethnicity and Class

Whether, as some have argued, ethnicity is a "myth" or merely "symbolic" or whether its emergence has genuine practical effects on politics, especially cultural politics, there is no doubt that for the last thirty years there is a new ethnic "question" that occupies both journalism and scholarship. The lines are drawn in two ways: In *Ethnicity*, Nathan Glazer, Daniel Patrick Moynihan, and Daniel Bell argued that ethnicity displaced class because in Bell's terms it combined interest with the "affective tie," while class as the repository of interest remained locked into the instrumental rationality of interest.[5] In a society where class lines are progressively blurred by the capacity of American capitalism to respond to demands on it from the margins and by education, while it has not disappeared, class seems to have declined together with Bell's celebrated "end of ideology." Others writing in the same anthology, such as Herbert Gans, for example, grant symbolic significance to ethnicity but find little or no evidence that ethnicity has retained the powerful political and social influence it possessed among first-generation immigrants. Perhaps with the exception of Chicago and a few smaller cities, the urban political machines have, in the main, broken down. Even when blacks have captured City Hall, they have been unable to consolidate power, as the experiences of New York, Cleveland, and Los Angeles demonstrate.

In the wake of the partial breakdown of nationality's ability to sustain consensus and class's inability to offer an alternative basis for solidarity, ethnicity refers instead to a subjective feeling of pride. Like Gans, Steven Steinberg in *The Ethnic Myth* finds assimilation remains the dominant mode of integration of the American population.[6] For Steinberg, the vagaries of assimilation may be ascribed to the persistence of the class system, of which racial oppression is an important part, rather than ethnicity. In his systematic refutation of the salience of ethnicity to such established modes of assimilation as education and work, Steinberg argued against "culturalist" explanations of why some groups attain levels of educational and occupational achievement disproportionate to their representation in the general population. For example, contrary to the widely accepted belief that the reason Jews are stunningly successful in the professions and in education is their traditional "love of learning," Steinberg showed that most immigrant groups have similar sentiments that have deep roots in their culture. Although most immigrant groups recognize the importance of education for social mobility, most also lack the means to achieve it, and some, especially those groups that were able to achieve secure berths in machine and construction trades, may not want it.

Steinberg attributes the difference between Jews and others to their experience in the cities of Eastern Europe where they were businesspeople and industrial workers, unlike the Poles or southern Italians who were chiefly peasants before their migration to the United States. Arriving in the United States with these skills and some capital, Jews were able to secure better economic niches in the emerging industrial system, from which their children were able to attend colleges and universities. This education *follows* attainment of economic niche rather than causes it. Armed with degrees, the Jews took advantage of the best mobility opportunity available at the turn of the twentieth century: school teaching. Contrary to expectations that credentials are all that are needed to gain access to the best and most lucrative professions, until World War II, Jews were mainly excluded from the professions, especially medicine and academia. During the 1920s and 1930s, most leading Jewish intellectuals were unable to find academic jobs; when they did, they were excluded from tenure by racial criteria.

The burden of Steinberg's argument is that economic rather than cultural advantages account for the differential gains among some ethnic groups in the United States. In his analysis, the race/class nexus is a far more reliable index of opportunity than ethnicity. In opposition to the profoundly essentialist explanations according to which culture—either of poverty or of learning—accounts for black failure or Jewish success, the articulation of blacks, Jews, and other groups with the class system may be a more reliable mobility indicator.

As William Julius Wilson reports in *When Work Disappears,* there are fewer black men working than are employed in the cities—black male unemployment in the cities reached 58 percent by 1996.[7] He contends that this is not primarily a function of the deficits of black culture, such as the absence of a two-parent household, lack of skills, or the absence of cultural values, such as adherence to family and work as desirable states of being. The "lack" is one of jobs. Blacks are barred from the trades for reasons of race, from industrial employment because factories have left the cities in droves, and from many retail establishments in the cities because of rank discrimination. Although black enrollment in institutions of higher education in the 1960s and 1970s rose rapidly, their numbers are dropping in a free fall from colleges and universities in proportion to the decline of student aid and the widening gap within black communities between a rising middle-class salariat and an increasingly proletarianized and unemployed working class.

Abandoned in the 1980s and 1990s by the government's renunciation of its own policies, by the labor movement, and by middle-class-led civil rights organizations, many black men have become attracted to "ethnicity." The famous Million Man March, organized by Muslim leader Louis Farrakhan, and the designation "African American" adopted by many intellectuals to replace "black" (which, in the wake of the black power movement, replaced "Negro") signified a definite cultural turn. Mass, primarily male, black pride rather than the struggle against discrimination and other forms of economic and political exclusion has taken front rank in black communities. Here the specificity of ethnicity may be a marker of despair and disbelief in the capacity of government and traditional civil rights organizations to wage a determined fight for jobs and income.

Despair was in evidence during the bleak summer of 1996 when, with a stroke of the pen, a Democratic president achieved what no Republican could have done: he signed away income guarantees for the jobless poor. To be sure, members of the Congressional Black Caucus joined by a shrunken corporal's guard of remaining white liberals voted against the "welfare reform" proposal, but neither labor nor the black civil rights groups were able, or even willing, to oppose Bill Clinton's capitulation in the midst of his reelection bid. Consensus in the form of the closed-mouth inaction overwhelmed the waning tradition of distributive justice.

The rise of ethnic discourse corresponds not only to the disaggregation of the consensual basis of nationality in the face of the emergence of stark inequalities as a visible feature of American economic and political life. It may be traced, in part, to the emergence of a minority, but sufficiently numerous, middle class among groups who have historically been excluded from the professions and from other segments of the salariat. Under pressure from a black freedom movement whose most militant detachment during the 1960s and 1970s was urban youth, government policy was directed less to addressing blatant economic inequality than to assisting in the formation of a new black and Latino middle class. Among policymakers and corporate leaders in the 1960s, there was a general consensus that the mass radicalization among black, Latino, white student youth (many of whom were allied to the black freedom movement), and women had to be redirected to acceptable American outcomes, especially mobility. The urban uprisings, antiwar demonstrations, and civil rights and feminist marches of the decades could be stemmed best not by police repression (although this method was always used) but by a systematic effort to promote, through ethnic identification, a series of measures the sum of which would generate a new class of managers, including politicians, whose main assignment would be to run the now decimated "inner cities"—welfare agencies, schools, and the criminal justice system.

Under the panoply of legislation and under the rubrics "antipoverty" and "antidiscrimination," gender, race, income, and ethnicity became the crucial criteria for opportunities in education, job training, public housing, and public job-creation programs. The most *successful* of these were the programs directed to increasing minority admissions into colleges and universities and affirmative action employment programs. The most *visible* of these were the programs directed to staff and supervisory positions that, with government prodding, were adopted by a large segment of major corporations. Open admissions in many state colleges and universities, according to which a student need only attain a high school diploma in order to gain admission, and stepped-up federal and state underwritten student loan programs were the chief staging grounds for the formation of the new middle-class salariat. In short, in proportion as social movements grounded in generational and class discourse waned, ethnicity waxed but not spontaneously. Ethnic identities became markers of state-sponsored opportunity.

President Richard Nixon's 1971 inauguration of an affirmative action program pegged educational, training, and job opportunities to various ethnicities. On the one hand, it continued certain economic criteria, namely, the poverty-line for school and training admission, but shifted emphasis to race and ethnicity, especially Chicanos, Puerto Ricans, and some Asian categories. The guidelines even specified which Latinos were eligible for affirmative action. For example, Colombians were in but Argentinians and Salvadorans were out, a blatant exclusion based not on need but on American foreign policy.

Needless to say, the adoption of ethnic identity by some racial minorities had a distinct classlike flavor. It was oriented largely to those who sought to achieve specific modes of class mobility, especially from manual labor, to the professions and to management. For immigrant and first-generation white ethnic working-class groups, ethnicity was a mechanism for establishing a unique form of working-class identities—whiteness—and had a specific economic goal, establishing monopolies over a particular segment of the blue-collar occupations or industries. Until the 1960s, black, Latino, and Asian working-class groups had had only limited success in deploying ethnicity for the purpose of forging their own economic niches. Even when they were able to establish hegemony over some occupations, it was primarily in the services and the second- and third-tier construction trades. Until the 1960s, most black professionals were trained for the clergy, medicine, and law in Negro colleges and universities. Their representation in engineering and the sciences was limited to biology and chemistry, and their presence in mostly white universities was negligible.

This pattern contrasts rather sharply with the experience of turn-of-the-century white working-class groups for whom ethnic identities were, to a large extent, vehicles for the expression of economic interest even as they increasingly were culturally assimilated into American society. Labor monopolies were formed under the sign of ethnicity rather than of the white race in general; "whiteness" defined the social and cultural position of these ethnic groups. Even in mass production industries such as steel and coal mining, "white" ethnicity played an important role in determining who was hired: Poles and other Eastern Europeans formed hiring networks and so did Italians through their social clubs and church organizations. During the successful effort to organize the Chicago stockyards and packing plants and again in the preparation for the failed post–World War I steel-organizing drive and the consequent strike, organizers were obliged to print union material in Italian, Spanish, Portuguese, and in nearly all of the Eastern European languages because "language" groups did not communicate in English and frequently did not understand each other or, as in the case of coal, worked in different parts of the mine.

Perhaps the most undisputed black success was in the sleeping car porter trade. In what was once a poorly paid form of servitude where the Pullman Corporation enjoyed unchallenged sway over wages and working conditions for some ten thousand black men in the late 1920s, the porters organized into a national union, The Brotherhood of Sleeping Car Porters, and became among the best paid and most respected members of many black communities. Their union and its longtime president A. Phillip Randolph were, until the late 1960s, among the most fervent supporters of the civil rights upsurges. The first evidence of this was in early 1941 when Randolph threatened a march on Washington unless President Roosevelt issued an executive order banning employment discrimination; then, during the 1960s freedom rides, sit-ins, and civil rights marches, regional leaders of the union often provided access to important elements in the black community, including the black churches where many served as deacons or lay preachers.

The Sleeping Car Porters organized in the tradition of social movement unionism. Acutely aware of their racial identity, they nevertheless saw themselves as participants in a struggle for class justice. They affiliated with the American Federation of Labor, and Randolph became the first black member of its executive council. Many of its leaders, including Randolph, were socialists and committed the union to the general labor struggle. By the late 1930s, Randolph was widely regarded as America's leading civil rights figure and its most prominent black trade unionist. His career embodied the fusion of class and race.

Unlike the sleeping car porters, domestic workers and residential construction workers did not achieve anything like the power and wage standards unionism could provide. These jobs were coded as semiskilled work even though they required considerable ability and training. Skilled black carpenters and bricklayers were able only to get rehabilitation and renovation jobs in the largely nonunion residential sector of the construction industry because of the refusal of white-dominated unions to organize them for fear they might successfully compete in the more lucrative commercial section of the industry. Even during World War II when severe labor shortages afflicted construction, black carpenters were limited to ship repair and other vital but marginal work in the industry. With few exceptions, notably the short-lived New York-based Domestic Workers Union of the war years, domestic workers remain unorganized.

Today, when these domestic skills are transposed to union-organized office cleaning, black women often do not get the jobs. In many large cities, those jobs are largely occupied by immigrant East European women who are abetted by employment networks reminiscent of earlier periods, and they enjoy union wages and benefits. Black and Latino workers in these occupations and industries are part of the large and growing race/class of the working poor, including Latino and Asian garment workers, who are increasingly choosing to identify with unions and neighborhood quasi-union organizations which fight for immigrant rights and against employer abuses of wage-hour standards and unsafe working conditions. Their ethnic identity does not disappear, but to the extent that unions of the working poor like UNITE (Union of Needle Industries and Textile Employees), the United Farm Workers, and the Service Employees International Union have organized among blacks and Latinos, their success may be attributed to their adroit fusion of class and ethnicity.

Many first- and second-generation blacks, Asians, and Latinos identify with their respective national cultures and often experience the United States as a diaspora.[8] They live in separate communities from those of the mainstream, occupy limited economic niches, and continue to speak their native languages. Moreover, their links to their countries of origin are still quite close, and even when they become citizens, they do not feel at home. Like the Indian untouchables, they have in some cases formed strong networks to ensure their positions close to the bottom of the job scale in low-wage factory jobs, as taxicab drivers, and in restaurants. For example, Dominicans have an elaborate system of labor contracting, especially in the Northeast and especially in industrial plants. Similarly, Indians are the largest group among newsstand workers, and Pakistanis and Indians are represented in large numbers in New York's taxi industry.

Succeeding generations have, typically, been culturally and sometimes economically assimilated. During the era of ethnic social policy, many recovered what might be termed "strategic" ethnicity because this path was the only one available for those who sought class mobility. Among the entailments of this strategic ethnicity was the reintroduction of the hyphen into cultural identity. There was little question that some sought as much integration into mainstream American society as educational credentials could bring. By the self-designation African American, Mexican American, or Chinese American rather than the more radical terms black, Latino, or Asian (which were distinctly diasporic terms), this fraction of racial communities announced its primary identification with the nation in which ethnicity was situated as a plural modifier. The fundamental individualist and consensual premise of American ideology was believed to be fulfilled by higher education or, in a relatively small number of instances, entrepreneurship.

New Directions: Beyond Ethnicity

The second feature of American ideology is the doctrine of the open society best enunciated by the philosopher Karl Popper, who spent most of his career in Great Britain.[9] As H. T. Wilson persuasively argued, the idea that America is "open"—in contrast to Europe—renders class theory entirely obsolete.[10] If on the strength of individual achievement anyone can climb the economic and social ladder, structural inequalities may be explained by reference to culture. If the overwhelming majority of blacks, Asians, and Latinos remained class-locked, this unfortunate circumstance could be ascribed to a culture of poverty, social disorganization, or any theory that avoids naming the class structure as the chief barrier to economic well-being. That the social structure proved capable of providing paths of mobility for some was sufficient proof of its openness.

Of course, the concepts of mobility and equality of opportunity imply inequality. Open societies must facilitate those with ambition to make of themselves anything their talents will permit. In open societies, limits are deemed entirely individual; societies must remove only those barriers that inhibit the individual from realizing her or his potential but should not put value on economic and social equality lest it degenerate by dull leveling. Inequality is an entailment of freedom that is preferable to an egalitarian society such as the former Soviet Union. Freedom—that is, market capitalism—is preferable to a society governed by the principles of central government and planning, both for the ethical reason that it provides more liberty to the individual and because the historical record demonstrates that the Soviet Union and its satellites were unable to provide high living standards for most of its professionals let alone manual workers.

Proponents of the open society never deny that some injustice still exists in democratic countries. Some, such as Samuel Brittan, are aware of the inherent inequalities of the market, do not countenance or ignore discrimination, and are sympathetic to reform.[11] What they disdain are claims that market capitalism may be convicted of structural inequality, which cannot be rooted out by piecemeal reform. Rather, according to Popper, open societies are capable of reforming themselves because they are democratic. Rejecting grand programs and comprehensive state planning, they are always subject to the pressures exerted by advocates or by aggrieved interest groups. Because liberal democracy rests on the consent of the governed when the governed speak, the representatives must listen. If change is too slow, this is the price we pay for freedom; the alternative, convulsive revolutionary transformation, frequently and perhaps inevitably leads to totalitarian rule.

Since radical change has not been on the agenda of American political life and seems to oppose the most fundamental precepts of its political culture, piecemeal reform rather than radical social change has been observed assiduously by social movements during the course of the twentieth century. This program has been reinforced by the impressive expansion of American capitalism after the two world wars. Among other features, it was marked by the emergence on a large scale of scientifically based production labor forces and administrative staffs in major corporations, the growth of public and private bureaucracies, and the expansion of health and educational services after World War II. Single-issue movements based on ethnicity, race, and gender were able to make substantial gains for a minority of their constituencies when they were militant and also because their demands did not entail the question of a zero-sum game. This is particularly the case for social movements that entail challenging religious-based conceptions of appropriate behavior, such as abortion rights. Although existing power is threatened, economic privilege is not, except indirectly. Similarly, during periods of economic expansion, blacks have demanded entrance into professions and skilled trades dominated by whites. Under these circumstances, the demand for access can be accommodated. Since power never concedes without a struggle and there was subsequently little room at the top, the middle seemed hospitable to pressure.

Globalization, downsizing, technological displacement, the emergence of temporary, part-time, and contingent jobs as the characteristic product of the Great American Job Machine and, equally to the point, the palpable overproduction of qualified educated labor are all straining the credibility of American ideology. As the labor movement attempts to rouse itself from its half century of slumber and reasserts class discourse, and the political embodiment of the open society (the Democratic Party and liberal Republicanism) adapts to a right-wing version of the consensus, the open society seems to have been relegated to the status of utopian hope. But if the open society was merely a product of the specific historical period of a lapsed American global hegemony, what are the elements for its rebirth? Can American capitalism renew its breakneck pace of economic growth? If not, what is the fate of ethnicity?

Clearly, regardless of the short-term economic forecasts, ethnicity has positioned itself and has been positioned by elements of the political and economic power groups to remain a major, if not *the* major, identity of groups struggling against exploitation of workers and other oppressed groups. Class appeals among the working poor have already coalesced with ethnic, racial, and gender identities, not only because "pure" class identities are rarely adopted by American workers or managers but because such barriers as the color line and the glass ceiling remain at all levels of the social structure, even at the bottom. The question that remains in doubt is whether "identity" politics will adopt a class dimension despite the overwhelming ideological campaign against class discourse.

Finally, we are in midst of a massive reevaluation by government and university administrations of the postwar program of expanded educational opportunity for traditionally excluded groups. To be sure, even in the halcyon days of the 1960s and early 1970s, colleges and universities were open only to the *deserving* poor and minorities—that is, those who made the grades and the test scores. "Open" admissions was never a policy of four-year public colleges, only the community colleges that, nonetheless, offered important transfer options to many students. Now as legislatures slash higher education budgets in the Northeast, California, and some Midwestern states, and as federal student aid withers, state as well as private school tuitions climb dramatically. Even as high-level politicians such as President Bill Clinton who, in his 1997 State of the Union address, proclaimed the centrality of education and training for America's economic future that reified terms of social policy, the market is beginning to take care of the educational surplus. In some universities, admission criteria have climbed beyond the reach of well-prepared middle-class students. In others, the deserving others may still gain admission but discover they are offered little more than vocational training, even at four-year colleges. The liberal arts institutions are in crisis; except for the elite institutions, second- and third-tier private school enrollments decline due to tuition hikes. Many schools, especially but not exclusively Catholic universities, are reducing their admission standards to high school diploma plus a regular heart beat. Except for community colleges, which many state systems use to fulfill the opportunity promise and keep a segment of the work force off the job market, state schools have raised admission criteria even as they increase tuition, a virtual move towards privatization, because state legislatures have caught the parsimony bug. In other cases, the college sells curriculum power to private corporations wishing to train its workforce and at the same time provide credentials to its employees. Of course, most famously, just as many research universities sold their wares to the Defense Department during the Cold War, they are rapidly shifting to becoming supplicants of the major pharmaceutical and electronics companies that provide research funds in return for patent rights.

Vocationalization and downsizing correspond to the scarcity of good salaried jobs. Administrators and many students are moving toward a regime of schooling in which education and training are once more conflated, and families are asking whether the expenditure in lost income as well as fees is worth the five or six years the average working-class student needs to complete degree requirements. Under these circumstances, the fight for higher education *as a right* takes on class rather than primarily ethnic significance, and no longer corresponds to the experience of the 1960s to early 1980s when educational credentials were reasonably certain rites of passage out of manual or low-wage service labor and a working life of frequent unemployment.

The remaining question is whether Americans will revise their ideology of individual opportunity, consensus, and the open society and recognize the limits of piecemeal reform, of which ethnicity and other forms of identity politics were symptoms. Needless to say, doctrine frequently maintains its effective power over experience long after the material conditions for its efficacy have passed. We can ask new questions because there are new circumstances to be faced. One is whether we are at the beginning of a new class discourse in this most classless of advanced industrial societies. Is it time to ask whether the best preparation for what Ulrich Beck has called "The Risk Society" is a critical education rather than career or vocational training?[12] These questions are posed against the grain of contemporary discourse, which is moving in exactly the opposite direction. Public universities are scurrying to vocationalize and privatize as fast as they can in hopes of minimizing the effects of state-mandated budget cuts, or even when budgets are stagnant, are convinced that the private sector holds the key to the future of education, especially higher education. Yet it must be apparent to all but the most blinkered observer that we are in the midst of a climactic turning point in the terms and conditions of our economic and political history. The outcome of these changes depends, in the last instance, on whether civility, a concomitant of consensus, yields to confrontation and difference from those who counsel complacency.

In this chapter I have argued that, as in its past, the future of ethnicity as a politics as much as a form of personal identity is inextricably linked to whether and how classes and social strata define themselves. Further, I have tried to show that in America, as well as in other countries, the categories of identity are always *displaced* and emerge in their own terms only for short periods. In essence, how people define themselves varies according to collective practices and the discursive terms that accompany them—whether identities are adopted by groups in political and cultural motion, whether the specificity of the economic is addressed or is institutionally displaced, for example, to education. Moreover, I have insisted on the concept of the *social* individual; when people adopt certain ethnic identities rather than those of race, gender, and class, they are often the result of how social movements and social ideas have moved them to make these choices. Some are based on interests—whether selecting one identity over another, for example, can make concrete gains. Others are based on much longer-range ideological formations. For example, one can see this process in the history of self-adopted racial identities: black, Negro, black, African American; black slave, Negro worker, black worker, and so forth.

We are in the midst of a sharp turn back towards conceptions of educational opportunity in which higher education as opposed to higher training is reserved for the few. Under these conditions, meritocratic replace democratic norms; we discover people are "hard-wired"—that is, intelligence is no longer described in sociohistorical terms but becomes a function of the DNA molecule and its codes—in which case, individuals "fail" but not societies. Under these conditions, the new terms of educational opportunity can be more frankly retrograde, as in Richard Herrnstein and Charles Murray's social Darwinist tract, *The Bell Curve.*[13] These new theoretical and ideological formulations may justify significant budget cuts in public education or, equally salient, the massive turn of public colleges and universities into trade schools, reserving what remains of the intellectual pursuits to a few private elite schools. This is the tendency, unless new discourses and movements emerge to oppose and reverse them.

IV

CHANGING THEORIES OF THE STATE

GLOBALIZATION AND THE STATE

At the turn of the century, in the shadow of the collapse of state socialism, "global" capitalism took center stage in world politics. For political forces—Left as well as Right—the decade of the 1990s marked a decisive turning point in the shape of economic, political, and social relations. Workers' movements were cut down to size, in some cases to impotence. The once-vibrant Green Parties of Germany and Italy seemed securely integrated into their respective electoral systems and now live on as a fig leaf, disguising the worst side of neoliberal governments. Not a few analysts proclaimed the triumph of world capitalism—some said it was irreversible—and many added the demise or at least the serious weakening of the nation-state. The unexpected emergence of social movements dedicated to, variously, throttling its power, overthrowing it, or reforming its more egregious features may be explained by the virtual free ride transnational capital has enjoyed in the 1990s.

Global capitalism was once tempered by the presence of Eastern European state socialisms which, despite their profound flaws, haunted the commanding heights of capitalism and played a large role in thwarting its most brutal features. It is arguable that, in the face of the partial deindustrialization of most advanced capitalist states, the specter of communism maintained, for a time, the historic compromise of regulated capitalism. This in no way diminishes the role played by national liberation movements in the colonial and postcolonial world, nor by still powerful working-class movements in advanced capitalist countries. Buttressed by a resurgent neoliberal ideology after the fall of its communist specter, international capitalism moved boldly in the 1990s to reimpose market-driven trade relations, to partially abrogate the prevailing postwar social contract that kept unions at the state bargaining tables, and to strip the state of many of its regulatory and social welfare functions. In the United States, the stripped-down state promulgated the rollback of welfare; for most intents and purposes, it became a national security state as a combination of internalized terrorism and the threat of external terrorism reinforced its most repressive functions. The internal terror was signaled by real and imagined crime waves that dominated public discussion; the revival of a clear antiyouth bias often took the form of blatant racism and xenophobia directed against the burgeoning immigrant populations.

In the 1990s, the role of once-hidden institutions of international finance and economic terror—the International Monetary Fund (IMF), the World Bank, and the World Trade Organization (WTO)—became, under pressure from labor and social movements, sites of political contestation. Once viewed by activists and intellectuals as a distant shore, internationalism gripped a wide array of trade unionists and social movements. To be sure, despite their vehement denials, the labor organizations' concern for world trade issues is often motivated by thinly masked protectionism Rather than identifying the despoliation of nature with rampant capitalism—either in its so-called free-market or state-socialist forms—some ecologists view industrialization itself as a scourge and propose to extend those regulations currently in effect and to strengthen the state's constraints on capital's ability to consume unlimited national resources. Yet the fact remains that after a decade of untrammeled attacks against living standards and on the material world in both advanced and third world countries, in Europe as well as the United States, international capitalism has, for the first time since the early 1970s, come under scrutiny by popular forces.

In December 1999, more than fifty thousand demonstrators—thirty thousand of them trade unionists—descended on a planned WTO meeting in Seattle; in the course of their protests, they effectively shut down the meeting and much of the city. As if on cue, a coalition of environmental, antisweatshop groups, some of the encrusted American trade unions, and an assortment of organized radicals turned their attention to the WTO and the other visible international institutions of global capital. By April 2000, the scene had shifted to Washington and London where similar alliances staged demonstrations against these institutions, which—unlike Seattle—were met with the full repressive force of the local state. Their demands ranged from the abolition of these organizations to a variety of reforms: that the IMF and the World Bank reduce or cancel the debts of developing countries; rigorous enforcement of fair labor standards; enforcement of environmental protections as a condition for making loans or awarding favored-nation trade status; and perhaps most significantly, transparency in their deliberations and democratic involvement of nongovernmental organizations in their governance. In contrast to the reform demands, some now openly identified as anarchists and affiliated with organizations such as the "Black-Bloc" named capitalism as the ultimate culprit, a step which went beyond specific issues and reform programs and, in turn, beyond the nonviolent strategic orientation of the reformers.

These events, which electrified the Left and scandalized the media and financial establishments, occurred against the backdrop of a major debate in state theory. At issue is whether what is variously termed the "new" imperialism or, in Michael Hardt and Tony Negri's terms, the emergence of a multinational empire in which national states play a diminishing role, or simply a new plateau of international economic and political integration under American and Western European dominance, signals the demise or (at least) the advent of restructured but stripped-down nation-states. Or, as some have vociferously argued, is all the talk of globalization so much global baloney with a serious ideological intent? Under the threat of capital flight and other forms of deindustrialization, including where to locate investment sites, is globalization a strategy to subordinate and otherwise contain working-class struggles? On this view, we have not left behind the era of sovereign nation-states or interimperialist rivalries. Accordingly, class and other social struggles still occur in a distinct national context.

Many questions arise from these developments. Perhaps the most important is, in the wake of the emergence of new forms of class power, whether the traditional context for social struggles, the nation-state, remains intact or must now turn to conceptualizing new formations specific to globalization that tend to dominate politics. As we shall see, for Nicos Poulantzas as much as Ralph Miliband, the early signs of globalization were occasions for profound skepticism. Undeterred, Poulantzas held fast to the effectivity of the national context for class struggles, indeed for all politics. After exploring Poulantzas's views in some detail, while recognizing the merit in his position, this chapter asks whether and how political theory needs to go beyond Poulantzas, indeed, beyond state theory as it emerged in the twentieth century.

1

Without denying the importance of internationalization, as the theoretical debate emerged in the 1970s, Nicos Poulantzas weighed in on the side of those who argued that the national state was not only alive but well and remained the principal site of class struggles as well as of international economic relations. Poulantzas's later work, *State, Power, Socialism,* and particularly *Classes in Contemporary Capitalism,* where he addressed the imperialism question explicitly and at length, may be read as attempts to integrate a distinction between passive and active consent with a more precise understanding of the state in the framework of internationalization. In *Classes,* Poulantzas aligned himself (but only partially) with the Lenin-Bukharin theory of imperialism as an extension of competing national capitalisms but added the salience of a classic interpretation of Marx's *Capital.* That is, in contrast to earlier periods in which capital investment and imperialist plunder were understood by many to be a consequence of the search for markets and for raw materials and tended to presuppose but not explore the sources of imperialism in the logic of capital accumulation and capitalist crises, for Poulantzas, contemporary imperialism stemmed chiefly from the internal contradictions—most notably the class struggle—within national capitalisms of the most developed countries. The export of capital, its economic expression, is seen as a solution to the falling rate of profit that, in turn, results from a rising organic composition of capital which Marx called a consequence of capitalism's attempt to solve problems of the wage relation, competition, and other pressures on profit by raising worker productivity, principally by replacing living labor with machinery. The falling rate of profit, then, stemmed indirectly as well as directly from the more or less successful economic and political struggles of the working class to raise living standards.

Thus did Poulantzas attempt to refute those like Paul Sweezy and especially Harry Magdoff (whose *The Age of Imperialism* dominated the American debate for two decades), who held to the view that imperialism results from the search for new markets and for raw materials and declared the more or less permanent mitigation of class struggle by consumerism, the production of waste, and the perfidy and institutional integration of the labor leadership. Nor does Poulantzas support the thesis of "super" imperialism, which derives in a large measure from Rudolph Hilferding's turn-of-the-century study, *Finance Capital* (1909), according to which international finance capital has become so organized as to eliminate, or at least seriously inhibit, interimperialist schisms. Owing to capitalism's ability to make concessions to a large fraction of the working class, it can reduce to the vanishing point prospects for world-transforming class struggles. In *Classes,* Poulantzas invokes uneven development, which is essentially a temporal category that Lenin suggested, to explain the persistence of these intercapitalist and international schisms in the late twentieth century. In Poulantzas's reflection, the United States emerged from World War II as the most powerful world power. At the same time, he argued, a newly united Europe emerged in the 1960s as a formidable although subordinate challenger, thereby setting the stage for sharper interimperialist conflicts. In short, while multinational capitalism developed into a world system under American hegemony, it is not without deep fissures.

I want to make two observations here. If, as Poulantzas says, the state displaces and "condenses" capitalism's own contradictions—namely, the permutations of class struggles—and has become, historically, the crucial mechanism by which capitalist social relations of production are reproduced, and class and other social and cultural movements are constitutive, not merely objects, of power relations on the terrain of the state, then we may say that, within the limitation imposed by its reproductive role, the state remains the chief arena of contestation rather than wholly an efflux of capital, let alone international capital. In fact, a corollary to this conception of state power is that its reproductive and consent functions may be in conflict. One of the crucial political shifts of the workers' movements in the past century has been to insist upon power sharing *within* the state even as they have deferred the quest for social power in their own name.

My second observation is that states are nation-states. There is, in Poulantzas's reprise of imperialism, no discussion of meta-states consisting of multinational capitalism's own institutions. Or to be more precise, in his critique of superimperialism, he implied that the thesis of the formation of an international capitalist class with effective political hegemony over national sovereignty was mistaken. However powerful the international capitalist arrangements, the nation provided the framework for their realization just as it did for accumulated capital. Despite the prattle about world government and the consultative institutions such as G7 and the European Union, which offer the shell of representative government but little substance, sovereignty is limited to national borders. Hence, until now, "politics" has remained national. In sum, the *social formation* always refers to the economic, political, and ideological relations of a specific geopolitical space whose boundaries of culture, language, and political forms define the nation.

Despite the *Manifesto*'s call for proletarian internationalism and its declaration that the working class has no country, we have no experience of citizenship that is transgressive of national states nor of an international working class capable of crossnational mobilization on a sustained basis. Whether the state is theorized as relatively autonomous, autopoetic (self-reproducing), or is held to be umbilically tied to capital as its economic, ideological, or repressive agent, all state theories presuppose these conditions. If these conditions remain despite evidence of increasing international coordination among national capitals of differential capacities, the emergence of a truly global capitalism may remain, at best, a tendency and always subject to the rivalries of dominant national capitals.

However, the question is whether this formulation is a theoretical proposition or one that is rooted in a specific historical period. Poulantzas insisted on the periodization and historicity of forms of internationalization as well as the state. Capitalism may have, relatively speaking, some transhistorical features (the profit imperative in any period, its tendency to expand beyond national borders, uneven development, and so forth). In this spirit, the question is whether the formulations of Poulantzas and Miliband hold in the period of deregulation, and especially in the era of global capitalism's ideological as well as economic triumph over its principal opponent, "actually existing" state socialism.[1] What may have remained ambiguous and tentative in the 1970s needs to be reassessed in the postcommunist era when neoliberal tendencies have become dominant in national and international economic and political affairs. While capital has always been, in part, international, and Poulantzas's claim that the United States' economic power has been increasingly challenged within the world system by competitors since the 1960s retains its validity (note well the division among the Atlantic powers on Bosnia, Kosovo, and the Gulf War), it would be erroneous to overestimate the significance of these differences and infer a profound political challenge to the U.S. program. Moreover, to ignore mounting signs that transnationalism is progressively weakening nation-states is to miss the significance of unmistakable power exercised by the key institutions of global capital and of the emergent opposition. Although it is true that the leadership of these institutions comprises finance ministers of the leading powers, including the United States, and it is, for the time being, inconceivable that the bureaucracy at the helm of the IMF and the World Bank would take steps that directly contravened the will of the ruling circles of these countries, the question remains whether these imperatives are a permanent feature of global arrangements.

Before proceeding, it is important to take into account the liberalization of virtually all Western European Socialist and Communist Parties in the 1990s. The Social-Democratic and Labor Parties have long fashioned themselves as parties of government by their broad abandonment of Keynesianism in favor of neoliberalism: they have signaled their willingness to consider measures to "reform" welfare state protections by reducing benefits, renouncing nationalization as a political program, and reversing their temporary anticolonial stance of the 1970s and 1980s (see especially the despicable conduct of French forces under the command of Socialist Lionel Jospin in Rwanda). The Communists, long the official opposition party in France and Italy and with significant forces in Greece, responded to the end of Soviet rule and liberal hegemony by renouncing their own revolutionary aims (even though it may be claimed that this renunciation in practice was effected shortly after World War II) and declared themselves parties of capitalist governments and, in the case of Italy, changed their name to signify their altered intentions to the Democratic Party of the Left and assumed its reins in the late 1990s.

Unless one identifies revolution with the parties that embrace its legacy, it would be inaccurate to declare the death of revolutionary socialism in a world dominated ideologically as well as politically by big capitalism. What seems to have died is the close link between the parties of socialism and communism with labor and social movements. The mass base of these parties is now purely elec-toral, and in this sense they have become bourgeois parties. In turn, while labor and social movements retain some ties with these parties and the state, and in the case of public employees, remain state-builders (especially at the local level), the struggle has partly shifted away from the state to the transnationals themselves; when the state is brought "back in" to their strategic agendas, it is mainly to mount actions against the state and its new global institutions. For example, the direct actions principally by public employees and students in 1995 in France were directed towards opposing efforts to rescind elements of the postwar com-promise between labor and capital in which workers renounced decisive politi-cal power in return for substantial money and social wages. The struggle against institutions of international finance focuses as much on their abolition or weak-ening as on efforts to reform them. In either case, the national state, whose ideo-logical and economic functions may not be diminished, are fundamentally dif-ferent than they were in the regulation era.

Today we are witnessing the merger of what Louis Althusser termed the ide-ological apparatuses with those of repression. The institutions of the old welfare state, private as well as public, are mobilized to discipline the labor force and to maintain order in the reserve labor army of the unemployed and the underem-ployed, rather than positioning themselves as advocates. In the United States, the role of the doctrine of law and order and the penetration of terrorism as the crucial element of the political unconscious underlie the apparatuses of the national security state that has a popular base of consent, a popular base that is race and class specific. Having certified youth alongside blacks and immigrants as "other" is, in addition, profoundly generational. Consequently, it is no sur-prise to discover that anarchism—the revolt against the state—rather than social democracy and its progressivist country cousin, has become cutting edge in this new struggle against global capitalism.

Unless a "united states" of at least advanced industrial societies is able to impose uniform taxes for the purposes of maintaining legitimating services (in the Althusserian mode, some crucial ideological state apparatuses such as Social Security take in the wider meaning of the term), the ideological appara-tuses of the state (for example, the social wage of which education and income guarantees are a crucial aspect) are everywhere in retreat. In order to maintain these functions, the tax base has to be relatively stable. This, of course, points to the link between accumulation and legitimation, even absent the state's interventionist role in the economic sphere that, in any case, seems to be increasingly confined to the manipulations of monetarism rather than of fiscal policy. Global capital has shown little taste for shouldering requisite tax burdens and instead has made reverse distribution away from the working class, including the working poor, a condition of maintaining a base within advanced industrial countries. More to the point, transnational capital, the characteristic mode of capitalism, has sharply challenged state sovereignty since the early 1970s.

Globalization signaled the more or less rapid dismantlement of most of the salient features of the regulation era: in many countries, this has led to the drive to "privatization." In the United States, we have seen the virtual end of major regulatory agencies such as the Interstate Commerce Commission, the Securities and Exchange Commission, and the antitrust division of the Justice Department (notwithstanding its recent effort to split Microsoft). French and British privatization are proceeding apace as state enterprises are sold off and neither labor nor socialist governments are inclined to promise to return banks and industrial plants to the public sector. The same is even more evident at the local levels within the United States. Although there are few publicly owned and operated utility companies, many states have deregulated electric and gas rates for commercial and home uses and have all but ended their once-ruling power commissions; rent control, never strong outside New York and some California communities, is under siege. Most of all, business regulations such as "insider trading" and other investment restrictions are rapidly eroding.

The ideological attacks against the welfare state institutions of the regulation era are no more powerful than in the United States and the United Kingdom. The question is whether the underpinnings are to be found in both the conflation by libertarians and conservatives alike of freedom within the market and diminishing funds for public services at the local level produced by the increasingly narrow tax base due to capital flight, legal limits on taxation, and the simultaneous reverse redistribution generated by inequitable tax cuts. Some, notably economist Doug Henwood, have argued that capital flight and internationalization generally are overstated and have been deployed by labor's enemies to disarm the workers' movement. Needless to say, there is some justice in this allegation, but it seems myopic to deny or otherwise dismiss the palpable evidence that globalizing tendencies, always a feature of capitalist reproduction and development, have not intensified in the past twenty years. It may be further asserted, as Negri and Hardt have argued, among others, that we are witnessing a veritable paradigm shift in the structure of global relations.[2]

In the first place, many more corporations have become transnational in the scope of investment, patterns of ownership and control, and the large number of mergers and acquisitions across national boundaries. National states are increasingly held hostage to capital. The price of retaining plants, and therefore jobs and taxes to run governmental functions, is to withdraw the state's regulatory functions and to shrink the social wage. The state is still recruited to provide infrastructural goods, such as roads and water, but not to own or regulate communications, including electrical and gas companies.

Secondly, the merger and acquisition movement has led to massive displacement of qualified labor since the stock market crash of 1987, a tendency that continued well into the 1990s. Unlike Western Europe, especially Germany and the Scandinavian countries (which still have extensive programs of education and retraining for some categories of administrative personnel as well as industrial labor), the United States has provided only minimal support. Even training and placement services are largely privatized. In this connection, the emergent federal programs of educational aid that were a characteristic feature of the temporary enlargement of the U.S. welfare state in the 1960s have been halted and reversed. As is well known, state and local communities are once more held responsible for education and training at all levels. With the decline of federally supported research, public universities and colleges find themselves at the mercy of an overtaxed electorate as well as right-wing ideologues who, in the shadow of the reversal of fortunes of Democratic state parties, have entered boards of trustees of state institutions on a large scale. At the same time, the local tax base is simply unable to address education and health needs.

Rather than focusing on the state's repressive functions, Althusser, Poulantzas, and the Frankfurt School emphasize the significance of the ideological apparatuses or, in another vernacular, the legitimating functions of the modern state in advanced capitalist societies. Whether derived from Gramsci's work on the theory of hegemony within a much expanded conception of civil society or from Frederick Pollock's, Franz Neumann's, and Otto Kirscheimer's investigations of the state in democratic and authoritarian political regimes, the argument about the modern state has decisively shifted to determinations of the conditions of consent rather than focusing on elements of force. In his final statement, *State, Power, Socialism,* Nicos Poulantzas declared, among other new features of late twentieth-century capitalism, what he called "the decline of democracy" and the emergence of "authoritarian statism."

> Probably for the first time in the history of democratic states, the present-form not only contains scattered elements of totalitarianism, but crystallizes their organic disposition in a permanent structure running parallel to the official state. Indeed

this duplication of the State seems to be a structural feature of authoritarian statism, involving not a watertight dissociation between the Official State and the structure in question, but the functional overlapping and constant symbiosis.[3]

Ascribing this development to the emerging economic crisis during the 1970s, and also to changes in the relations of production and the social division of labor that, among other things, is marked by capital's strategy of maintaining profits by an aggressive attack on working-class living standards, Poulantzas points to a steady shift in the state from its "popular democratic" features to its more authoritarian elements. In contrast to the binary formulation of many state theorists, we may designate his position a "dual" or parallel theory according to which the authoritarian and democratic states exist in the same social space. That is, the formal popular democratic features of the modern state do not disappear in advanced capitalist societies even as its authoritarian features emerge as, perhaps, dominant. Among these, he emphasizes the widening gap between political democracy and socioeconomic democracy, in particular the rise of poverty in advanced capitalist states, the increasing role of the national state in favoring transnational rather than domestic capital, especially smaller business and the agricultural sector. To which might be added—from the United States' perspective—the rising authoritarianism of the ideological apparatuses, particularly education and the fierce politicization of the so-called private sphere, notably the family, which is now subject to the intervention of courts and other repressive authorities.

These judgments are more than twenty years old, but we can see their salience in the United States today. Signaled by the so-called Welfare Reform legislation of 1996 and especially by the balanced budget consensus between the two dominant parties, the socioeconomic commitment of the state to alleviate the effects of the economic crisis for those most aggrieved has declined precipitously. At the same time—to borrow the formula of Habermas, Offe, and O'Connor—the outcome of this shift is the discernable decline in the legitimating functions of the state in favor of its repressive functions. In the cities, where jobless rates are as much as twice the national averages and black and other racial minorities suffer three times more unemployment, the criminal justice system has risen to new prominence. Spurred by a series of Supreme Court decisions, police have gained wider powers of arrest and surveillance. There is a two-fold increase in police forces; the prison population has risen to more than 1 percent of the population, or two-and-a-half million. One of three black men will, during his lifetime, be subsumed under the criminal justice system either by incarceration or official surveillance in forms such as parole and probation.

Indeed, the idea of the political machinery as such suggests an indeterminate relation between social reproduction and consent. It is difficult to institute practices of political participation, including its most elementary form, voting, without risking (at least putatively) that citizens will not overflow the boundaries between private and public and thereby insist on public voice, if not expropriation, in matters of accumulation. In this connection, we may cite, not the labor movement (for unions seem appallingly incapable of offering resistance let alone any alternative to the drift toward modern authoritarian statism) but environmentalists and urban activists who, more than other sectors, have contested capitalist priorities.

There is a neglected but strikingly parallel perspective to that of Poulantzas: Marcuse's theory of fascism, which was developed between 1937 and 1948 in a series of articles and reports written mainly during the period when he was employed as an analyst for intelligence agencies during World War II and then the State Department. In Marcuse's view, the liberal capitalist state at its best is a "mediator" between the individual and the enormous economic power accumulated by the modern corporation. Through the judicial system, legislation, and political parties that are broadly representative of social groups and, in some countries, of formal constitutional rights, the state provides individuals with the means to vindicate their grievances. "The *rule of law* has, to an ever increasing extent, become the medium through which the state operates as a system of national administration," a formulation strikingly close to Poulantzas's insistence that law cannot be reduced to its role as an adjunct to capitalist interests.[4] But, far from agreeing that national socialism is characterized by the emergence of a totalitarian state which, against the will of corporations as much as society as a whole, plays the decisive role in capital accumulation and rules, exclusively, by terror, Marcuse advances the original thesis that under national socialism the state loses its autonomy and, therefore, its ability to mediate through its political and juridical functions.

> National Socialism has done away with the essential features which characterized the modern state. It tends to abolish any separation between state and society by transferring political functions to the social groups actually in power. In other words, National Socialism tends toward direct and immediate self-government by the prevailing social groups over the rest of the population.[5]

Marcuse points to practices that have accompanied the precipitous decline of the labor movement and of movements of the poor in large U.S. cities. In the aftermath of the notorious air traffic controllers strike in 1981, capitalism extracted a series of compromises from once powerful unions, not only or even primarily on wage issues but perhaps more importantly on questions of work rules. Backs to the wall and increasingly isolated from a public that had been taught to despise them in contract negotiations, steelworkers, autoworkers, and many others conceded shop-floor control to management, including the right to discharge or otherwise discipline workers for various infractions of management-imposed rules. In a remarkably parallel thesis to that of C. Wright Mills, but written a decade earlier and published nowhere, Marcuse claimed that, under fascism, society is ruled by a triumvirate of big capital, the army, and the party, whose collective will is mediated by, and concentrated in, the leader who symbolized the drive toward homogeneity and harmony among the various elements of society. Yet, contrary to the usual views, according to Marcuse, however much the individual is deprived of the mediating role of a now totally instrumentalized and subordinated public bureaucracy, individualism is not, thereby, destroyed. Fascism

> manipulates the masses by unleashing the most brutal and self instincts of the individual. The National Socialist state is not the reversal but the consummation of competitive individualism. The regime releases all those forces of brutal self-interest which the democratic countries have tried to curb and tried to combine with the interest of freedom.[6]

Social groups are replaced by the *crowd*.

Marcuse draws a parallel to the early days of capitalism when the ideology and, to some extent, the practices of the free market reduced the state to what Adam Smith termed a Night Watchman. But even as private corporate power grew by geometric proportions, the

> social division of labor and the technological process had equalized individuals and their liberation seemed to call for a union of men acting in solidarity of a common interest which superceded the interest of individual self-preservation. Such a union is the opposite of the National Socialist mass.[7]

In opposition to this tradition, the Nazis organized the masses guided by the "principle of atomization," within production as much as within civil society. Like advanced capitalist societies today, fascism was guided by what one Nazi edict terms "that mental and physical condition that enables him the highest efficiency and this guarantees the greatest advance for the racial community."[8]

It is not difficult to observe the same tendencies in the United States today. Capitalism has spared no effort to configure technology so that production units are smaller, spatially divided from each other both within national borders and throughout the world, and the individual worker more isolated. On the threat of discharge or capital flight, the worker is pressured to achieve more efficiency and to work longer hours to the extent that, for many, the weekend has all but disappeared. Moreover, the labor movement (reduced and made timid by industrial terror, the promotion of fierce competitive individualism, and the "unleashing" of an ethos of self-preservation over solidarity) has produced conditions in which the mediations between the individual and representatives of capitalism have all but disappeared in the preponderance of workplaces. We have witnessed the decline of the job, if by that term we designate a position that brings with it the amenities of paid health care and work rules that are shaped by labor, management, and procedures that ensure employment security.

The more labor becomes temporary and contingent, the more the individual seeks "security" through identification with the company. The terror associated with losing a relatively well-paying job tempers the militancy that in unionized workplaces is associated with being mistreated. Instead, the union counsels what the worker is often ready to hear: keep your head down and keep your job. In these times, the state has retreated from its mediating role. Any employer wishing to break a union organizing drive need only fire a few activists to show the rest the price of resistance. The union files unfair labor-practice charges with the Labor Relations Board, but the employer has many avenues of delay. Meanwhile, the campaign peters out and workers learn that to raise their voices leads only to retribution. As every organizer knows, the rule of law has given way to the almost unfettered rule of capital.

This is not to say that America has entered a fascist era. For example, in recent United States history, even as legislatures have become less responsive to the popular will and have revealed their own subordination to corporate interests, it is still possible, through the judicial system, for individuals and the state (that is, local governments) to sue tobacco companies and other manufacturers of unhealthy goods, enter small claims against recalcitrant merchants, and obtain cash settlements in cases of race and sex discrimination. Even if seriously weakened, health, labor, and other laws and institutions (such as labor unions) dedicated to ensuring their enforcement still afford some redress. These protections are, however, conditioned by social struggles and are dependent on maintaining the separation between the state and society, where a public bureaucracy retains sufficient autonomy to act against the most wanton impulses of capitalism, the reckless and irresponsible use of police power, and hate crimes perpetrated by citizens against each other.

In the 1990s, we have witnessed growing public heteronomy; the state and its institutions are pressed into the direct service of capital when, for instance, the American president becomes little more than a trade representative and, in the Clinton era, an effective means by which discontent was dispersed to the margins of politics—in the manner of C. Wright Mills's observation—that increasingly public issues were coded as private troubles. In a period of intensifying international economic instability, when capital threatens to massively withdraw from Asia, Eastern Europe, and Latin America unless its profit margins are ensured by the state, the American president and his treasury secretary are dispatched to conferences with the world's financial leaders to deliver a single message: don't try to interfere with the free flow of capital by introducing measures to regulate currencies, restrain large-scale capital flight, and so forth. At the same time, at home, antitrust enforcement, one of the more contentious features of the regulation era is, with the except of the upstart computer-mediated information industry, assiduously ignored by the administration, even though it is still legally charged with responsibility.

As a result, mergers and acquisitions reached a new historical high during the 1990s. In the midst of a much-heralded economic "boom" in the 1990s, hundreds of thousands of production workers, technical and professional employees, and middle managers were laid off each year (the operative term is "downsized"), and many had little or no severance pay, found themselves without health insurance, and, if over fifty were, for all intents and purposes, retired without pension from their careers. In many instances, downsizing is the result of transnational mergers. Not only are production workers laid off but administrative, low, and middle managers—and even some professionals—may find themselves on the job market.

If capital demands the state stand aside in the economic sphere except to fulfill its function as a valorizing agent, it calls upon government to strengthen its police forces at home as well as abroad. In 2000, President Clinton and Congress agreed that while there were no funds for expanding the social wage—indeed, many groups were struggling to prevent further cuts—there was money for only two initiatives: paying down the trillions in national debt to the banks and a small increase in the huge military budget that, in the absence of a credible enemy, had to be increased anyway in order to sustain the small wars that continually crop up, especially in the periphery and semiperiphery of the great capitalist states.

Although it is still possible for a victim of police brutality to get his day in court in the United States, in the name of public safety, elected officials such as Rudolph Giuliani, the New York City mayor for most of the 1990s, flagrantly defended the right of the police to terrorize blacks and other minorities. Many cities have become exemplars of the garrison state. In public schools, many kids, particularly in black and Latino working-class neighborhoods, are forcibly restrained from leaving the building during school hours, even if they have free periods. Armed police roam the halls to make sure kids are in class and, on occasion, administer corporal punishment to offenders, even when the law prohibits such behavior. In New York and the Midwest, elected officials threaten to withdraw public funds from museums that dare to violate the canon of conservative morality by staging art that offends religious and sexually repressive sensibilities.

While it would be overly schematic to attribute these developments to shifts in the character of the world and national economies (indeed, ideological conservatism has a long history even in the era of capitalism's steep ascent), the specificity of the latest attacks on the social wage and on freedom is surely linked to shifts in the relations of production and the social division of labor. Rather than seeking to generate a new power bloc to thwart capitalism's offensive based on alliances with other classes and social movements, despite the originality of the Seattle events, the labor movement has generally shown tendencies to draw closer to dependency on its "own" transnational capital, an ominous development in the shadow of globalization when what Poulantzas calls "domestic" capital has steadily retreated.

This pattern of dependency is thrown sharply into relief by the ominous silence of most of the leading production unions in the wake of capital's economic and political offensive against living standards and hard-won union protections at the workplace. Many sectors of the constantly shrinking industrial working class and its decimated unions despair that they can generate significant offensives on the wage front, against enforced overtime, and for the preservation of contractually negotiated union control over the terms and conditions of work. Under the shadow of capital flight, many have settled for job guarantees for the existing workforce and have willingly given up their rights to prevent permanent shifts of jobs away from union control. Moreover, workers accept, sometimes eagerly, overtime work assignments on the theory that they must grab whatever benefit they can before the plant shuts down or, alternatively, have become more submissive to management's initiatives as a means to keep the plant from leaving town. Nor, in the United States, does there exist a shorter-hours movement parallel to those of France and Germany. Instead, working hours are actually increasing, and despite economic expansion, employers brazenly, if unsuccessfully, proposed eliminating premium pay for overtime. Most controversially, many contracts negotiated from the early 1980s through the present day establish two- and three-tier wage systems and permit management to hire nonunion contract labor to work alongside the shrinking unionized workforce. In the face of these concessions, capital is emboldened. It was no accident that the leadership of the United Steelworkers, one of the more compliant industrial unions, was among the more aggressive participants in the

Seattle and Washington events. These developments form the backdrop for comprehending the apparent upsurge in labor's response to globalization and, in contrast to most of the postwar era where unions were allied with the state and the liberal political parties in opposition to social movements, the willingness of some unions to ally with environmentalists and students. Despite signs of labor's newly crafted outreach, it still appears umbilically tied to hopes for the return of regulation-era benefits, not the least of which is the eroded, but publicly sanctioned, right of workers to organize freely and without employer intimidation. The AFL-CIO rewarded the neoliberal Democrats with tens of millions of dollars in workers' money to elect its presidential and congressional candidates and has refrained from proposing to organize its own political party, even as pressure on the wayward Democrats. These choices reveal the extent to which one of the more challenging of Poulantzasian concepts, trade unions as an ideological state apparatus, retains its validity even in the midst of some signs of revival of labor militancy.

The validity of theory is by no means assured by algorithms of falsification conducted in the manner of an empirical test. Whether capital becomes more globally coherent and intervenes directly in the affairs of nation-states is a settled historical question. If the IMF and the WTO are coalitions of autopoetic national ruling circles—always constituted by an alliance of leading sectors of capitalism with the political directorate and key intellectuals tied to them—the institutions nevertheless act in accordance with both the collective interests of national states and of transnational capital, the identity of which is mediated by internal difference. Thus the institutions of world order are constituted by difference, always subject to tension and even fissure. These institutions are anchored to states that provide the military and ideological means that are the precondition of their ability to impose regimes of austerity, sanction authoritarian and totalitarian political and military directorates in developing countries, and maintain capitalism's world dominance.

One might speculate that the relations of dominance in these alliances between transnational capitals and national states are never determined a priori. In the first place, interests vary and even collide and the relation of forces tends to produce shifts; second, the intervention of social movements that, in relation to capital, are really class signifiers insofar as the struggles increasingly take on a class character. As a condition of the renewal of their mandates, political directorates must be sensitive to popular protests, lest they be replaced—or even worse, provoke radicalization. In turn, if political and social movements within, say, developing countries, influence the investment climate, capitalism may insist on military and diplomatic policy changes in order to stabilize conditions for business.

We can see the operation of this principal in relations with Cuba. After forty years of embargo, repeated attempted assassinations of Fidel Castro, and economic and political isolation of the regime, significant capital factions have concluded that their interests suggested a policy shift to which a section of the political directorate is willing to accommodate. Yet other corporate interests and the political leadership to which it is tied resist major changes in the relationship with Cuba. The rule of modernization and normalization, which has guided some aspects of U.S. foreign policy in the Clinton era, suggests an earlier rather than later agreement. But like the Middle East and former Yugoslavia where America's allies on many issues have diverged from U.S. direction, the outcomes remain indeterminate, precisely because of the continuing appeal of nationalism in these semiperipheral areas and of the resistance of European states to armed intervention.

Needless to say, our estimates of the current period are conditioned by theoretical perspectives as well as by historical evidence, by the concepts that guide our understanding of social practice, and by the level of abstraction we employ in the analysis of the state and globalization. For example, what I have just described can be dismissed by the superimperialism theorists as a glitch, and confirmed by those who follow Poulantzas as evidence of the importance of interimperialist differences in helping to produce stalemates in international affairs. Against inevitabilists who have noted China, Vietnam, and Eastern Europe's partial submission to the terms of empire, one must note that the capacity of the Cuban regime to mobilize its own people to endure adversity, their ability to improvise a new economy after the collapse of the Soviet Union, and their refusal to submit to neoliberal solutions must be accredited in helping to explain the bend in U.S. policy. With Poulantzas, I argue that the agency of those bearing the weight of empire is constitutive of its trajectories. At the same time, one must reject every attempt to reify the present as illustration of ineluctability. Only by maintaining the historicity of social structures based on the vicissitudes of class struggles is this possible.

CAPITALISM AND THE STATE

MARCUSE'S LEGACY

1

Nineteen ninety-eight is the one hundredth anniversary of Herbert Marcuse's birth. After decades of teaching and writing for relatively limited, mostly academic audiences, he became a figure of international renown in the sixties and some of his books were bestsellers. But it seems that he had just fifteen minutes of fame; his work is now out of fashion and virtually unread by students, activists, and academics, save for the narrow circle of those who work and teach in the tradition of the Critical Theory of the Frankfurt School. Nevertheless, due to one of those mysterious conjunctions of history and thought, Marcuse was one of the figures from which Russell Jacoby derived his model of the "public" intellectual. A philosopher who never ceased to remind his readers that he was an "orthodox Marxist," Marcuse borrowed freely from the phenomenological tradition (especially its Heideggerian spin), from sociology (mainly Max Weber), and most famously, from the metatheories of Sigmund Freud regarding the relation of individual to society.[1]

His conception of theoretical and political "orthodoxy" was in the direct line from Marx to Rosa Luxemburg and, except for a brief period immediately after World War II, did not extend to the Leninist tradition. His political position was consonant with the small anti-Leninist communist movement that broke from

the German and Dutch Communist Parties in the 1920s known as "councilists," so named because their conception of the new society was based on
workers councils.[2] In this respect, Marcuse once remarked that the best critique
of his work was that of one of the movement's founders, Paul Mattick, whose
virtually unknown book *Critique of Marcuse* (1971) took him to task for failing
to pay sufficient attention to the contradictions of the processes of capital accumulation, and for ignoring the implications of capitalism's crisis tendencies.[3]
Marcuse was always opposed to a conception of the revolutionary goal of seiz-
ing "state power" and in this respect was closer to his critic (Mattick) than to
many of his admirers. His conception of a new society was one in which the producers controlled production and popular organs such as councils exercised
power over public life. He scorned notions of revolutionary "dictatorship," even
as a transitional measure.

Even as many complained that Marcuse's prose was difficult to read, his writing and his political interventions animated the "generation of '68" like no other
social theorist. He was celebrated and widely read by New Left activists
throughout the advanced capitalist world, but also in countries like Mexico and
Brazil where student movements challenged the status quo. Although Marcuse
was vilified by communists and social democrats alike for the libertarianism of
his Marxism and its lack of programmatic specification, students and others in
the once-massive independent Left knew somehow that he meant for them to
flesh out the solutions for which he could only suggest problems. Perhaps more
important, together with Henri Lefebvre and the Situationists in France, and C.
Wright Mills and Paul Goodman in the United States, he held up a mirror to
their lives by articulating the banality and boredom endemic to late capitalist
everyday life. While he was closely identified with Critical Theory (the version
of Marxism associated with the so-called Frankfurt School) and unlike the two
other prominent figures in the movement, Theodor Adorno and Max
Horkheimer, the object of his investigation and reflection was praxis, a perspective eventually renounced on empirical and historical grounds by the others.

Marcuse was a student of Soviet ideology and a severe critic of Stalinism—
indeed his *Soviet Marxism* (1953) may be the most insightful study of the subject—but he never took the road of others of his contemporaries whose anti-
Stalinism often led them to veer rightward towards liberalism and beyond. Both
Marcuse and the group of Americans known as the New York Intellectuals
began from political premises informed by their judgment of the Soviet Union
as the leader of an authoritarian power bloc within the system of world domination. There the similarity ends. He wrote in some of the leading journals of
anti-Stalinist liberalism, including *Partisan Review,* the most influential among
them, but never associated with these ex-radicals who, after World War II, trav-

eled together to the political center of democratic liberalism, at different paces. Unlike Daniel Bell and others whose anti-Stalinism ended in despair and, eventually, in the ambivalence of neoconservatism (an ambivalence that led Bell, for example, to disdain the chance that, in a period of unparalleled capitalist prosperity, anything was possible save more of the present), Marcuse exemplified Gramsci's dictum, pessimism of the intellect, optimism of the spirit. More to the point, while his hopes were utopian, unlike the party Marxists and those whose radicalism gave way to a grudging or blinkered reconciliation with the liberal democratic capitalist order, his specification of the conditions of advanced capitalist societies was brutally concrete and his commitment to ending capitalist domination unwavering.

Marcuse remains a "name" but one that is distinctly of the past. To the extent that the Frankfurt School still enjoys some cachet, attention focuses on Adorno for reasons that are entirely understandable. Adorno's work on literature and on aesthetic theory remains compelling, and he is, arguably, the best theorist of twentieth-century music. The plain fact is that the term Gramsci applied to Marxism in a period of political terror, "the philosophy of praxis," has fallen on bad times, even into disrepute, since the collapse of the Berlin Wall and the consequential political disasters for state socialist regimes which ruled "under the banner of Marxism."[4]

A second factor that has produced indifference towards Marcuse is the ascendancy, in academic circles, of diverse post-Marxist discourses, roughly corresponding to the crack-up of the ideological hegemony of the communist movement. On the one side, some, including a number of erstwhile Marcuse admirers, have seized on Jürgen Habermas to provide permission to abandon what Mills once called the "labor metaphysic" in favor of a much less precise search for the possibility of perfect communication in a mythic "civil society." For class struggle they have substituted "communicative action." On the other side, there remains the mélange of literary critics and philosophers who followed Michel Foucault, Jacques Derrida, and Jean-François Lyotard into the territory characterized as "poststructuralism" which, among other moves, renounced all possible master discourses, especially Marxism, and marked the project of emancipation as hopelessly essentialist.

It is true that some in this camp, notably Ernesto Laclau and Chantal Mouffe, attempted a radical renewal from within a Nietzschean/Derridian framework and based their hopes on the vitality of the "new" social movements of sex, gender, and ecology. But notions of structured social relations were jettisoned or collapsed into "discourse" or, following Foucault, "discursive formations." While some gave lip service to the mantra of "class, race, gender," class was, for practical purposes, left by the wayside along with historical materialism that, in turn, is condemned as an a priori and metaphysical ideology. Imagine their surprise when Derrida wrote of the "specter" of Marx and Gilles Deleuze, who, although anti-Hegelian, was neither poststructuralist nor post-Marxist, and was reputed to have prepared most of a Marx book before his death in 1997. One wonders whether Derrida's book on Marx will, in academic literary circles, receive the attention lavished on the rest of his work or whether it will provoke the embarrassed silence that has attended the political writings of Deleuze and Guattari. Nor have Foucault's numerous acolytes explored the implications of his comment of 1983: "If I had known about the Frankfurt School in time, I would saved a great deal of work. I would not have said a certain amount of nonsense and would not have taken so many false trails trying not to get lost, when the Frankfurt School cleared the way."[5]

Another reason for Marcuse's declining influence is that the postcommunist era has witnessed not merely the virtual disappearance of movements and ideologies that, despite their reformist practice, declared systemic opposition to capitalism but also the catastrophic decline of trade unions, the feminist movement, and the integration of environmentalism into social democracy as its loyal "left wing," especially in Germany, Italy, and France. Witness, too, the political diminution of the great Italian Communist Party which, shortly following the collapse of the Soviet Union changed not only its name to the Democratic Party of the Left but watered down its program to get votes. The party gets more votes but has less intellectual and spiritual influence in Italian society. No longer committed to socialist transformation, it has abandoned the traditional distinction between immediate demands and the socialist goal and has, instead, merged with democratic republicanism. Following the pattern of European social democracy, it became a "party of government," a term which signals the Left is prepared to manage the capitalist state and to respect liberal democracy as a permanent and irrevocable achievement. First proposed by Eduard Bernstein in 1899, the parties of the European communists have universally followed this example. Lacking the framework once provided by Soviet state socialism and by revolutionary Leninism, let alone the Luxemburgist conception of workers' self-management, their long-term practical resemblance to postwar social democracy has now been inscribed in their doctrines as well.

In sum, it may have turned out that Marcuse's political philosophy was ensconced in conditions that are now surpassed, especially the regulation era of world capitalism and its companions, consumer society and the welfare state. Whereas Marcuse announced capitalism had solved most material needs for those he called "the underlying populations" of advanced capitalist societies, the reappearance of manufactured scarcity, with a vengeance, has resuscitated free market ideology and also the nostalgia for a return to what cannot be resuscitated, the welfare state. Hence, the resurgence of social-democratic parties that paradoxically seemed to have lost their reformist voice. In a period of rapid dis-aggregation of nation-states and the emergence of three major global economic power blocs to partially replace them, is Critical Theory obsolete?

What Marcuse himself had posited—the disappearance of the political dialectic, if not systemic contradictions—in advanced capitalist societies may be the chief reason his philosophy no longer resonates with a Left; its intellectual minions have generally disdained any politics save those of reform, which takes the form of rear guard actions in defense of past gains. Or, in its degraded man-ifestation, many believe that politics consists of internecine warfare in academ-ic departments and disciplines. The question he posed at the end of World War II and reiterated with searing force in the early 1960s is whether, in the wake of the incorporation of the uprisings in colonial societies by capital's main institu-tion of imperial intervention, the International Monetary Fund, the suppression of the insurgencies in the metropolitan areas and in the schools, we may speak of a viable movement of political opposition. Or, as Paul Piccone once argued, is what passes for oppositional politics merely so many forms of "artificial" negativity?[6]

Some of the American "generation of '68" have rediscovered liberal democ-racy, the virtues of incremental reform as a political ideal, and have urged those still loyal to the "new" social movements, especially those of freedom, sexual and otherwise (an important element in the Marcusian legacy), to abandon their frivolity and return to the fold of plain—read white male—class justice. Between the second demise of intellectual radicalism (the first, embodied in the New York Intellectuals, followed World War II) and the disappearance of the rheto-ric, if not the practice, of the opposition, what Marcuse has to say may be viewed by those who have reconciled themselves to the "given" and only seek to improve or fine tune it, as irrelevant. If his words sound strange to a new gener-ation trained to adapt to the prevailing social order and its technological appa-ratus, those who have not surrendered, and are interested in finding ways to address it, might find his work still compelling.

There is, of course, one more element of his relative obscurity: the tendency of what remains of radical politics to focus on single issues, identity domains, and intrainstitutional combat. This observation should not be interpreted as an attack on the inevitable (and generally healthy) dictum that all politics is local. The sites are not in question nor is the imperative to, as one writer has urged, "dig where you stand."[7] But the distance many activists and intellectuals alike have taken from "theory"—to find the categories that enable us to grasp the dynamic of the world system, the links between the contradictions of capital accumulation, culture, and politics—vitiates radical possibility. Sometimes this refusal takes the form of blatant anti-intellectualism, and since Marcuse was a consummate intellectual, he is readily identified with the enemy. This is a factor, but not the main response to the project of which he was a most eloquent tribune. Instead, I suspect that some who chose to remain politically engaged, but only at the level of immediacy, have abandoned hope that the intention of theory, to find the basis for global solidarity, is possible. If we are condemned to work in our backyards without forging intellectual and political links with others and have forgone the search for solidarity and for historical alternatives, is this not a backhanded version of the social-democratic compromise of the postwar era? Does this not expose the newer movements to nationalist incorporation, just as the trade unions were brought to heel in the 1940s?

2

The publication of the first of a projected six-volume collection of Marcuse's mostly uncollected essays is an opportunity for a new generation of readers, and some of his older interlocutors as well, to make acquaintance with his writings.[8] These pieces, written in the decade between the late 1930s and 1949, are almost all "occasional." They were composed for specific purposes, some of which had to do with Marcuse's role as an analyst for the Office of Strategic Services during the war (these concerned with the nature of the Nazi economic and political system and its mentality) and for the State Department in the immediate postwar years where he began his studies of the Cold War. The volume also contains, among other articles, "Some Social Implications of Modern Technology" (the precursor to *One Dimensional Man*) and a remarkable summa of his aesthetic theory, "Some Remarks on Aragon," where the theme of the subversive nature of romantic love is evoked, later to be expanded in his *Eros and Civilization* (1955) and in his final book, *The Aesthetic Dimension*. In addition, the reader will find two essays, coauthored with Franz Neumann, on theories of social change that may be the most cogent and concise history of modern political theory available.

Reproduced in the first volume are letters to Max Horkheimer from whom Marcuse (futilely, as it turns out) sought a permanent position in the relocated Institute for Social Research, and a brief correspondence with his former teacher, Martin Heidegger, in which Marcuse reflects on Heidegger's refusal to renounce his association and complicity with the Nazi regime. Marcuse reminded him that "you never renounced any of the actions or ideologies of the regime" and wondered how his mentor could be silent in the wake of a regime that murdered millions of Jews, to which Heidegger replied that after 1934 he "recognized his error" in regarding Nazism as a means to "spiritual renewal" but admittedly refrained from taking issue with the regime. There follows an astounding comment on Nazi murders:

> to the charge of dubious validity that you express about a regime that murdered millions of Jews, that made terror into an everyday phenomenon, and that turned everything that pertains to the ideas of spirit, freedom and truth into its bloody opposite, I can merely add that if instead of "Jews" you had written "East Germans" [that is, Germans of Eastern territories] then the same holds true for one of the allies.

Of course, the "ally" in question was the Soviet Union.[9]

Two points: Heidegger's statement of the "dubious validity" of Marcuse's remark concerning Nazi terror is a refrain of the European Right since the war and a fairly solid indication of his enduring sympathies. Heidegger's equation with the Holocaust of some Soviet atrocities against Germans undoubtedly occurred in conquered territories. Moreover, in the same paragraph, Heidegger repeats the well-known contention that the "bloody terror of the Nazis in point of fact had been kept secret from the German people," which was a major bone of contention among postwar intellectuals, especially in the debate between those who would hold the whole of the German people responsible for the terror and those, like Dwight Macdonald, who argued that the terror was an aspect of a war spirit for which human life had become expendable and of a new system of technological and bureaucratic power which routinely hid information from the people and deprived them of sovereignty, and also of responsibility. Chances are, according to this point of view, most did not know of the Holocaust, and the rank-and-file perpetrators of the Nazi crimes, down to the technicians who operated the ovens, could, with some justice, claim they were merely following orders. Hannah Arendt was to call this outcome the "banality of evil." However, with their silence, those capable of escaping banality, especially the intellectuals, bore some responsibility for what transpired. In a letter dated May 12, 1948, in using Heidegger's own categories (*Logos, dasein,* and so forth), Marcuse decisively convicted him of betraying his own philosophy and remaining ensconced in the zeitgeist of 1933, and ended their correspondence.

3

He began as a scholar, a designation Marcuse never ceased to mock because, in his eyes, scholarship without a *telos,* lacking what I shall call an onto-historical purpose, became, in his words, *scholarshit.* In contrast to Adorno and

Horkheimer, Marcuse was a philosopher of praxis; he was forever searching for the openings for revolution and believed that theory was intimately linked to action. Having written his doctoral thesis on aesthetics in 1922, three years after participating in the ill-fated Spartacus revolt of 1919 against the social-democratic retreat from the German revolution, he went on to study with Martin Heidegger in Freiburg. His *habilitation*, an advanced degree required of all who sought permanent university positions, a Heideggerian reading of Hegel's ontology, was submitted in 1933 to Heidegger, already on his way to joining forces with the Nazis. Despite interventions by others of his committee, it was not accepted and remained unpublished until well after the war.

Shortly after Hitler's rise to power, the Institute for Social Research (the academic embodiment of Critical Theory with which he was affiliated) temporarily removed to Paris on its way to New York. After a brief stay in the Institute's Geneva branch in 1934, Marcuse left for the United States and helped set up its new center at Columbia University. Until the war, he was "the institute's philosophy specialist" and during the 1930s wrote a brilliant study of authority that was published in 1936 as part of the celebrated sociological work directed by Horkheimer and Erich Fromm, *Studies in Authority and the Family*. His first major work in English, *Reason and Revolution: Hegel and the Rise of Social Theory*, appeared in 1941. In the 1960 preface, Marcuse wrote:

> This book was written in the hope that it would make a small contribution to the revival, not of Hegel, but of a mental faculty which is in danger of being obliterated: the power of negative thinking. As Hegel defines it: "Thinking is, indeed essentially the negation of what is immediately before us. . . ." Today, the dialectical mode of thought is alien to the whole established universe of discourse and action. It seems to belong to the past and to be rebutted by the achievements of technological civilization.[10]

Four years later he was to publish his most famous book, *One Dimensional Man*, which resumed the themes that had occupied his thinking since the early 1930s.

From World War II, when he served various U.S. governmental bodies, especially the newly formed Office of Strategic Services (OSS), the predecessor to the Central Intelligence Agency, as an analyst, to his last years ending with his death in 1979, his writings, teaching, and public expressions were directed to achieving human emancipation, first from the Nazi terror and then from one-dimensional society and thought, which he believed had permeated advanced capitalist societies as a consequence of the inversion of reason from its critical function.[11]

Several of the papers were written as reports to the directors of the OSS. They deal with the cultural and ideological aspects of Nazism, but also forge a highly original theory of fascism that differs rather sharply from some aspects of Horkheimer's, especially the idea that fascism is chiefly an authoritarian state form in which the state takes the role of capitalist. Marcuse disputed the prevailing Communist view that, in the words of Georgi Dimitrov, general secretary of the Communist International, it was "the open terroristic dictatorship of the most reactionary sections of finance capital."[12] Nor did he hold that fascism was chiefly a form of racist ideology and terrorist political practice in which the state occupied the central position. Rather, he argued rather convincingly that it was a new structural relationship between economic and social power and the individual, in which the state has lost its autonomy and thus its mediating role.

In the years immediately following the war, Marcuse occupied a singular political and intellectual position. His anti-Stalinism pervaded the pages of his articles and of his study of Soviet ideology of this period, *Soviet Marxism* (1953). Yet, despite the fact that he worked for the State Department until 1951, he remained loyal to the premises of Critical Theory and to Marxism: there is no question of joining in the celebration. In fact, however pessimistic his assessment of the practical chance that the working class might shake its lassitude and act as a catalyst for revolution, in this period he sharpened his critique of capitalist politics and culture and of the Cold War. However, in contrast to the anti-Stalinist Trotskyists, Marcuse remained an unrelenting critic of state socialism and also of voluntarism, expressed in Lenin's declaration that "politics takes precedence over economics."

Marcuse's most salient contribution to Critical Theory was to have shown the subsumption of reason under advanced capitalism to what he described as "technological rationality" and demonstrated its profound implications for praxis. The project of developing the theory of technological rationality may be traced to his essay "Some Social Implications of Modern Technology" (1941). From his early study, "The Foundations of Historical Materialism" (1932), a pioneering commentary on Marx's *Economic and Philosophical Manuscripts of 1844* which had recently been published as volume 3 of the *Collected Works*, his thinking never wavered from the task of discerning the agents of historical transformation that, in his view, were always located in social groups standing in a definite relation to the social structure. Marcuse found it increasingly difficult to maintain the standard Marxist hope in the agency of the working class, its trade unions, and its political parties.

Yet he constantly reiterated that human liberation, of which the abolition of capitalism was the first step, was unthinkable unless theory could specify material conditions for its realization, including those of culture, and identify and assess social forces capable of making change. He was keenly interested in the labor movement, not in the spirit of romantic nostalgia but because, in his thought, its fate was a barometer of political prospects. So, in the light of what Critical Theory believed to be the fateful "incorporation" of the proletariat by the apparatuses of advanced capitalism, Marcuse acknowledged that liberation was, for the time being, relegated to utopian hope but declared that his was a "concrete" utopia whose chance of realization was contingent on whether it was rooted in the very apparatus that constrained it.

It is relatively easy, in retrospect, to account for the unforeseen civil rights, student, antiwar, and feminist movements of the 1960s. We can now discern that the 1950s were years of seething discontent. In the first place, blacks took Roosevelt's wartime promises to mediate the blatant inequalities of the post-Reconstruction era seriously. When succeeding governments failed to deliver, the black church, returning veterans, and other organized forces began to mobilize and, in time, produced a mass insurgency that assumed the face of a movement of mainly southern black students. We trace other sources of discontent to middle-class discomfit with the American celebration that accompanied U.S. postwar hegemony. We discern an "existential crisis" of a relatively affluent middle-class generation which recognized, despite the surfeit of goods and artificial pleasures, that everyday life in late capitalism remained empty, even "boring." Students rebelled against the technicalization of their own education and demanded a voice in university curriculum and pedagogy.

Little of this was apparent at the time. The Beats and other literary movements notwithstanding, radical thought seemed cranky and hopelessly out of synch with the times. Yet even as ex-radical Daniel Bell was confidently pronouncing the death of radicalism, the writings of the few intellectual radicals were eagerly read and assimilated by a new generation poised to rebel against the consensus, the peace movement had amassed a broad cross section of the liberal middle class, and reform movements were rearing their heads in the universities and urban neighborhoods.

Perhaps the most influential books in the late 1950s and early 1960s among dissident students, intellectuals, and political activists were C. Wright Mills's *Power Elite* and Paul Goodman's *Growing Up Absurd*. Published in 1956 as the deep freeze of the postwar era was melting around the edges, Mills's study of the commanding heights of U.S. society provided for a largely inchoate new radicalism the terms with which to carry on a critique. Departing from the conventional Marxist category of a "ruling" class of industrial and commercial capital, Mills argued that social power was composed of the elites of three institutional orders: the corporations, the military, and the political directorate. In turn, drawing from earlier depression-era studies of trusts and monopolies, Mills found they were interlocked; except for the military, which flowed outward but did not accept civilian leadership, members of one order routinely served in one or both of the other two. Thus, for example, Dwight Eisenhower, a solid member of the military high command became, as a civilian, a member of innumerable corporate boards and president of the United States. Similarly, the leading corporate lawyer John Foster Dulles was Eisenhower's secretary of state. A succession of secretaries of the treasury, from Roosevelt's Henry Morgenthau and Eisenhower's C. Douglas Dillon to Clinton's Robert Rubin, and secretaries of state and defense have traditionally moved back and forth between financial and industrial corporations and the government. Mills made the ineffable visible; he codified and verified what every critic of liberal democracy suspected but could not articulate in concrete terms: that the notion of "one man, one vote" was only a—not the—political reality. The more salient reality was that a mostly unaccountable small group of rich and powerful men from corporations, the military, and the political elite made most of the decisions that affected the lives of ordinary people.

Published in 1960, Goodman's rant was directed against images of the 1950s as a decade in which people were, in the words of satirist Ira Wallach, "deliriously happy." Although Mills focused on the system of economic and political power, Goodman examined two of the crucial institutions of social reproduction, family and schools. Goodman's ideas—some of which recalled themes of John Dewey's educational philosophy, others derived from the anarchist school experiments of the earlier years of the twentieth century, and still others from that peculiar combination of Reichian and conventional Freudian concepts that underlay his own psychology—remain controversial and salient to a new radical movement. He confirmed the feelings of many children that, notwithstanding the postwar prosperity, theirs were lives of nearly unrelieved psychological and social bondage. Whereas Marcuse argued that the authoritarian father was the condition for youthful rebellion, for Goodman and for Wilhelm Reich, patriarchal authority stifled children's creativity and individuality.[13] Schools were mostly a continuation of this authority. They believed that schools were not only a waste of their intellectual energies; in addition to being places of intellectual conformity, they were constituted to impose conventional morality, sexual and otherwise. Goodman's cry for freedom—that schools should be places where the student could explore her own needs and inclinations—tried to shift the center of the educational ground from curriculum and teacher to the kids.

Before politicians and school authorities openly proclaimed it as official policy, the identification of education with training remained an unacknowledged practice and Goodman labeled such conflation "miseducation." *Growing Up Absurd* might have been dismissed by many educators as utopian loony-tunes and attacked by conservatives as dangerous to the prevailing order, but kids—especially young adults—found it a justification for dissent and for hope that a different future could be forged in the present. In the sixties and seventies, every educational reformer invoked the slogans derived from the libertarian program of Goodman and educator A. S. Neill of "child-centered" education, of individual development and choice. Needless to say, in the Anglo-American context, the anarchist content was, in translation, watered down. Goodman argued that state education was *inherently* authoritarian. Nor was Goodman's sexual libertarianism taken up by educational reformers. Mindful of the puritanical zeitgeist, even progressives were cautious. In the first place, most of them favored the concept of a progressive public bureaucracy to foster the interests of those traditionally excluded from educational opportunity. In the service of widening access to working-class and minority students, they put aside their own critique of state institutions such as schools. As for sexuality, the furthest they were willing to travel was to undertake timid programs of sex "education," in which sexuality was made procedural and, more egregiously, framed as discourse of a social problem to be overcome by the judicious use of contraceptives or, worse, by abstinence.

In this most open of all advanced industrial societies, notwithstanding the sexualized emanations of popular culture, sex still lives an underground existence. In a rebuke to the judgment, promulgated most recently by Foucault, that sex is no longer subversive because it has been co-opted by the dominant culture, after a period of what Marcuse termed "repressive desublimation," teenagers are again punished for practicing it. The view of children as sexual beings is no longer vilified as the ravings of psychoanalytic pornographers, but the fact has now become the occasion for a new repressive era in schooling. Schools now admit that their object is to foster the child's adaptation to conventional morality and are prepared to expel or severely discipline those who refuse to toe the line. In some parts of the United States, a regime of expulsion and other severe punishments for what is termed " inappropriate behavior" (read sex and fighting) has become one of the accepted routines of school life. For their indiscretions, young single mothers are pressed into forced labor if they stay on public assistance. Once protected by the press and now routinely exposed as adulterers, politicians may fall, and a whole new category of law enforcement, the sex police, has been brought into being and counts among its cadre parents and teachers, politicians, administrators, cops, and judges.

For the intellectual Left and many activists, Herbert Marcuse's *One Dimensional Man* was the defining treatise of the late 1960s. Whether they read it or not, those who identified with the "movement" took its descriptions of the flattening of everyday existence as a personal testament. Even as millions took to the streets protesting the war, racial, sex, and gender discrimination, and the destruction of the physical and social environment by commercial and military interests, Marcuse's pitiless analysis and gloomy prognostication of the possibility for radical social change, in Lenin's words, became a material force because it "gripped the masses," or at least, intellectuals and activists. The irony was lost neither on Marcuse nor his readers. Composed from materials culled from contemporary journalism, Mills's descriptions of how corporate and military power is wielded in the United States and in the world, and from Marcuse's own earlier work on technology and ideology reprinted in Kellner's collection, the book became a reference for precisely those whom Marcuse had proclaimed hopelessly integrated by consumerism and by liberalism into the prevailing order.

Marcuse's orthodoxy consisted in this: he said he "presupposed" Marx's critique of political economy, especially *Capital*'s imminent critique of categories such as the free market, the theory according to which, in a free market, supply, demand, and profits were generally in equilibrium, the bourgeois supposition that profit inhered in the risk of investment, and so forth. The task of Critical Theory was to "extend" the Marxist analysis to crucial spheres which arose in the twentieth century as a consequence of the passage of capitalism from its competitive phase to that of what he described, following the denotation of his day, the "monopoly" stage. Concretely, with the Frankfurt School and following Georg Lukacs, Marcuse located the source of bourgeois ideological hegemony in commodity fetishism but, through his critique of rationality, concluded that if "commodification" was the necessary condition of domination in advanced capitalism, it was no longer sufficient. Marcuse radicalized Heidegger's critique of technology; for him it became the sufficient condition for domination.[14]

In time, Marcuse came to terms with the social movements of the 1960s and took pride in his own role, even if unintended, in fostering them. The burden of his thesis was that the revolutionary opposition had not only been defeated in the interwar period and by the domination by the two great power blocs of world politics, society and its components, but that human beings had been unalterably transformed by advanced capitalism. His metaphor that technological society produced a somatic change that ultimately affected the genes underlined the gravity of his judgment. The explosive thesis of *One Dimensional Man* was to have freed ideology and critique from the mental realm and to endow it with onto-historical status. Technological rationality, which is inherent in nineteenth-century utilitarianism and in twentieth-century natural science and social theory, has penetrated every fiber of social being; not only has negation become literally unthinkable but liberal capitalism, no less than fascism, fixes limits so that alternatives which are not instrumental to systemic reproduction are silenced, not merely relegated to the paranoid margins.

However, in some ways, "Some Social Implications of Modern Technology" (1941) is the most succinct and illuminating introduction to Marcuse's thought on technology. For him, the question concerning technology is not entirely answered, as Heidegger claims, by making the distinction between the Greek meaning of the term *techne* as the activity of "uncovering" or disclosing nature, and holding nature in "reserve" for human ends. Marcuse distinguished between technology and technics. According to Marcuse, "technology is a social process," whereas technics is a "partial factor" that could "promote totalitarianism as well as liberty." In the name of efficiency and progress, technology's imperatives subsume individuals and other social processes.

> Under the impact of the apparatus, individualistic rationality has been transformed into technological rationality. It is by no means confined to the subjects and objects of large scale enterprises but characterizes the pervasive modes of thought and the even the manifold forms of protest and rebellion. This rationality establishes standards of judgement and fosters attitudes which make men ready to accept and event introject the dictates of the apparatus.[15]

The leading theme of the essay, one that is reiterated throughout the rest of his work for the next twenty-five years, is that technology, as Heidegger claimed, "enframes" social relations but leaves little, if any, room for difference. As Lewis Mumford argued in his earlier study, *Technics and Civilization,* intelligence has been transferred to the machine process that, in turn, sets its limits. Technology's criterion of efficiency, as defined by capitalism's requirements, enframes human activity through the mechanism of introjection (which here appears as "introjection"). In short, it becomes increasingly difficult for us to separate ourselves from the machine since we have identified with it, a theme reiterated within a different framework by, among others, Donna Haraway. Marcuse altered the well-known formulation that social reproduction required the individual to adapt, and to internalize, the normative order. Technology is not introjected by means of the mechanisms by which beliefs and values are assimilated. Reproduction no longer requires "ideology" in the traditional sense if rationality itself is identical to technology and the imperative of efficiency that demands only that our activity be subject to ratio, to measurement.

4

Critical Theory is unified by its appropriation of Weber's concept of instrumental rationality as domination, and Marcuse's early paper on technology provided one of the key texts. What Horkheimer called the "end" or "eclipse" of reason and its transformation into an instrument of capital's domination over labor became, during the interwar period, Critical Theory's sufficient explanation of how the leading capitalist powers have, against all predictions, managed to stave off collapse in the wake of wars, economic crises, and revolutions in the periphery as well as the center of the world system. For Critical Theory, domination entails the social and psychological subordination of the underlying population to class power by the reconfiguration of art into the culture industry, the emergence of consumer society (at least in the most developed capitalist countries), the suppression of any conception of the rational except the "given" reality, and the replacement of religion by science. Whereas science initially conceived itself as a critique of religion's domination over human knowledge, as it is integrated into production and becomes the central productive force, the scientific establishment is seen and sees itself as identical with the system of power. As science extends its purview, the domination of nature leads to the domination of human nature. This human domination is exemplified in the distortions capitalism has effected in the universal quest for happiness.

The dawn and youth of capitalism is marked by the ruthless exploitation of labor. It was also a period of mass workers' movements which sought ameliorative measures to relieve suffering and recognized the imperative of fighting for a new society in which the producers would have decisive power over social life. But, in the shadow of the rise of workers' movements and, especially the socialist revolutions of the post–World War I period, capitalism revealed its capacity to "learn" from history. Technology, once regarded as merely a tool of industrial production, now became a crucial cultural, as well as economic, weapon of capitalism's systemic reproduction. In time, science and scientifically based technology took on all the trappings of a new religion and became one of the crucial instruments of domination. We are admonished to "believe" in science as the moral equivalent of salvation. In medicine, for example, it promises, and sometimes delivers, a "magic bullet" to cure diseases, whether in the form of developing vaccines and other medications or, in recent years, by means of genetic alteration. Equipped with new biotechnology, science brings back the once-despised doctrine of eugenics and envisions human perfection, as well as a world of mass surveillance. In this sense, science is the vehicle for the obliteration of the boundaries between private and public, and thereby deprives the individual of the last vestiges of protection.

At the practical level, capitalism mobilizes scientifically based technology and is able to deliver many of the "goods" revolutionaries always believed must await a communist future. The conflation of one of the main elements of happiness— freedom from want—in advanced societies limits the horizon of possibility by "abolishing" or, more accurately, marginalizing and exporting material scarcity to the developing world. At the same time, as Marcuse pointed out, individuality no longer means self-development but the relentless pursuit of personal interests. This, for him, became vital for understanding of the nature of fascism.

What divided Marcuse from the Frankfurt School, of which Horkheimer (its director) was well aware, was their different perspectives on the possibilities for politics. For Adorno, praxis (that Greek term for a reflective political practice) was all but foreclosed by the integration of the putative agents of historical transformation, the working classes of the most advanced industrial societies, into the system of power and also by the intellectual hegemony of its most persuasive ideology, positivism. Capitalism had, in his view, secured its domination not by terror alone, although state repression was one of its time-honored tools. It had completely subsumed any possibility of critical thought so that the great category of emancipation, negation, had been driven from the vocabulary, thereby depriving us of the means by which to think behind the "given" social and political reality. The capacity of the capitalist order to close the gap between representation and reality, to find the means to heal the rift between consciousness and society, left only avant-garde art and the homeless mind to oppose it. Thus, Horkheimer and Adorno stopped at critique because, for them, genuine opposition existed only in theory; the empirical and historical opposition had effectively disappeared.

Of course, Marcuse recognized this loss and its consequences. His intellectual pessimism was tempered by what the philosopher Ernst Bloch termed the "principle" of hope, a principle because it is the a priori condition for intervention into the social world; without hope, intellectual pessimism degenerates into quietism and thereby becomes an agent for the naturalization of the given society. In the words that French Marxist sociologist and philosopher Henri Lefebvre used to describe the May 1968 events in Paris, Marcuse believed that "events belie forecasts."[16] As Adorno and Horkheimer carefully distanced themselves from the student movement, suspecting it was little more than a return to barbarism in revolutionary garb—or worse, grist for strengthening the social machine, Marcuse, already seventy years old, rarely refused an invitation to speak at a demonstration or lend his name to a petition or an appeal.

His activism helped convince the UC-San Diego administration to force him to retire in 1975, but Marcuse only ceased to teach classes for credit; throughout the 1970s, he participated in study groups, engaged in informal discussions with students and colleagues, and continued to write and speak to large audiences. One study group, conducted in the late 1970s with a few graduate students in literature, was on the writings of Walter Benjamin. Marcuse found himself at odds with the text, "The Work of Art in the Age of Mechanical Reproduction," and also with his fellow students. For him, the idea that the mechanical reproduction and dissemination of "great" art could lead to its democratization was ludicrous. He never came to terms with film and other forms of popular, especially visual, culture and regarded them as instances of anti-aesthetic. But, influenced by his wife Erica Sherover and other women who were close to him, he came to understand the radical implications of contemporary feminism and also the salience of new social movements towards the end of his life. Subject to adulation but also to rebuke, he opened himself to criticism because, despite his intellectual gloom, he believed in the redemptive power of love.

5

Marcuse's theory of fascism entails a theory of the modern state, but it is not consonant with the prevailing theory of the state developed by Horkheimer in collaboration with Frederick Pollock, for whom fascism was an authoritarian form of "state capitalism." Horkheimer's powerful article "The Authoritarian State" (1940) summarizes this position.[17] In Horkheimer's view "those who would not speak of capitalism should keep silent about fascism." This aphorism signifies that fascism's characteristic forms of authority inhere in capitalist social relations. For far from being governed by the free market, advanced capitalist societies have long since entered a period of permanent state intervention into the economy that, in its most extreme manifestation, takes on more than a regulative role. According to Pollack and Horkheimer, even before the advent of militaristic/fascist societies, the state tended to take on many of the functions of private capital, and frequently displaced private property to a subordinate role.

The integration of the state and finance capital was first theorized by Rudolph Hilferding, who also developed the core ideas that became the basis of Bukharin's theory of imperialism, of which Lenin was the main publicist. With the onset of the economic crisis and of the Great Depression, it was Henryk Grossman, briefly associated with the Institute for Social Research, and a leading Marxist economic theorist who offered the view that monopoly capitalism within the liberal democratic state has already eliminated its "relative autonomy." By the mid-thirties Pollack was writing his "state capitalism" thesis, and several years later, Horkheimer argued that fascism was "merely" a continuation of state capitalism, already evident at the dawn of the twentieth century in the advanced countries.

Marcuse departed from this perspective when he insisted on the salience of the relative autonomy of the liberal state, even in the wake of the rise of the large corporation, the trusts, and financial capitalism. Thus, instead of emphasizing the continuity between the monopoly phase of capitalism and fascism, he focused on the break. In this view, at its best, the liberal capitalist state is a "mediator" between the individual and the enormous economic power accumulated by the modern corporation.

In February 1947, five years after the paper "State and Individual under National Socialism" appeared, Marcuse wrote what Kellner has called "33 Theses." When I mentioned to Peter Marcuse, the literary executor of his father's papers, that I was writing this chapter and would address these theses, he replied that they were a bit "dated." It is not difficult to come to this conclusion if statements such as this one are taken at face value.

> After military defeat of Hitler-Fascism (which was a premature and isolated form of capitalist reorganization) the world is dividing into a neo-fascist and a Soviet camp. What still remains of democratic-liberal forms will be crushed between the two camps or absorbed by them. The states in which the old ruling class survived the war economically and politically will become fascicized in the foreseeable future, while the others will enter the Soviet camp.[18]

On the surface, this prediction appears to have turned out to be wrong on two counts: liberal democracy remains the state form in all advanced capitalist societies and, within severe limits, has diffused to the ex-communist states, such as Russia, Poland, Hungary, and the Czech Republic, and to developing countries which were formerly military or one-party dictatorships, such as Argentina, Mexico, and Brazil. Moreover, although China and Vietnam experienced communist-led nationalist revolutions and Cuba underwent a parallel revolutionary process, liberal-democratic forms have not been instituted to this day, but their social systems are not forged in the Soviet model, except insofar as they are party dictatorships. However, state ownership of key production and distribution industries is disintegrating in favor of massive private ownership and capital investment. With this shift, the working class experiences an unprecedented level of exploitation.

But consider how Marcuse's conception differs from the accepted views of fascism. Of course, United States society is not marked by a program of *systematic* terror against racial minorities, although we have seen that the number of police violations of the rights of black men has escalated in proportion as poverty and unemployment deepen in the cities. But, in other respects, such as the intensification of individualism, the decline of the labor movement and other social groups, and the emergence of a cultural environment of puritanical antisexuality, we can find the earmarks of a growing authoritarianism. At the same time, as it observes the rituals of parliamentary democratic processes, have not the mediating functions of the state gradually receded? Are not the imperatives of global and regional capital taken as priorities by legislatures and public bureaucracies to the detriment of the social wage? Does the "general welfare" regulate state functions or is the state systematically constrained to cut back education and income supports to the poor and the aged, and reduce health care to the aged and to the poor to bare minimum levels? Finally, to what extent does the individual have recourse to institutions of justice, and to what extent are social groups disintegrating and being replaced by atomized individuals who fiercely assert their own competitive interests?

The second theme of the theses is by now familiar: "outside the Soviet camp there is no workers movement capable of revolution." Assessing the communist movement, Marcuse found the Trotskyists too weak and, in any case, hopelessly divided, and as for the Communist Parties, while they are capable of revolution, their subordination to the Soviet politics which is committed to détente on the basis of a balance of terror with the capitalist powers makes them hostile to revolution (thesis five). Besides, Marcuse argued, "The societal tendency of state socialism is anti-revolutionary. . . . The direct producers do not control production (and with it their destiny) any more than they do in the system of liberal-democratic capitalism."[19] Prefiguring what became painfully apparent in the 1960s, he wrote, "the communist parties are becoming more social democratic themselves," signaling that Social Democracy had "monopolized" the workers' movement after the war.[20]

Finally, fighting defeat with hope, Marcuse outlined a revolutionary Socialist program: the socialization of the means of production and their administration by the "immediate producers"; the abolition of wage labor; and, after taking control, shorter working hours. Nearly thirty years after the decisive suppression of the soviets (workers' councils) in Germany and Hungary by the counter-revolution and in the newly created Soviet Union in the period of "war communism" by the revolution itself, which devoured its own children, Marcuse insisted upon the councilist program. He did not end there. The last four theses are a critique of the Soviet experience as a prelude to what he argued was the imperative of fleshing out a new revolutionary theory. In these paragraphs, Marcuse focused on the "problem of preventing a state-socialist bureaucracy" where workers exchange one set of masters for another. Marcuse argued that bureaucracy is "an economic" problem rooted in "the technological structure of the production apparatus." It took another twenty years before labor process theorists caught on to this issue. Alfred Sohn-Rethel formulated the question in terms of the division of intellectual and manual labor; the bureaucracy as a managerial class monopolized technical and organizational knowledge, and, as Harry Braverman argued, relentlessly "deskilled" manual labor, rendering the possibility of workers' control less likely.[21]

So, whereas under capitalism, the disaggregation of the public bureaucracy is an authoritarian measure because it leaves the individual helpless before the superior forces of corporations and of the market, the industrial bureaucracy is inimical to workers' interests under socialism as much as under capitalism. For Marcuse, the trade unions are the best workers' defensive organization under capitalism; but they are hostile to socialism. Thus "the political workers party remains the subject of revolution," unlike Marx's view that as soon as conditions are present, the workers' "knowledge of its own interests" is sufficient for revolutionary action. According to Marcuse, the Leninist vanguard is made necessary because monopoly capital has found the means to "level" the proletariat and deprive it of the collective knowledge by which to lead itself. Despite his critique of the communist parties, they remained the only possible source of revolutionary theory and practice. Needless to say, in his moment of despair, Marcuse was driven to an uncharacteristic endorsement and one that he lived to renounce.

In these essays, one can view the dialectic at work as both method of analysis and description of social reality. For this reason alone, they have more than purely historical interest. If some of his political judgments are of their time and, in the post-Soviet era, surpassed, what remains is a highly provocative and creative Marxism in which the simplicities of inherited views are constantly challenged. Marcuse's acute understanding of the relative autonomy of technological domination, his insistence on the salience of theory as both a tool of practice and a site of opposition in a time of conformity, and his unsurpassed explorations into the culture and politics of authoritarianism and of its outcome, fascism, are as fresh today as they were a half century ago.

13

ONTO⊖HISTORY AND EPISTEMOLOGY

There are two logics of scientific discovery that correspond to fundamentally divergent theoretical approaches. The first, emanating from Kant and elaborated in a variety of ways by realists and antirealists alike, is keyed to what Ian Hacking termed "representing and intervening." This tradition is chiefly concerned with issues of (1) what scientific knowledge is, in itself, and to what it refers, and (2) how we know what we know. The second framework—whose sources are as diverse as Spinoza, Hegel, and Marx—addresses three closely related questions: the onto-historical aspects of science, especially how scientific knowledge derives from industrial and technical practice, much of which bears on issues of ideology and politics; the cultural environment within which knowledge is produced, including what might be termed a scientific culture; and the "effects" or "leaks" of science on social institutions and practices. Needless to say, these leaks backtrack and have effects on science.

Characteristically, many practitioners of what might be termed the epistemological logic of science are preoccupied with Fregian language games, while others who are also interested in language try to evaluate the relation of theory to observation—often distinguishing between them—and ask, like Carnap, whether science depends on induction; still others might claim that all observation and experiment is, in Norwood Hanson's or Willard Quine's terms, theory loaded, in which case the idea of induction—that theories and other generalizations derive, in the last instance, from experience or data—is absurd. Some follow Popper's notion that experiment is not about verification but is concerned with a method by which falsification of theories is possible.

Of the influential philosophers of science, Popper has, perhaps, gone furthest in conceding that culture, ideology, and social relations are, inescapably, part of the conjectural apparatus of scientific discovery. He acknowledges that a scientific culture exists which encourages or discourages scientific progress. He is willing to grant that observation is, indeed, theory laden, but he insists on the primacy of method as the key cleansing device that will factor out the messiness of culture. Although there is no possibility of verifying scientific propositions since, along with the best anti-empiricist positivists such as Quine, Popper disdains the crude versions of the reflection theory of knowledge and the correspondence theory of truth. Scientific propositions are not a "copy" of nature. But he rescues positivism by insisting that, by algorithms of falsification, science is able to arrive at a provisional truth that, even if it does not mirror nature, provides scientific propositions a high warrant of assertability.

Thus we have the preeminence of epistemology in the dominant logic of scientific philosophy and frequently also of science and technology studies in the sociological or anthropological modes. Underlying this approach is the distinction between the subject that knows and the object that is "given" to observation and to theorizing. Although some, like Hacking, recognize that science is always an intervention and suspect that its objects are constituted rather than "given," the epistemologists remain within the bonds of Cartesian presuppositions and positivist protocols. Even many engaged in science and technology studies, which are based on the controversial idea that the material practices of science shape its results, tend to render an essentially internal account of shifts in scientific knowledge. While science studies is attentive to the role of conversation, machinery, and what Latour and Woolgar call "inscriptions" in determining the results of scientific discovery, they tend to reify the laboratory as the exclusive site of investigation. Perhaps, at the end of the day, they share the empiricists' suspicion of speculation and theorizing.

To be sure, some—like Latour—recognize the social nature of scientific work; with his collaborator Woolgar, he showed that laboratory life is implicated in the process and in the results of inquiry. The social nature of scientific work is more concretely involved in the relation, in turn, of observation and experiment to machinery, inscription (the accounts of scientific experiment), and talk, which, he argues, ineluctably mediate knowledge. Or, in its stronger program, Sharon Traweek and Andrew Pickering, among others, take a step beyond the ambiguous term "implication." The burden of the argument that arises from their investigations is that the social relations of the laboratory are constitutive of knowledge: relations of authority as well as collegiality, the process of deciding what investigators have "seen" when they use machine indicators to signify observation, and the selection of information that goes into reports of observation and result. Latour has argued that the laboratory is a model, perhaps *the* model of the "world," a euphemism for social relations.

But many ethnographers like Latour remain within the microinstitutional framework of scientific discovery and in this sense have not broken with the tradition of the sociology of science established more than a half century ago by Robert Merton. Far from opposing epistemological investigations they have, in Steve Fuller's terms, produced a social epistemology that, in most respects, is enframed in the Cartesian premise of subject/object relations, each term taken as an actor in the unfolding of discovery.

The twentieth-century work in the onto-historical paradigm, the second major approach, is mainly found in the Marxist traditions of the Frankfurt School and Althusser, and is more recently taken up by the Deleuzians, of which Foucault is both historian and philosopher of science. Since knowledge, including scientific knowledge, is not lodged in a sovereign "subject" but is, itself, a part of being (in these investigations one makes no fundamental distinctions between the social and natural), there is no inside and no outside to processes of scientific discovery. Taking a cue from Vico, we know the world because we are rooted in it and make it, where "making" is not a reference to consciousness but to material practices, of which the production of language and culture is an aspect. The "truth-value" of propositions is neither the focus of inquiry nor apposite to the problematic of the onto-historical paradigm. Thus, the problems of representation and its corollary correspondence are indeterminate because scientific objects are never "given" but are presumed to be immanent in modes of scientific inquiry.

This is not a statement of social constructionism, which derives its fundamental inspiration from Kant because it claims that meanings in the world are the complex emanations of consciousness. The onto-historical proposes a different understanding of objectivity. Being is the case, not the divided subject/object.

The story of the division begins with the dialectic of the Enlightenment. Although the project of Enlightenment science was to free itself from the thrall of religious belief and to know the world through fresh eyes, it was also implicated, and implicated science, in the bourgeois project of nature's domination to meet human needs. Recall Horkheimer and Adorno's argument: it is not that science is a form of ideology if by that designation we mean it is false. Horkheimer and Adorno note science's ability to predict and control nature, which among other benefits to humanity augurs well for the end of backbreaking labor and, perhaps

most of all, the possibility that labor as such (not work, because the former signifies compulsion while the latter is a category of self-directed activity) would all
but disappear through scientifically rooted technological innovation.

Despite these advances, science is one-sided. Science is the keystone of the
larger Enlightenment enterprise of the domination of nature and of humans.
While the Enlightenment aimed to liberate humankind from the thrall of superstition and dogma, it generated new dogmas; while its concern was to separate
knowledge from the control of religious institutions and establish science's sovereignty, it succeeded in establishing a new religion among whose salient elements was the primacy of "observation" as the source of legitimate intellectual
knowledge and, perhaps most of all, its claim that the book of nature is written
in the language of mathematics, a language which facilitates nature's subordination. As Husserl demonstrated, the crucial move is the separation of quality
from quantity; being is being measured. Mathematization of nature enhances
nature's predictability, makes it fungible—to which may be added that under the
power of Cartesian science, nature's totality is parceled out between physical,
chemical, biological, social, cultural, and psychological domains as if these divisions inhere in the natural order itself. These are arranged hierarchically and
ultimately reduced, in recent developments, to the primacy of physics because,
until the advent of molecular biology, it was indisputably the most mathematical of all the sciences. Math and physics became the models for all forms of
being. And, of course, Cartesian epistemology is the master discourse of domination. Its posit of subject and object as two quite separate entities drains the
subject of nature and drains the object of culture. They face each other as antag-
onists, but nature is constructed as object, devoid of any of the presumed qual-
ities of the subject, especially agency.

What can be shown to be a cultural posit becomes naturalized. Historically,
one of the more ubiquitous leaks from science to institutions was the adaptation
of the theory of biological evolution to the development of the concepts associated with inherited intelligence—the nefarious proposition that differences in
what might easily be shown to be culturally constituted are, on the contrary,
intellectual performances taken to be genetic. During the progressive era, this
doctrine, although still firmly implanted in schools, suffered considerable erosion in science and in the public. From the earlier work of Ashley Montagu to
the later refutations by Stephen Jay Gould, the idea that intelligence was subject
to quantitative measurement and a natural property that could be correlated
with conditions of birth and inheritance was widely condemned for its race,
gender, and class biases by, among others, scientists. However, in the wake of the
exhaustion of liberal and radical ideas and social movements, enter molecular
biology and its companion, sociobiology, which have become the scientific

authorities for the astounding revival of all manner of genetic determinism whose leaks are today among the leading ideological weapons of the latest attack on equality.

The complicity of scientists and of scientific institutions is, in this respect, an important political question, just as was the relationship between physics and the development of atomic weapons in the 1940s and 1950s. Since scientific culture entails, among other elements, a brutally imposed doctrine of professionalization and its concomitant, the separation of values from facts, scientists have little alternative but to consider that even if the uses to which their work is put may be reprehensible or salutary, their task is to do science, a decision which, except after the fact, precludes considerations of effects or consequences as possible determinations of whether and what kind of science they are prepared to do.

From the perspective of the social theory of science, these are interesting but subordinate questions. More to the point, what counts is the ways in which scientific discoveries and the ideas derived from them become social and political questions, how they leak from the initial context from which they were generated to institutional and discursive sites. The statement that nature is culturally constituted refers, then, not to questions of the existence of an external world or even of the existence of nature as a given "object" of investigation, but to the historical and social conditions of its existence. On one hand, the selection of scientific objects cannot be separated from the economic, social, or ideological context within which they are identified, isolated, and investigated. On the other, the results of science, unknown from the perspective of the studiously naïve investigator, can be known by anyone who understands the nature of social and political things.

Objects are selected in three distinct ways. First, as Thomas Kuhn theorized, they can be chosen from anomalies appearing in some previous theory or paradigm. Although Kuhn did not deny that culture permeates the paradigm, the appearance of anomalies occurs in the process of doing what he calls "normal science"—solving the puzzles generated by the prevailing paradigm, the function of which is to complete it. This is consistent with, but more sophisticated than, most "internalist" accounts, and I want to affirm its effectiveness, yet these inherited puzzles are themselves not free of presuppositions. Second, and on the other end—crude as it might appear—objects are selected by the conditions of funding and other institutional controls. Accordingly, since he who pays the piper calls the tune (and modern science requires huge inputs of capital, such as machinery and full-time practitioners), contemporary science is ineluctably in the thrall of the state and the large corporations that set the agenda and establish boundaries of research. Third, modern science is technoscience; what is "seen" is characteristically mediated by machinery, without which observation even of effects cannot be fostered. In a word, in science, the naked eye no longer (if it ever did) directly observes nature without the help of technology (machines) whose configurative role is central. So, in order to make "observational statements," still the legitimating presupposition of theoretical as much as empirical science, the selection of objects must fulfill the criterion of visualizability, even if mainly by means of technology. Needless to say, the imperative of visualizability becomes increasingly problematic with respect to processes investigated by microphysics and microbiology. There is no longer an "object" so to speak, only relations and inferences.

Scientific sovereignty is interpolated by these requirements—which is not a moral comment. It refers to the prevailing context of technoscience and of cyberculture. Although the production of scientific knowledge presupposes machinery, it is important to remember that many scientists are, by necessity, machine inventors. Much of the scientist's job is devoted to designing, adapting, and modifying machines produced for other uses to the specificity of their own projects. Thus, the machine mediates observation, but the observer creates the machine as a fetishized object. That is, the scientist is dependent for observation and experiment on the machine she or he has constructed.

2

Technoscience, constituted by the imperatives of measurement, observation, and experiment, and deriving in a large measure from the craft and organizational traditions of the industrial revolution, has, in turn, penetrated all corners of the social world. We have already seen the influence of biology on issues of educational access—to which we might add its growing centrality to what counts as schooling; its influence over the curriculum; the degree to which scientific methods and mathematical algorithms have overtaken all other forms of knowledge and displaced them to the margins; and the relation of what counts as "science" to employment outcomes.

Consider what might be the most outstanding example of the leaks emanating from science: the broad influence on contemporary culture of the scientifically wrought knowledge that some sixty years ago produced the modern computer. For the moment, let us concede its applications to certain problems of calculation, or even as a word processor, such as the one used in writing this chapter. These applications would have ensured the indispensability of computers for many businesses and for writers. Almost no field of human endeavor has been spared the technological leak. Most ubiquitously, computers have, in

the hands of capitalism, altered most of the world's regimes of industrial production as well as the services, and in its wake, tens of millions of jobs have been
consigned to historical memory.

Although not "caused" by the development of electronic technologies, mergers and acquisitions on a world scale—perhaps the most significant event in
contemporary business history—are facilitated by computers. Under the impact
of computer-mediated communications technologies (which make possible
instant business orders and fulfillment), there is a sharply reduced need for
branch offices, except for sales; even here, telecommunications and the Internet
are taking ever more space in the sales effort. At the same time, the relentless
application of these technologies to management and organizational regimes
results in a quantum leap in the centralization of control. The consequence is
that middle management, the bedrock of the salaried middle class, is rapidly
becoming an endangered species.

Science is most unwittingly recruited in one of the major political events of
this century: the erosion of nationhood under the force of transnational capital.
For the computer and its miniaturization by means of the inventions derived
from solid-state physics, communications technologies especially have made
possible transnational capital's permeation of national borders by the occular-
ization and aestheticization of the commodity as a cultural ideal. For the purposes of this chapter, I am not demeaning this cultural ideal but use it only to
illustrate thereby the broad significance of the concept of "leak." In its com-
pressed form, a leak is the way knowledge overflows its purposes and inten-
tion(s) and spreads quite independently to other territories.

The leak surely results in new products, but computer technology transforms the nature and the quantity of work, not only manual labor. Everyone is
familiar with the consequences of computer-mediated robotization and of
numerical and laser technologies in basic production industries such as oil
refining, chemical processing, auto manufacturing, and steel processing. Less
familiar is the extent to which computers have affected professions such as medicine, engineering, and the professoriat. Many technical and professional occupations have either shifted to accommodate the computer or have been eliminated by it. For example, the occupation and the function of mechanical drafting have virtually disappeared as an independent occupation, and thus the
entire profession of design engineering has been radically transformed. With
the advent of computer-aided design (CAD), using computer graphics and
mathematical menus, the design engineer performs few, if any, of the routine
tasks associated with drafting and calculation. Physicians increasingly depend
on computer-aided diagnostic and prescriptive information. In the case of medicine, the transfer of professional scientific knowledge to the computer has

played a large role in reducing the physician to a dependent variable in the health care process. In many managed care organizations, they must justify their judgment not to follow the prescribed computerized treatment. As a result, we have seen a new surge in union organization among physicians; even the American Medical Association, once an elite conservative professional organization, has sanctioned unionization among medical doctors.

The computer displaced the beaker and the test tube as the fundamental tool of inquiry. Ask a molecular physicist where his laboratory is located and he will point to his computer. Computer-mediated simulations in physical and biological science stand in for observation. "Observational" statements derived from three-dimensional graphic models are as far removed from the act of "seeing" as is any mathematical model. That propositions based on model-building "work" simply indicates that they yield plausible "pictures" and explanations that can be transformed into technologies. In the visual arts, we may observe the "the end of painting" and the rise of computer simulation. A recent Colorado Springs exhibit featured visual art entirely done through "new" media. All of the works were computer-based. Similarly, the emergence of electronic sound simulations has overtaken all but some die-hard classical and folk musicians.

Solid-state physics' most striking achievements, the theoretical basis for technologies such as digital television and Internet communications, have given rise to new pedagogies such as distance learning, which, in time, may end the concept of the professor as we know her or, at a minimum, may require most professors to teach on the Internet. The effects of this pedagogical regime on learning are as yet not fully known. A mad race to use distance learning as a means to achieve cost-cutting in education and other services is likely; the use of computer applications by management to eliminate intellectual labor, perhaps the most labor-intensive and expensive of all of labor's forms, is perhaps even more likely. What does it mean when the president of the United States, in his State of the Union speech, promises a computer in every classroom as his main educational achievement? What is the relationship between this remarkable objective and the simultaneous call by educational reformers for a national curriculum, one of the United States' most controversial educational issues?

The point is not that these changes are made inevitable by computers, but that scientifically based technology is not divorced from regimes of capital accumulation, management, nor from the humanities or the arts. The technological and scientific imperative is woven into our cultural imagination. We see the world through the lens of this imperative; we can no longer envision a future that is, in any significant way, separate from the tools at hand, no more than science itself can conceive even a theoretical (let alone experimental or observational) practice that is bereft of computers and other machine technologies.

Clearly, the instruments of discovery are not separate from its representations any more than observation and theory belong to different domains.

The machine is the body of science and also its head. Dijksterhuis's *The Mechanization of the World Picture* and Sohn-Rethel's *Intellectual and Manual Labor* showed the dependence of scientific knowledge on industrial practice not as an epistemological question, but a historical one. Sohn-Rethel argued that as intellectual labor developed with the help of machines, it acquired, sometime at the turn of the twentieth century, a nearly complete dependence on advanced mathematics—which was relatively autonomous from manual labor. Science as discourse and institution is consistent with the progressive division of labor that produces wider distance between intellectual knowledge and the craft traditions that spawned much of its early discoveries. The concept of "theory" as distinct from the philosophy or speculative tradition that, in many ways, came to an end with Hegel (analytic philosophy is a gaggle of scientifically dependent "theories" seeking to clarify the remaining linguistic ambiguities of scientific practice rather than of speculations, in the Hegelian sense) is itself a measure of the degree to which positivism, a mechanical concentrate of scientific practice, leaks into scientific knowledge. Theory is the pinnacle of scientific labor, but it is always constrained by the invocation against speculative reason or metatheory, since these are presumed metaphysical. Thus "logic" is said to be a discipline that generalizes scientific practice rather than, as in Hegel, a self-critical reason without which science cannot overcome the world of appearances.

While Popper acknowledged that science cannot be done in a vacuum and is therefore subject to cultural, political, and economic influences, he attempts to refute these arguments by advancing the idea that experimental falsification of propositions is the self-reflection of scientific theory, its self-correction in the light of cultural constitutions of all sorts. Moreover, he claimed that the procedure of experimental falsification is the road to transform conjectures, whose necessary presupposition is culture, into warranted assertions of the case. The warrant is the conjecture that has met the challenge of repeatable experiment and cannot be refuted within the algorithms of approved scientific method.

Thus method is advanced to the premier place in the pantheon of scientific knowledge. The problem with this formulation is that the experiment itself is framed by the rules according to which prediction and control are the goals of the scientific enterprise and criticism is constrained by notions of correspondence of propositions to objects which remain unquestioned either from the perspective of their "origin" or from their effects. Science is said to be hermetically sealed in the laboratory, and neither the material context of experiment nor the broader discursive field can penetrate this chamber. But if scientific knowledge may be said to be inseparable from the contexts within which it has been constituted or from its often-unintended effects or leaks, then the task of reflection is to treat of the totality of the process in and outside its experimental or theoretical laboratory.

This raises the question of science as power. Following the objectivity of science as a machinic or complex of social and cultural relations, the power of science consists not in the will of its individual subjects but, to the degree that scientific knowledge and its practices are onto-historical, in how they displace one side of the cultural imaginary. Its power manifests itself in the first place as a common sense to which all of us are subject; secondly, in its influence over most of the institutional life of society; and thirdly as the privileged and authoritative mode of knowledge (in comparison, say, with everyday knowledge such as gossip and stories, literature, visual forms, and so forth). The power of science is implicit in what we mean by Western civilization on all of its sides. Although reason may be understood as prior to the current forms of institutional science, it has almost no extant exemplars. Institutionalized science has taken over the territory of reason.

At stake is nothing less than the status of natural science as the undisputed common sense of our age at a time when government funds dry up, skepticism in the larger polity is at a new height (witness the United States Congress's refusal to fund the superconductor), new public challenges to the ethics of cloning and other products of bioengineering have appeared, the enormous hand-wringing by some that the condition of continuing the scientific enterprise is increasingly tied to private funding (the price for which is the surrender of the very sovereignty which scientists so militantly defend against its cultural critics), and activists in social movements concerned with AIDS, breast cancer, and other highly charged illnesses linked to sex in its multiple forms are generating considerable attention.

Of course, the crisis in science has other aspects: have we arrived at a moment when, having conquered the last frontier, science "as we know it" has come to an end? Is the vaunted neutrality of science a not-so-believable fig leaf of an increasingly compromised scientific enterprise? Is science's historic proclivity for attaching itself to capital and the state finally becoming evident to everyone, even scientists themselves who, for the most part, plead with us to ignore their alliances on the ground that, as the state gradually withdraws its support, capital has become the only game in town? And if science is ineluctably political, that is, intertwined with power, and itself a form of knowledge and power, can it switch sides without losing its means of production? And what is the other side to which it might ally?

V

JOBS IN A
GLOBALIZED TECHNOCULTURE

14

OΠ UΠIOΠ DΣMOCRACY

In 1956, Arthur J. Goldberg, general counsel of the newly formed AFL-CIO (he later became a UN ambassador and Supreme Court justice), published a book in which he drew the labor movement in the image of a military organization. Just as one would not demand of an army that its generals be subject to election and recall by the dog soldiers, so labor leaders should not be held to the standard of direct democracy in which the rank and file held actual sovereignty in union affairs. In order to accumulate the necessary experience and strategic knowledge, the union had to function as a hierarchy of power and of opportunity. The labor leader had to be a relatively permanent fixture in the union, his subordinates subject to command, and, most of all, he had to be granted maximum tactical flexibility in an increasingly complex and dangerous industrial relations system. Among Goldberg's more persuasive arguments was that the unions had to mirror the powerful corporations against which they were arrayed. Since corporations were organized hierarchically and had a fairly rigid chain of command to allow them maximum maneuverability, unions had no choice but to mimic them. Any breach in the ranks that might result from contentious internal debate might be suicidal for a labor movement that, even in its "golden age," seemed chronically besieged.

Indeed, despite unparalleled economic prosperity and, in many production industries, high union density, the mid-1950s were by no means calm times for America's unions. Even as unions maintained a continuous effort to persuade capital that unions should be considered a permanent actor in the labor relations system, and many union leaders were anxious to collaborate with the employers, internal fights raged throughout the decade. The profound ideological struggle between "Left" and "Right" in the electrical industry had left both sides considerably diminished in the wake of one of the most anti-union of American industrial corporations, General Electric, and some CIO unions such as the Steelworkers and the AFL Tobacco Workers spent more time raiding left-wing adversaries than fighting employers. Coming on the heels of the CIO's near rout in Operation Dixie, its textile-oriented Southern organizing campaign, the Textile Workers Union underwent a leadership split that left the union severely weakened after the flop in the early 1950s. The auto union's rank and file chafed under a five-year no-strike contract, a ball and chain which led to shop-floor rebellions over work rules; UAW president Walter Reuther was unwilling to counter the effects of automation by putting shorter hours at the top of the union's bargaining agenda. In the same period, Goldberg's client, the Steelworkers' leadership—perhaps one of the most authoritarian among the industrial unions—was being seriously challenged by a Pittsburgh area local union official, Pat Rarick, and Buffalo district director, Joseph Maloney.

No sooner had they managed to come to terms with the crippling Taft-Hartley amendments to the labor relations law by capitulation under the premise that, whatever its faults, it had the virtue of driving the communists out of the movement, unions faced a new political attack. Although the Democrats nominally controlled both houses of Congress, the liberals were hopelessly outnumbered by the alliance of Republicans and the large contingent of Southern Democrats. On the heels of Dwight D. Eisenhower's reelection, Arkansas Democratic Senator James McClellan began hearings into union corruption that, two years later, resulted in the Labor-Management Reporting and Disclosure Act of 1959. Among other provisions, this legislation contained a union member's bill of rights, elements of which confirmed Goldberg's worst nightmares. Although not guaranteeing such reforms as direct election of union officers, it gave dissidents access to union membership lists, required officers to hold regular meetings, and mandated international union conventions at least every five years. It also gave individuals the right to grieve arbitrary and undemocratic actions of union officials to a special bureau of the Department of Labor. The overwhelming majority of union officials were enraged by this legislation because it required regular reports of union finances and of health and welfare funds and, most of all, because of the bill of rights. The AFL-CIO lobbied hard against the bill and worked to soften its most draconian features. In the end, it passed and Eisenhower signed it.

Now, after forty years of steady trade union decline, comes Steve Fraser's neo-Goldbergian "Is Democracy Good for Unions?" which repeats the military metaphor but, more to the point, without evaluating the costs for the labor movement, apologizes for the consolidation of the entrenched bureaucracy in much of American Labor.[1] Goldberg's plea occurred during a period when unions were under attack from within as much as from without. Fraser's diatribe, set against a background of organized labor's virtual free fall, argues in the vein of House Speaker Thomas Foley who, on the eve of the Panama invasion, told his colleagues, "This is no time for complicated debate." While ostensibly directed against what he called a "procedural" approach to union democracy that would subject union leaders to openness and consultation with the membership about negotiations and other union affairs, the burden of his argument is that unions are not best conceived in the model of voluntary organizations. Instead, in light of the largely anti-union American industrial relations system, the model of an army fits better. Leaders must be freed from internal conflict and especially liberated from the insistence of their critics that it retrieve its lost credentials as a social movement. Indeed, Fraser infers that rank-and-file rights need to be restricted in order to perfect labor's capacity to "soldier on." He accuses the union democrats of, perhaps unwittingly, sacrificing the "union" to "democracy" and to its role as a social movement. And he cites some of the most effective union leaders who, in his account, "don't care a rat's ass about union democracy; indeed consider it an actual hindrance."[2]

There has never been a time when some version of Goldberg's and of Fraser's arguments could not have been offered on similar grounds. Indeed, since the inception of the modern labor movement in 1881, except for the brief periods of labor-management collaboration during the two world wars, its corporate and political enemies have been legion. Radical versions of union democracy, which were usually accompanied by criticism of the business model in which the role of the leaders as labor contractors took precedence, have always been faulted on debilitative grounds. Conflict, it is said, weakens the fighting capacity of unions.

The radical retort has rested on two foundations: the pragmatic argument is that unions are best able to wage class warfare when the rank and file has sovereign control over its basic decisions; and the ideological contention, in opposition to the tacit authoritarianism of liberal democracies which reduce the polity to acts of consent, believes the labor movement should be a model of participatory democracy. Moreover, it can be shown that, in one of the most rowdy periods in labor history, the 1930s, when ideological as well as interunion rivalry was intense, union expansion was unprecedented. Workers did not recoil when the AFL charged the CIO with communist domination nor when the CIO termed many AFL affiliates company unions. They joined in the millions. In one of the most ideologically cleaved industrial unions, the Auto Workers, a coalition of socialist, communist, and career trade unionists unceremoniously threw out a sitting president who enjoyed the support of some Catholic members and other rabid anticommunists. Amid the turmoil, the union conducted some of its more historic struggles and managed to organize the bulk of the industry.

This chapter will defend the two poles of the radical argument, but introduce a third and perhaps more controversial claim: as long as unions accept the prevailing system of labor relations, participatory democracy is structurally undermined, and the consent and overtly authoritarian variants of current practice seem necessary. For this reason, I claim that only in the event unions are freed from their functions as bargaining agents and insurance companies can union democracy flourish.

1

Meeting in New Orleans, on July 5, 1998, delegates to a special convention of the National Education Association (NEA) decisively rejected its leaders' recommendation to merge with the American Federation of Teachers (AFT). For some, especially the association's southern locals, the merger was objectionable because it would have entailed affiliation with the AFL-CIO, thereby ripping the fig-leaf belief that the NEA was primarily a professional group, not a labor union. Others voted "no" because they did not like some of the details, but, by far, the largest group cited the two organizations' different political cultures as reasons for opposing the merger.

The AFT and the NEA are representative institutions in the American labor movement. Unlike the Teamsters, Carpenters, Laborers, and a handful of other unions, neither is tainted with racketeering or other forms of overt corruption. Each has a governance structure that provides mechanisms of consent: leaders duly elected by the membership for specified terms of office, rank-and-file approval of negotiated labor agreements, and representative bodies such as delegate assemblies to provide consent for the day-to-day decisions of elected leaders. Each claims to practice democratic unionism, but there the similarity ends.

For the past thirty years, since its key organizer, former president David Selden, took office, the AFT has belied its name: it has been less a federation than a strong national center modeled on the industrial unions, especially the United Auto Workers. This reflects that fact that, like many industrial unions that emerged in the 1930s, the AFT has been organized and led by professional unionists since the late 1950s, rather than by people on the job who formed and ran their own organization. The NEA roughly conforms to the typical AFL mode. It is a federation of independent local organizations that, because their trade union styles and ideologies were often different, contrived to keep their national leadership weak. The AFT—although, like the industrial unions, it relished its reputation for militancy—is in the mainstream of the former CIO unions in exercising strong control over its locals. In Fraser's terms, most of its officials "don't care a rat's ass about democracy." It requires a local affiliate to procure strike authorization from the national office; employs a large national and state staff to keep tabs on them; and, perhaps most significantly but less tangibly, makes and breaks its rules when rank-and-file insurgents threaten incumbents. For example, when insurgents captured leadership for high schools of the large New York affiliate, the United Federation of Teachers (UFT)—about a third of the membership—the election procedures were changed so that all officers were elected at large. Naturally, the insurgents lost the next election.

The AFT corresponds to what C. Wright Mills once described as typical of postwar unions: although ideologically liberal, they are "political machines" in the old-time Tammany tradition. AFT confers support and patronage to loyal locals, tends to slight the rebellious among them, and even works towards defeating disloyal officers for local union office. As an organization with a permanent leadership and affiliates that depend upon the national union for funds, organizational support, and patronage—such as staff jobs for local officials, trips to Europe and other exotic places, and other benefits—when the merger deal was negotiated on the top, there was never any question what the AFT delegates would do.

In contrast, the NEA, which (unlike the AFT) began as a professional association and still retains some of the features of that model, is a decentralized union with strong local organizations that fiercely defend their autonomy. The organizational structure mirrors the positions and orientations of its local affiliates, rather than being greater than the sum of its parts. Its national leaders, and many of its local officers as well, are subject to term limits. The national office and most of its state associations are chiefly educational and lobbying organizations. Unlike the AFT, which despite the decentralized American education system retains tight reins on its affiliates, collective bargaining and union governance in the NEA are very local matters. Many of its leaders return to the classroom after their tour of duty is completed.

The NEA national convention is usually alive with debate because most delegates are not career officials who, in the typical AFL-CIO international union, are subject to the discipline of the center. Few local officers seek full-time staff jobs, so they are more likely to exercise independent judgment on matters before the convention. As the merger vote showed, even though the NEA officers and the press were reasonably confident of victory—an illusion born of increasing bureaucratization of the center—it was not entirely surprising that delegates voted otherwise. Said one opponent of the merger, "we did not want to become the AFT."[3] Plainly, this leader of a powerful state association believed that the issue of local sovereignty overrode the costs of refusing organic unity with the smaller, but more visible, AFT.

Insofar as the NEA has become a trade union in the legal meaning of the term, in relation to its own doctrine of participatory democracy, it shares an inherent limitation with all other collective bargaining agents: it is both a democratically constituted voluntary organization and an agent of the state. I want to defend the proposition that these roles are incompatible; in the end, as Fraser astutely observes, the role of the union as a labor contractor predominates over its broad, democratic purpose. Until unions are freed from the responsibility of direct contract administration, they will remain agents against, as well as of, the rank-and-file members.

2

In the post–World War II era, many of the most celebrated fights for "union democracy" were conducted by rank-and-file movements against oligarchies which were often, if not always, controlled by racketeers. Reform movements were numerous. The New York Painters District (a rank-and-file group led by Frank Schonfeld), assisted by the Association for Union Democracy (an independent organization), ousted the mob-connected leadership. The Teamsters for a Democratic Union's successive campaigns for rank-and-file determination of contracts and its dramatic effort to force a secret-ballot direct-membership vote for national leaders entailed the intervention of the federal government and the courts. As with several other parallel cases, the dissidents availed themselves of the "notorious" Labor-Management Reporting and Disclosure Act and, especially, the RICO law, which gave the federal government extraordinary powers to intervene when a "private" organization, such as a labor union or a business, is suspected of racketeering. Needless to say, the reliance by the rank-and-file union democrats on the government was an object of derision by the entrenched leaderships who, in their defense, often cited the AFL's traditional opposition to government control over unions.

Although there have been many victories for the reformers, the question of democracy is not resolved when the membership cleanses its union of leaders who steal from the treasury, bilk the members' health and pension funds, and commit acts of overt violence and other types of repression against union dissidents. Or when, however free of racketeering, they have ended practices such as when the leadership pays itself two or three salaries, fails to hold regular membership meetings, discriminates against dissidents by refusing to make membership lists available to them, silences their voices at contract ratification meetings, or deprives them of their livelihoods (or, on occasion, their lives).

In most cases, cleaning up a union results in a liberal democratic model of governance such as that which pervades the majority of unions. Members may gain the right to approve contract settlements and directly elect national as well as local officers by secret ballot, and these are by no means small gains in organizations where these rights have been systematically denied. In the Brooklyn Local 1814 of the legendary business union, the International Longshoremen's Association (ILA), after the government set severe limitations on intimidation, the once-underground rank-and-file opposition caucus was able to function openly, even though subtle forms of discrimination against caucus leaders persisted; local union meetings, especially at contract ratification time, were often raucous. The same is true of more socially liberal locals, such as New York's Transport Workers Local 100, but the transformation does not resolve the fundamental issue in the battle for union democracy.

Stated simply, the issue is: should the rank and file be content to designate full-time officials to represent their interests on the shop floor and at the bargaining table, as well as to do organizing and educational work? Democracy, in this model, consists in conferring or withdrawing consent for others to act on members' behalf. Or should the union be a participatory organization in which the members control their union's everyday affairs—at the bargaining table, in grievance handling—and be the core of its organizing, political, and educational activities?

The consent model of union governance mirrors the American political system insofar as voting is the substance of its definition of democratic participation. Like any politician, the union official rarely, if ever, calls upon the membership to act on its own behalf, except when the representatives have exhausted their own means of obtaining agreement from the employer or from the legislature. In this mode of operation, direct action by the membership is, under ordinary circumstances, disdained by officials as "a hindrance." A hindrance of what? Strikes and demonstrations may antagonize the employer or mass lobbying might enrage the legislators. To the demand for open, transparent communication during contract negotiations, the leadership defends the need for secrecy on the argument that too much information will create divisions in the ranks and weaken the union's position by undermining the employer's confidence that union bargainers can deliver the membership's agreement to the result.

The permanent leadership is skilled at negotiations and compromise and, increasingly, has no experience, let alone talent, for social movement unionism. They are proud to be successful labor contractors, to which all other considerations should be, and are, subordinate. In fact, the preponderant definition of the "labor movement," one that is accepted by most labor leaders, is its ability to bid up wages and benefits. Recently, however, in the face of their growing inability to achieve these goals, some have revised their definition: the measure of success is whether the union survives and whether workers keep their jobs in this era of corporate hegemony. In this view, all other activities, including politics, are placed within the same defensive framework.

In the consent model, union democracy can never be an end; at best, and only under unusual circumstances, it may be justified as a means towards the goal of saving the union. At the core of the permanent leadership's hostility to participatory democracy is the belief that membership mobilization may create a threat to their own control over the union's affairs. As every official knows, just as trade union demands escalate the longer workers are on strike or when they take an active part in protests and demonstrations, you can't turn the membership on and off like a water faucet. Once turned on, the water overflows with expectations borne of the rank and file's own participation. As crazy as it seems, some union officials prefer to watch the union's power erode and the membership decline as long as they remain at the helm.

The American version of the liberal-democratic system underlies the law of labor relations as well. Only those who choose union representation and succeed in obtaining a contract have collective bargaining rights. All others must apply through the submission of representation cards, signed by at least 30 percent of a unit of employees deemed "appropriate" of a covered employer. If a majority has signed, the union usually demands recognition, and in most cases, the employer uses its legal right to challenge the union claim. The issue of representation is then settled by means of a government-supervised secret ballot election. If the union wins a majority of votes, it gains *exclusive* bargaining rights. It becomes the only legally designated agent for a given group of employees, even if a rival union has obtained a considerable minority of the votes. The employer is now obliged to bargain in good faith, but not to conclude a contract. Workers who have not chosen to undergo this procedure have no bargaining rights under the law, nor do they have contractually guaranteed job security in cases of discharge, nor seniority rights in matters such as promotion and transfer unless they can prove the employer's intent in matters of race and sex discrimination.

Because the American system regards property rights as sacred, in violation of one of the key principles of American jurisprudence, the employee is guilty until proven innocent and the burden of proof is on the union under most union contracts. The limits of other employee rights are specified under a contract, one of whose staple (although not legally mandated) provisions is that management has the prerogative to direct the workforces, including the right to lay off workers (subject to seniority provisions) and make investment decisions without worker interference. Although the law imposes sanctions on the union as an institution, particularly its obligation to maintain continuous production, and although the union can be punished for failing to do so—despite the rhetorical guarantee of the preamble to the National Labor Relations Act, which recognizes the right of workers to form unions of their own choosing—in practice, this right is observed by its abrogation more than its enforcement.

Of course, insofar as the labor leader is a "labor contractor" (negotiates and administers a collective bargaining agreement that protects certain wages and benefits, working conditions and individual job security), her or his integration is always incomplete. Enforcing the contract works both ways. Often the representative advocates on behalf of worker grievances and is especially effective when management unfairly disciplines union members. Although the union leadership's role at the bargaining table is more ambivalent because, as a part of the labor relations system, she or he is prone to take the standpoint of management as well as of union members, good union bargainers may help gain genuine benefits even as they concede management's prerogatives on many fronts.

In the American system of labor relations, the official must bear responsibility for discipline against workers when they have violated the terms of the agreement, and especially when their infraction disrupts production. The National Labor Relations Act, its Taft-Hartley amendments, and state public labor relations laws make the union responsible for the administration of the collective agreement. As the recent suit by General Motors against the UAW demonstrates, unions are liable for infractions (such as disruptions of production) resulting from strike activity, if such strikes are not specifically sanctioned by the agreement. Similarly, the union may be fined, under court injunction, for having failed to stem unauthorized strikes and other job actions. Like lawyers, union officials are, first and foremost, officers of the courts and of the law upon which their authority—and liability—rests. Consequently, union officials become workers' leaders rather than contract enforcers mainly when the contract has expired and, at least in the private sector, so have their obligations to enforce it on behalf of the employer.

In the liberal-democratic (consent) model, the career trade-union official tends to be separated from her or his constituency. Even when salaries are modest (in contrast to some unions where they are often two to four times that of the highest paid worker in the industry or occupation), the permanent officials tend to be integrated into the political class. They tend to share the political class's outlook and methods. It's not primarily a question of lifestyle or even associations, both of which can be criticized on other grounds. Instead, the issue is whether the trade union apparatus is part of the system of political and legal control—whether it is, primarily, a defender of workers' interests or of those of the state.

3

If the greatest barrier to participatory, direct democracy resides not so much in the preferences of certain leaders or the bureaucracies they control but in the institutional role of unions in American economic and legal relations, movements for trade union reform that fail to go to the root of the problem are fated to prove inadequate to the task. Even when a disgusted rank-and-file movement succeeds in "throwing the rascals out," they are often chagrined to discover—as did the Teamsters' rank and file—that a broom, even a vacuum cleaner, is not enough to wipe the slate clean. Things may improve, but the tendency of even the most radically democratic of the new leaders to recreate the machine and become integrated with the political class, be forced to act like cops against the membership, and become more distant from the rank and file is virtually certain.

Perhaps the rise and fall of Teamsters President Ron Carey is exemplary of this problem. After he was elected in a classic rank-and-file insurgency, the twin pillars of his program were militancy at the bargaining table and grassroots democracy. Even as he organized and led the most successful strike in recent memory, the 1997 UPS struggle, he became so entangled with the Washington political class that, in order to finance his reelection campaign, he abandoned his own pledge to seek funds only from the rank and file and engaged in a sordid money-laundering scheme. The root of the problem is not to be found in Carey's character but in the contradiction between unions as state institutions and their role as voluntary, democratically run organizations.

We may view the process of democratization on a continuum. At a minimum, union democracy means that the rank and file has the right to refuse contract settlements negotiated by its representatives, and also is freed from the crippling no-strike provision of over 90 percent of collective bargaining agreements and the almost-inevitable management prerogatives clause, to which must be added the tendency for unions concerned with their survival to sign long-term agreements. Internally, officials should be required to hold regular membership meetings, conduct frequent elections for top officers, and, on the principle that only an informed polity can make informed decisions, maintain regular channels of information about bargaining and grievance issues to the rank and file.

At the next level, the steward or shop chair should, as in the older and virtually expired industrial union tradition, be not only the first step griever but the primary griever. In turn, rank-and-file negotiators at other levels of the grievance procedure should have the ultimate power; if the no-strike clause were eliminated, arbitration would also play a much-diminished role, if any at all. A rank-and-file committee, assisted upon request by career staff, should conduct contract negotiations. This step is necessary to ensure the needed two-way communications channels with an alerted rank and file, which the doctrine of secrecy subverts. In that doctrine, communication is virtually one way, from the top down, especially after negotiations have begun. As a result, members are usually left in the dark until the contract has been negotiated. They are asked only to approve or disapprove but not even on the basis of full access to information.

Within the union local, active rank-and-file committees on finance, education, political action, membership welfare, recreation, and other activities should be formed on the premise that the union is not only a business and insurance organization but social and political as well. The organizing committee should be fully responsible for setting recruitment goals, supplying funds, and developing materials, as well as being the primary vehicle by which the union reaches out to the unorganized.

The AFL-CIO merger deprived workers of one of their most precious tools: competitive unionism. Under Article 20 of the federation's constitution, competition is banned except for unorganized units. A group of workers seeking redress from what they perceive to be poor representation (or, in some cases, none at all) by the incumbent union, has few options. They can decertify the existing union, form an independent organization, and seek recognition by their employer, if and only if they petition for the same unit under which the original petition was filed. Under such conditions, if the majority of workers in the shop are demoralized by the union's prior malfeasance, they may end up with no union. They can overthrow the existing shop leadership but if they are in an "amalgamated" local of many, and often diverse, shops, this solution may prove futile. Or, as in the case of rank-and-file movements in New York's transit industry, the huge Service Employees International Local 32B-32J, or the union of City University faculty and professional staff, they can try to gain leadership and proceed with a more militant program. In most states, public employees lack the same rights as workers in the private sector, such as access to membership lists or a procedure to appeal decisions by union officials regarding grievance handling. Even if they win, while the victory might improve the quality of representation, it is not likely to solve the problems associated with the former leadership.

In the absence of broad, competitive unionism in the American labor movement, the existence of political parties within unions is vital to provide members with genuine choices in the selection of their leaders. On the concept that democracy always entails the presentation of, and free choice between, different views and ideologies, the right of rank-and-file caucuses to form should be guaranteed by the union constitution and bylaws. These caucuses or internal political parties should have full access to membership lists, union files, and other documents in order to get their message out, and since most incumbents find ways to pay for their campaigns by using membership dues, their campaigns as well should be funded by the union treasury. The union constitution should bar discrimination against opposition groups and the individuals within them.

The concept of a party is not identical to that of a caucus, the life span of which usually ends when the opposition caucus attains union power. In contrast, the party is always nominally independent of the officers; it can replace a candidate or slate and offer a new one without dissolving the party. Some caucuses are composed of the "outs" who want power because they want jobs. Caucus movements for which the content of unionism is at issue in their opposition might consider the consequences of forming permanent political parties within the unions as an alternative to the caucus, since these do not entail maintaining an active rank-and-file group if the opposition wins local union office. In many cases, the caucus dissolves after opposition victory or when it is integrated into the established leadership by giving some of its leaders official positions. In the case of the Typographical Union, the existence of a permanent two-party system enabled the rank and file to maintain discipline over its officers, whose natural tendency is always to drift.

None of these changes addresses the structural inequalities of the labor relations system. How to address the union-throttling characteristics of U.S. labor relations law? Some have argued for reforms that would only restrict the employer's capacity to intervene in elections by speeding up procedures by requiring them to accept evidence of majority union representation without recourse to elections, but would preserve the basic structure of the law, especially its piecemeal, winner-take-all approach. If union democracy were to become a central criterion for the law, the best solution would be to remove the union from direct responsibility for negotiating and administering contracts, and from dispensing health and pension benefits under the contract, since these practices undergird the power of the permanent officialdom. The best chance for rank-and-file control is to define the basic unit of representation as *every group of workers* in worksites with more than twenty-five employees. These groups would have the legal right to bargain over wages, hours, and working conditions, and the law would provide for the formation and for the training of workers' councils or enterprise committees to be the primary vehicle for workplace rights. This would have the advantage of eliminating what every organizer knows: the cards are stacked as long as employers have the right to "free speech" (read intimidation), to delay elections and good faith bargaining by using their right to appeal, and by unfair labor practices which take months to resolve. It would cut down, if not eliminate, regional competition for industrial investment by tending to reduce wage competition between North and South, city, suburb and rural areas, and union and nonunion shops. It would reduce the size and power of the permanent union officialdom by transforming the role of the union to recruiting members rather than administering contracts.

It would also provide a much-needed incentive to the labor movement to fight for better, publicly funded social insurance because unions would no longer have a fundamental interest in maintaining the private welfare state which evolved out of the failure of national health insurance legislation in the late 1940s. In the first place, not content with fighting for a patients' "bill of rights" directed at HMOs (a tacit recognition that health care privatization does not provide good services), the AFL-CIO might renew the fight for "single payer" or socialized medicine. Second, instead of being obliged to protect negotiated pension plans with private employers, unions might once more turn their attention to improving Social Security, the federal pension system. Since private supplementary pensions such as those provided in union contracts are not available to the vast number of nonunion workers, but are receding as a viable collective bargaining demand or are frozen for millions of union members as well, unions would, under a system of universal bargaining, have to advocate a significantly beefed-up Social Security system that provides a living income for retirees. Of course, this reform would entail a major revision of the tax base of the system. Relieved of their obligations to pay into retirement systems, many employers might actually save money by this reform, even if their taxes would increase.

In some European countries, notably France, Spain, and Italy, labor relations law provides for mandatory bargaining for enterprises over a specified size and social benefits are provided, in a large measure, by legislation and not by private contract. In these countries, competing unions contest seats on the shop or enterprise committee on the basis of their program and their broad ideological orientation. Selection is based on proportional representation rather than the principle of winner-take-all. For example, if three federations offer slates, they receive a proportional number of seats on the committee and are required to poll only a minimum percentage of the vote in order to achieve representation. Independent slates may run as well. In these systems, the union participates— but only indirectly—in the negotiations. Although it has been true that the largest federations in France and Italy, those close to the Communist Party, have tended to dominate the enterprise committees in the past, the relative decline of the party's traditional social base (industrial and rail workers) has shifted the balance of power in some worksites to the other federations and to independents. In these countries, even in some old communist strongholds, the other federations have been able to gain control for shorter and longer periods and have demonstrated greater strength among the newer sectors such as banks, professional organizations, and especially technical groups. The federations remain powerful in national bargaining in multiworksite corporations on the basis of their respective programs and relative strength.

Although collective bargaining is a key element of the union federations of these countries, since membership is voluntary—maintaining union membership is not a condition of continuous employment—the rank and file consists largely of activists; union staff members are freed from administration to put their energies into the main tasks: recruiting members, education and research, and program planning and execution. As a result, union density—the proportion of union members to the labor force—is not an entirely accurate measure of union power. Consequently, although the French unions represent no more of the workforce than their U.S. counterparts, for example, their political weight in society is much heavier, in part, because they are ideological formations which act like political parties among the workers.

When the right-wing government threatened to cut social welfare benefits, public employees, including French rail workers, blocked transportation; truckers, seeking workload and hours reductions, blocked roads. Although no less bureaucratic than American unions, as voluntary organizations that are constantly contesting for power against other groups within the workplace, French unions are more subject to rank-and-file pressure from their constituents as well as from their own members. For example, bank employees, members of the smallest federation, led the social welfare protests together with the rail workers, who had to drag their own union, the communist-led CGT, into the fray.

4

To evaluate the alternatives of liberal versus participatory democracy, of a politics of consent versus a labor politics of social movement, it is necessary to ask what the goals inherent in these alternatives might be. For Steve Fraser and others who are not sure that openness rather than secrecy, and participation rather than consent, are not hindrances, the goal of union organization is chiefly to raise wages, win more benefits, secure job security from the private welfare states that are the consequence of labor's failure to expand public goods, and help labor gain the "right to organize" within a rigged labor relations law. In short, like most liberals and leftists, despite evidence to the contrary, they place their strategic emphasis on the state, including the trade union leaders, to deliver the goods. Few participatory or radical democrats in the labor movement would renounce these objectives, and none would accept the either/or characterization that pervades the market-oriented and statist views of unions. There is, however, no question that most advocates of rank-and-file union democracy view democracy as an end, a goal in itself which, and only under very special circumstances, should be abrogated. The differences between the two views strike to the question of what the labor movement is.

Rank-and-file democratic versus bureaucratic, business unionism cuts across traditional ideologies. Stalinists and democratic socialists can agree that "ultra" democracy is a hindrance and that, at best, the membership ought to have the right to confer consent on union governors; membership should be prepared to take its place in the eternal traipse toward better living standards and "social justice," that term that connotes the demand of workers to be treated "fairly" by employers and protected by the government. Some from these backgrounds, as well as radical democrats, including many reared in the New Left, have come to believe that, far from being an question of sacrificing a living wage, the condition for achieving the most basic tenets of union power is a strong, democratic rank and file. They argue that even the most talented and devoted leadership cannot, by itself, hope to reverse the decades of concession bargaining, workplace repression, and runaway shops that together have depressed wages by creating a two-tier wage system. Nor, after decades of compromise and retreat under Democratic as well as Republican administrations, can unions depend on the government to protect them. Just as workers have to assume primary responsibility for running their own unions, no less than in the 1930s, the task of union revival is in their own hands.

Even more to the point, the question of union democracy as an end strikes to the differences between those who believe working people are exemplars of "economic" man and those who insist that economic and cultural issues are inextricably linked. The "economic" unionists regard democracy as subordinate, even a hindrance, to achieving clearly defined bread-and-butter ends. For the cultural radicals, means and ends are not separate. The question of social rule, including unions, is not a matter of indifference to whether workers can win higher living standards. It goes to the core of what the labor movement should be and especially whether it can survive, let alone prosper, without transforming itself into a broadly democratic movement that might prefigure the kind of society it seeks. The program of the economic unionist with his rhetoric of fairness and social justice presupposes acceptance of consent as the farthest horizon of a democratic polis. Such an economic unionist would argue that unions are constituted as organizations to achieve highly limited, narrowly construed economic ends. If rank-and-file union members have despaired that their unions can be anything else but insurance companies, this judgment does not prove that they are inherently passive policyholders; it simply confirms the program of business unionism over the past fifty years. Absent a lively debate about what unions should be, what they have become seems a force of nature.

The organizing experience of the contemporary labor movement belies the conservative pessimism of those who would defend things as they are. Every good organizer knows that the strength of the union drive, especially in the current historical moment, is in the in-worksite committee rather than in the literature or the organizer's charisma and wisdom. The best way to ensure that a committee consisting of the most respected workers in the shop is formed is to convince key individuals that they will run the campaign, and when the union is certified as bargaining agent, the full-timers will be available to assist, not control, them. Those who don't "give a rat's ass about democracy" are either bad organizers or liars. They know that unless they make the fundamental promise of democratic unionism, today's rank-and-file workers will turn their backs on the union.

The reason is fairly simple. In most cases, the days when a union can promise a first contract, let alone substantial economic gains, are long gone. The image of the union as a powerful, feared figure in U.S. labor relations faded nearly twenty years ago when, in lightning-like rapid succession, the coalition of conservative politicians and large employers humbled some of the most powerful unions, forcing them to make an apparently endless series of concessions. Even then, many workers knew that union promises were to be taken with a grain of salt. In today's environment, what any good organizer says is that if workers stick together and are prepared to take the risk of a long fight and even risk job loss, they can win. Nor do good organizers trumpet, as they once were prone to, the protective shield of the law. In any case, the union presents itself, not as an ATM (an automatic dispenser of benefits) but as a vehicle that is of and by, as well as for, the membership. How many times have we, the organizers, informed prospective members that the union is not a magic wand? We say, no institution can do it for you, "you are the union." I am not so naïve as to ignore the fact that most unions refuse to obey the invocation to build the organizing campaign and the consequent union from below. I also know that, with some exceptions, many of them, having made promises that the leadership can "deliver" hefty benefits, have fallen on bad times—in part because they can't.

If unions can't deliver as they once did, they will fail unless they adopt a new goal: to create a movement that has a vision of the Good Life, one that recognizes freedom, equality, and happiness for working people as well as individuals among them as an ideal. Having a fighting spirit on behalf of a series of ideological goals, however, is a necessary condition for labor's revival. Such ideals include building unions that value membership participation as well as mobilization and, for this reason, regard democracy as an end. Surely, such a perspective would stand in stark opposition to our prevailing plebiscitary or liberal democracy, but it might convince the vast numbers of skeptics in the ranks of labor's potential, unorganized constituencies that joining the union is worth risking one's job, an almost invariant eventuality in every private sector organizing drive. It might persuade the millions in organized labor's rank and file to defend their unions from becoming skeletons or from obliteration.

15

UNIONS AS A PUBLIC SPHERE

Since the end of World War II, United States trade unions and their leaders have come under heavy fire from two quarters. From the Right came the criticism that unionized workers had become "too greedy." For most of this period, unions drove up wages to the detriment of economic growth. Conservatives have blamed labor for the loss of well-paid factory jobs in the most developed capitalist societies since 1973. In their view, higher wages combined with lackluster productivity gains caused major inflationary trends in the 1970s and, even worse, drove investors to seek other outlets. Attracted by the plentiful low-wage labor supply offered by developing countries in Latin America and Asia, rampant capitalism accelerated offshore investment.

The Left weighed in on several levels. While refuting neoliberal accusations that labor is largely responsible for the worldwide economic crisis that has afflicted most countries for the past twenty years, the Left accuses unions of timidity in the face of capitalism's assaults on wages and working conditions when not outright guilty of class collaboration. In the United States, the Left criticizes unions for becoming, at best, service organizations in the model of insurance companies rather than remaining social movements and, at worst, sitting on the heads of a restive rank and file in the process of implementing bargaining and other policies that, taken together, constitute an accommodation to capitalism's program of globalization. More particularly, the Left holds the leadership responsible for going along with capitalism's program to transfer the burden of the world economic crisis to working people in the form of a long-term reduction in real wages, cuts in the social wage, and increasingly, tendencies towards the creation of a two-tier wage system in many production and service industries.

Consequently, on a dual program of union democracy and revived militancy to reverse labor's free fall in membership and in economic and political power, the Left has helped organize rank-and-file movements to oppose established leaderships during the past two decades, notably in the corruption-ridden Teamsters, the formally democratic but hierarchical United Auto Workers, and at the local level, in unions such as the once-progressive New York Municipal Employees District Council 37, teachers' unions, and the blue-collar dominated Transport Workers. In the main, these efforts have been narrowly focused on the pressing economic problems faced by groups who have suffered deteriorating living standards and increasingly onerous working conditions, and on violations of the democratic rights of dissidents.

In the first contested election in the federation's forty-year history, John Sweeney, president of the million-member Service Employees International Union became AFL-CIO president and, since 1996, has undertaken some major initiatives to reverse organized labor's apparent free fall in membership. He has openly advocated that affiliated unions adopt an "organizing model," according to which the emphasis of "service" yields to "organizing." This shift would be reflected in the allocation of union resources, the degree of rank-and-file mobilization to play a large role in organizing the unorganized, and a call for more activism on political and legislative issues of concern to organized labor. Make no mistake, Sweeney is no radical democrat—if by that phrase is meant a social movement model in which members' sovereignty is not confined to union elections and to contract approvals and where union issues are no longer narrowly construed. Instead, in the social movement model, the rank and file runs the union from top to bottom, both at the level of decision making and in administration, and the labor movement allies itself with movements of feminists, racial minorities, environmentalists, and for sexual freedom.

On the whole, rank-and-file trade union movements have experienced mixed results. The most successful of them, Teamsters for a Democratic Union (TDU) recently suffered setbacks after entering into a coalition with the traditional (although militant) leader of a local union of United Parcel Service drivers, Ron Carey, who went on to win the union's presidency in 1991. In 1997 after his reelection for a second term, Carey led the most successful national strike in recent memory to reduce gaps in United Parcel Service's two-tier wage system. Three years after his successful reelection bid, Carey was forced out of office after charges were brought that he had allegedly used members' dues money to finance his campaign. Although TDU disavowed Carey, its candidate to replace him went down to defeat in 1999 at the hands of James P. Hoffa, son of the famous Teamsters president.

There are encouraging beginnings at the local level. It was a rank-and-file leader in the Municipal Employees District Council 37 who blew the whistle on union corruption at the highest levels, including leaders of DC 37's largest locals. A number of dissident local union presidents, mostly of smaller groups, quickly gathered together to form a Committee for Real Change. They exposed corruption and, equally importantly, made union democracy the cornerstone of union reform. More to the point, they tried to establish a link between the leadership's accommodationist collective bargaining policies and the corruption among its leadership after it had negotiated a five-year contract with no raises for the first two years and had perpetrated contracts with similarly paltry increases over a twenty-five-year period. A New York rank-and-file municipal workers' coalition soon emerged and won the affiliation of about a dozen rank-and-file groups whose unions bargain with city government, all of whom were fighting the twin objectives of democracy and renewed militancy.

Yet none of the leading forces behind union renewal—Left as much as progressive—have addressed one of the underlying issues in labor's decline: the virtual disappearance of a labor *public sphere*. Although there is a large labor press—indeed every major national union publishes a newspaper which appears at least monthly—and some unions have used the Internet to post web sites which offer organizing information and news—labor opinion is not a staple of the airwaves, nor is there a national labor newspaper. Moreover, the labor press is little more than a public relations vehicle for the established leadership. Photos of union presidents and other officers regularly adorn the pages of these publications; in only a few instances do they print dissenting or alternative opinions, mostly in the letters column. In New York, with the sole exception of the Transport Workers New Directions caucus, the insurgent caucuses offered the membership no means by which to communicate with each other over the heads of the leaders. New Directions publishes an impressive tabloid that appears regularly, but most of the other rank-and-file groups content themselves with newsletters and periodic letters and leaflets to convey their message. The once-ubiquitous union hall where members congregated, socialized, and discussed union and political issues is all but a relic, as the union "office" offers little space for conviviality.

Raymond Williams has insisted that trade unions are sites of working-class culture as well as instruments of struggle and collective bargaining agents. He insists that their character as bureaucratic organizations does not exhaust their cultural importance. Williams's declaration probably derived, in part, from his long experience as a workers' education teacher but also from his boyhood experience in Wales, the site of the most militant miners' movement in recent memory. Williams's father was a railroad worker albeit in a rural setting. As he relates his father's experience, it is clear that in this predominantly farm community, despite their minority status, "the political leaders of the village were the railwaymen." The social ties of these union men translated into public activity, and such instances were by no means a rarity in early twentieth-century Great Britain, even in rural precincts. In the most industrial of European societies, the workers had a cohesive tradition of struggle and cultural solidarity that dated from the enclosures and the corn laws, which drove millions from agriculture to the sixteenth- and seventeenth-century cities.

Similarly, in smaller communities in the United States as much as big cities in the nineteenth century, when the country made its turn from agriculture to industrial production, the craft unions of the American Federation of Labor, many of which were still ensconced in the old artisan mode of production, frequently built "labor temples" that housed the offices of affiliates of the local trades council and also provided space not only for routine union meetings but also for public lectures and discussion groups. During the great industrial union upsurge of the 1930s and 1940s, unions of semiskilled as well as skilled workers in mass production established their own union halls. The Auto Workers, the Electrical Workers, Textile Workers, and the older needle trades union halls, among others, were sites of public and social life for hundreds of thousands of workers. In New York, Local 65, a manufacturing, retail, and wholesale union that organized small shops and large department stores, had a restaurant, a bar, and a large hall that featured concerts, dances, and other cultural activities as well as mass membership meetings.

Local 65 built the union and sustained considerable rank-and-file activism by maintaining close contact with its members. For decades after World War II, when most unions had resorted to the automatic "check-off" method of collecting dues (dues, like taxes, deducted from wages), Local 65 maintained the archaic practice of collecting dues "by hand." Every member in good standing appeared at the union hall at least once a month to pay his dues, grab a snack or a full meal, and attend the mandatory local union meeting. On occasion, they could attend a lecture or an art exhibit; on Saturdays they might take classes in painting and drawing, creative writing, photography, or crafts. During its fifty-year existence, Local 65 sporadically offered its members a children's program as well. In 1989, under clouds of corruption and membership erosion, the union dissolved into a series of Auto Workers local unions; one of the more striking instances of a working-class public sphere is now nearly forgotten, except by the mostly retired members who had been among its beneficiaries.

There is a scene in Orson Welles's film *Lady From Shanghai* depicting a hall similar to many maintained by the Seafarers and National Maritime Unions in the 1940s and 1950s. Since the contract obliged employers to fill jobs by using a union hiring hall like Local 65's, the hall in Welles's film had a dispatcher who sent workers out on jobs. Members spent the time waiting by playing cards and shooting the bull. In many industries, such as maritime, construction, musicians and other artists, and urban retail and wholesaling, where the workforce was otherwise widely dispersed, the hiring hall was the glue that held the membership together. It was both a culture in the highly specific sense of bringing people together on the basis of their common occupational and work experiences and a public sphere to the extent that it was a site of conversation about politics and personal lives. The demise of the hiring hall may be attributed to many influences having to do with the differential restructuring of U.S. capitalism, but the consequences for the loss of working-class movements were epochal.

1

If you take a ride south on New Jersey's Route 1 past Elizabeth and into the city of Linden, within minutes you will notice, on your right, a modest sign, "Linden Assemblers." There is an oddly shaped parking lot and two buildings: the credit union and the union hall of Local 595, United Auto Workers. As you enter the union hall, you are assaulted by a distinctive musty, slightly alcoholic, smell. The fragrance is that of a poorly ventilated tavern, and for good reason. The union offices sit on a slightly elevated street floor; walk a little further down the corridor and you cannot miss the meeting room that can hold about 200 people cheek by jowl, maybe 150 comfortably. The room is used for the local's regular monthly meetings, larger meetings such as that of the shop committee (the smaller meetings are usually held in one of the offices), the monthly retirees' meeting, and the occasional social event or conference.

The basement is the real center of the local union. On the right side is a long bar which is usually full during the hour and a half after the two shift changes; on the left is a large space where, after meetings, several members of the union and their families cater a Southern dinner of ribs and chicken and the usual "fixin's." On ordinary occasions, people take their meals in this room, mainly because of the proximity of the bar. During a conference I helped organize, the relatively large attendance made the upstairs space more feasible.

What goes on here is talk: people watch sports on TV and have the usual arguments about teams and leading figures in the game; since almost every union election is contested three or four months before the vote, people debate the relative merits of the candidates; and because this is a relatively active union, national and state politics are often on the informal agenda. The retirees are forever discussing their health problems, sometimes relating the usual health care atrocities to anyone who will listen. During the Social Security scare of the late 1990s, retirees debated issues such as whether there was a real crisis (most were skeptical of politicians' claims). Like most everyday communication, almost all of the talk is personal. The working members of the local average about forty-seven years old and some are starting to have grandchildren; their children are getting married or graduating from college, and many are sweating the problem their noncollege kids are having getting good jobs. In New Jersey, high school graduates and dropouts are having a tough time, even in the midst of the so-called prosperity.

The sixty-year-old General Motors plant in Linden once employed some 6,800 workers; in 1999, employment barely reached 2,600 because the company has introduced "lean production"; the vehicle design combines parts in order to save labor. Lean production means parts are delivered to the assembly line "just in time"; there is virtually no inventory. The result is that hordes of off-line jobs once done in the plant, such as welding fenders, bending sheet metal, and producing small parts, are now "outsourced," sometimes to domestic and foreign nonunion plants that pay a fraction of the basic auto wage of more than $20 an hour. As a result, save a few hundred temporary workers who were offered permanent jobs at the end of 1998, there has been no appreciable hiring since 1982. This accounts for the middle ages of most of the workers. In March 1999, some of the talk at the bar turned to rumors the plant, which assembles Chevrolet's main sports utility vehicle, might eventually shut down if they do not get another "product." Members hoped that by that time, a considerable fraction of the labor force would be eligible for the "thirty-and-out" provision of the union contract, which enables workers at age fifty-five who have thirty years on the job to retire at $2,200 a month. Those who choose to work or are ineligible for retirement would be offered jobs in other GM plants, a right guaranteed by the contract. In fact, some members had recently entered the plant when the company shut down the Tarrytown, New York, and the Trenton, New Jersey, facilities.

In any case, there is strong evidence that if the Linden GM plant survives, like similar assembly plants in the industry, it will produce vehicles by means of a relative new technology called modular production. In this technology, parts are preassembled and delivered to a nearby shop, which "stuffs" them inside a module, a method that copies containerization, the automated process of long-shoring introduced on the waterfront some thirty years ago. The whole-car assembly would entail putting four modules together; at the same time, the plant's workforce would be reduced by half. At least, that is what some local unionists believe—the union hall and the shop floor are sites of incessant rumor and speculation. Contrary to newspaper reports of a booming economy and a bright economic future, most plant workers here agree with the assessment that, whatever the outcome of the fight for new product, they are "doomed." Their kids are not finding jobs that pay as well as those they hold—in 1999, an average of $65,000 to $70,000 a year, more for skilled trades—and their own prospects over the intermediate run are uncertain, to say the least. Many are hoping to hang on long enough to qualify for the thirty-and-out provision of the UAW-GM contract. Although the contract also guarantees relocation rights to laid-off workers, many fear that there will simply not be enough jobs in the company, even if they are willing to move to faraway places such as Texas and Oklahoma.

Local 595's hall is one of the premier remaining, but rapidly disappearing, working-class public spheres. It is not a space of cultural development as some radicals and progressive labor educators might wish it to be. Nor is it a place where the discourse of common ground is articulated among competent speakers, in the middle-class sense. What goes on is a lot of informal talk, mostly routine union and retirees' meetings, and some political and trade union education—hardly enough to qualify by standards that prevailed until the 1940s, when many single-plant or neighborhood-based industrial union locals maintained lively halls that offered a variety of educational and social activities as well as the staple of a meeting hall and a bar.

Since World War II, when the auto, steel, electrical, and textile corporations abandoned the cities and moved to suburban locations, the old labor temple or craft-based hall in which hiring was done, union business transacted, and social life organized, gave way to the union hall of a large local representing workers in a single or a fairly small number of large industrial plants. Many union halls were built next to the plants on the highways. Because many traveled as much as one hundred miles round trip to get to and from work, for most the connection between home and work was irretrievably broken. For employees of large enterprises, the union hall and bar provided for many a major site with which to forge friendships, enjoy a sense of community not available elsewhere, watch the ball games, or relax with a game of darts, pool, or shuffleboard.

As goods production increasingly employs fewer workers, as plants are scattered and smaller, and because there are fewer of them, the industrial union halls are closing. In steel, for example, when once a typical mill had thousands of workers, the newest technology, so-called mini-mills (which now account for half of the country's steel output) often employ fewer than three hundred workers, and are typically located in anti-union areas. Under the impact of similar technologies, many union plants across industries are now closed or have been reduced to hundreds rather than thousands of workers. Hurting for money to support their large headquarters, local unions tend to sell their valuable property to real estate developers and move their operations to suburban office buildings where, along with other locals, they become administrators of the contracts, and little else.

In short, many of the older industrial unions have been hollowed out by the transformations that have afflicted the manufacturing sector. After a prolonged period during which unions were the track upon which the corporate locomotive traveled, with few stops in recent years, some have regained their taste for industrial combat. Strikes in auto and trucking industries have increased over the issue of capital flight, and in private mail against the perpetuation of the two-tier wage system. With diminished power at the bargaining table has come another loss: the disappearance of a specifically labor and class culture. As workers have been riven by consumerism (which drives many to seek as much overtime as they can get), separated by the chasm between workplace and living space, and estranged from their unions by pervasive bureaucratic practices of both their leadership and those dictated by collective bargaining and by the law, the bonds of solidarity have gradually loosened. Under these conditions, there is a dramatically reduced time for conviviality with fellow workers.

The underlying motifs of the disappearance of working-class public spheres are the rearrangement of space by the dispersal of physical capital and the narrowing of time available for anything but paid labor. The failure, even refusal, of unions to address the issues of hours, industrial location, capital flight, and the configuration of everyday working-class existence has had enormous consequences for their own survival, and for the ability of labor to have a voice in reshaping its own future. Since 1975, membership of industrial unions has fallen off by more than half—and this statistic does not tell the whole story. The decline would have been greater if many of them had not organized in the public and service sectors. For example, membership in the Auto Workers is down by nearly 50 percent from its apex of 1.4 million, but in the last twenty years it has gained some hundred thousand members in such occupations as clerical workers and graduate teaching and research assistants, health care employees, and thousands who were members of the defunct District 65, which had organized in retail and wholesale as well as the nonprofit sector, such as universities. As its strength in the auto, agricultural implement, and aircraft industries diminishes, increases in the service sector have partially hidden the true extent of its decline.

The past thirty years are marked by a decisive shift in the social composition of trade union membership. In broad strokes, this period is marked by the emergence of public employees' unionism and by the growth of unionism in the private services sector. Today, these unions constitute more than half of labor's diminished legions, which highlights the steep decline of labor's industrial backbone—"backbone" because the giant industrial unions were once the core of the labor public sphere, the place where, on the basis of shop-floor and union-hall communal life, organized labor once flexed its political and economic muscle, forced a dramatic rise in living standards for large chunks of the population, and played a vital role in the communities within which they lived and worked.

Public and service unionism has introduced new traditions into the labor movement.

The older craft and industrial unions were built around the concept (even if not always faithfully followed) that the organization was of, by, and for the members; newer unions are constructed on a "service" model. Except for the Teachers Union, which was built on the industrial union model of aggressive bargaining and membership sovereignty in the liberal democratic model (which emphasized bureaucratic administration rather than rank-and-file control over everyday union affairs), many of the largest units of public and service unions regard the members as *clients* to be served by a staff of professional representatives, lawyers, teachers, and counselors.

Take New York's Municipal Employees' DC 37, for example. With 120,000 members in fifty-six locals, representing employees in almost every branch of city government except the uniformed services, the union became one of the more potent urban political machines in the United States in the 1970s and 1980s; according to a former executive director, it was the "best service organization in the labor movement." Its members—preponderantly black and Latino women—work mostly in a wide variety of low-salaried jobs as cafeteria workers, crossing guards, nurses aides, housekeeping and dietary employees in hospitals, clerical workers in nearly every city agency, and blue-collar parks workers. Another substantial group, caseworkers in public welfare agencies, professionals such as engineers, librarians, and nurses and technicians in municipal hospitals and public health centers, is a fast-growing section of the union, accounting for some one-third of the membership, in the wake of sharp cuts in relatively well-paid blue-collar and clerical jobs.

Since the 1970s, the union has offered an array of services to individual members. Its legal department handles a myriad of civil cases associated with typical problems faced by low-income people: tenant-landlord relations, especially evictions and rent increases; disciplinary issues of members' children who attend public schools; matrimonial disputes; and problems associated with bank loans and time-payments on various consumer goods. Like many other unions in the not-for-profit sectors, DC 37 has taken a great interest in providing its members with academic credentials, since these are often requisite for achieving higher pay and a notch on the promotion ladder. The union main-tains a branch of the College of New Rochelle, a regional Catholic college, on its premises and through arrangements with other local colleges and universities sponsors a number of short-term training programs. The union, rather than the employer, is the administrator of the benefits programs that obliges many mem-bers to consult with the appropriate program administrator to obtain reim-bursements or deal with their retirement plans.

DC 37 is a leader in the transformation of many unions into a private welfare state. Like the public agencies that deal with the unemployed, the union tends to view its members as clients rather than acknowledge their sovereign power in the organization. Its mode of operation is marked by relationships that are clos-er to those of the old urban political machine than to those of a democratic pub-lic sphere, let alone anything to do with the concept of counterpublic (consti-tuted by itself in opposition to the mass public, which is created by the media and other mainstream institutions). The everyday life of unionism, in addition to attending to the highly formalized grievance procedure of which its members must avail themselves in order to get a measure of job justice, may be character-ized by the serial nature typical of banks and insurance companies—there are numerous interactions, but they are largely confined to those between profes-sional servants and clients to whom they dispense benefits and whom they rep-resent on the job. The shop chair or steward—the staple shop-floor leader of the union—is relegated to agent or reporter of problems rather than problem solver. During the twenty-five years this regime was (and remains) in force, the idea of the union headquarters as a public sphere, either in the industrial union or labor temple model, has been unthinkable for two reasons.

The first has to do with the specific history of the New York public and serv-ice sector unions. The key organizers (who generally became the key leaders of these unions) were not rooted in the occupations and work sites that made up the membership. Many were imported from political groups with ideological and power perspectives; whether of the social democratic or communist variety, they were "sent in" either as staff members or as rank-and-file workers for the purpose of building, then leading, the union. The second reason has to do with the legal framework of public employees' bargaining, which places severe con-straints on a compliant union leadership.

Perhaps the most famously militant among them, Local 1199 of the New York-based 100,000-member Hospital Workers Union, illustrates the folly of deriving unwarranted conclusions from ideological premises. Low-wage black and Latino workers largely perform the New York City Voluntary Hospitals' patient, dietary, and housekeeping services. The union had been organized by a small, 3,000-member local of pharmacy workers—some professional pharma-

cists, others retail clerks. Organized and led since the early 1930s by communists who were indigenous to the occupations within large drugstores, Local
1199's leadership became persuaded in the mid-1950s by one of its own, phar-
macist Elliot Godoff, to tackle the unionization of New York's nonprofit hospitals. With hefty appropriations from the union's treasury, volunteer organizers'
contributions by members, and substantial financial and staff support of Local
65 (by then a fairly large union of more than 35,000 members), Godoff, who
had had a long and frustrating experience trying to organize hospital workers
since the late 1930s, assembled a small organizing staff supplemented by the
volunteer rank-and-file organizers. Brandishing the banners of economic justice
and also of the civil rights movement and its icon, Martin Luther King Jr., and
with strong support from the Central Labor Council and its president, Harry
Van Arsdale, the union wisely chose to disregard legal avenues to gaining union
recognition. Instead, it mounted a series of demonstrations, job actions, and
strikes against the key hospitals in the vast medical empire of New York: Mount
Sinai, Montefiore, and Maimonides, as well as others such as Beth Israel and
Flower-Fifth Avenue. The strategy of combining direct action, the symbolic language of social liberation, and of wage justice, to recruit thousands of workers
with adroit political maneuvering among the city's establishment institutions
and politicians paid off handsomely. Within a decade, Local 1199 had driven a
wide berth in the once-impenetrable wall of hospital management, and began to
organize the non-Jewish voluntaries such as Lenox Hill and Columbia-
Presbyterian (which proved far more difficult). By the1970s, the union widened
its purview to New Jersey, Pennsylvania, Massachusetts, and Connecticut.

For two decades after its initial victories, the hospital workers were led mainly by those who had organized the union—white leftists. By 1975, those leaders
had forged a solid trade-union mass base and created a new language and culture of militant unionism that was reminiscent of, but not identical to, labor's
pre–Cold War era strategies. Race, nationality, and the traditional leftist vocabularies of class exploitation were represented both visually in murals and other
art works and in the rhetoric of liberation, rather than merely invoking the
promises of business unions to deliver only wages and better benefits. What was
missing was a new generation of black and Puerto Rican hospital floor leaders.

By the early 1970s, the turbulence of the organizing phase was over.
Although maintaining the rhetoric of social change, the union adopted some of
the business union practices of the old AFL: reliance on full-time business representatives to handle small and large grievances and, in tandem with management, to act as a disciplinary agent over the workers. Like DC 37, but with far
more panache, Local 1199 members were transformed into clients and the leadership into a service bureaucracy whose main task was to administer the contract

and to serve members. By the mid-1970s, black staff members were chafing under the benevolent but nonetheless paternalistic leadership of the white progressives who ran the union. They began to demand a succession plan because the union's leader, Leon Davis, was already well into his seventies.

Like Local 65, whose social composition was similar to that of Local 1199, the leadership did little to anticipate the inevitable transfer of power and the equally probable turmoil that might accompany it. There was no real education program for rank-and-file leaders or for the members; most staff members were hired from other unions, from its large professional membership of social workers and technical categories, or from a coterie of eager college graduates. Within a few years of consolidation, the union staff was a professional cadre similar to that of any social service agency. They were poorly paid, at least by general union standards, but despite being treated as employees rather than a part of the movement, many organizers and staff members stayed as long as the work was exciting. Local 1199 never ceased to organize the unorganized and did not hesitate to "mobilize" its members around contract issues and political questions such as the Vietnam War and civil rights, and most recently, it brought out its members to protest the murder of Amadou Diallo, an unarmed peddler of West African origin, by New York police.

At Local 1199, the union's organizing and mobilizing model was not enough to prevent searing conflict when Leon Davis announced his retirement in 1982. His handpicked successor, staff member Doris Turner, a union vice-president, moved rapidly to distance herself from the union's mostly white and Latino inner circle. Within a few years, the union was embroiled in a raging internecine struggle between the two factions. Davis's coterie backed Dennis Rivera to run against Turner and he won a relatively narrow victory. Although charismatic and politically sophisticated, Rivera has maintained the service model. After the defeat of President Bill Clinton's national health care plan, when an austere cost-cutting program was implemented by the hospitals, the union was unprepared to deal effectively with the changes. Anticipating thousands of layoffs, new affiliation agreements, and massive changes in job titles and descriptions, Local 1199's solution was to demand early retirements, a large-scale training program for displaced members, and political mobilization to force the city administration to pour money into the hospitals. Absent from the union's response was a concerted attempt to rebuild union culture and to finally build a base of rank-and-file leadership.

2

The prevailing service model of unionism has been particularly strong in the public sector. Although the fact that many of these unions are dominated by paid professionals may be due to specific histories, among its elements are the historical circumstances that framed public labor relations law. While the organizing phase of state and local public unionization occurred before legislation to enable these unions to enjoy recognition for the purposes of collective bargaining, the most rapid growth followed passage of these laws in many instances. Many state legislatures restricted or banned the right of public employees to strike, and eager to obtain bargaining rights, many union officials accepted this constraint. Beyond collective bargaining, some struck a Faustian bargain with lawmakers. In return for accepting arbitration to settle contract and grievance impasses, the legislation provided the unions with control over part or all of the social wage package: health and pension benefits, funds for legal services to members, training and education funds, and with them the choice of training and educational institutions to provide these services.

While public sector unionism is marked deeply by legalism, public sector unions took a page from the book of industrial unions that grew up in the shadow of the New Deal. Rank-and-file insurgents had been successful in three general strikes in 1934. It may be argued that the National Labor Relations Act (NLRA), one of the crucial "achievements" of the New Deal of Franklin D. Roosevelt, was intended to regulate what his administration considered a runaway radical movement. Organized labor gained from the procedural democratic provisions of the NLRA. Workers could now vote for unions of their own choosing rather than relying on the strike weapon to achieve union recognition. The new contract unionism successfully replaced direct action with a bureaucratic grievance procedure, however, and thereby relegated the strike to an occasional tool, used only within legally restricted limits. As a result, direct action at the workplace and in union bargaining went underground.

Thus, the bureaucratic organization of public employees and many private sector unions that adopted a similar model followed from the tacit decision to put members to sleep except on relatively rare occasions when mobilization was deemed necessary to win expanded wages and benefits or legislation. Newer unions also followed the decision (whether from the legal or implied agreement) to forgo the use of the weapons of direct action, only some of them connected with strikes. Needless to say, in recent years, the union bureaucracies are under increasing pressures from rank-and-file organizations and from widespread member discontent with their performances at the bargaining table and in the legislative arenas.

In effect, if not intentionally, the emergence of the rank and file as a potent economic and political force is producing the simultaneous development of labor counterpublics. To be sure, much of the counterpublic is the result of sustained protest against the leadership's accommodationism in this era of crisis, rather than seeing itself as an alternative to the current worldview of the prevailing bureaucracy, but there are exceptions to rule. Movements like the Teamsters for a Democratic Union and the Transport Workers New Directions caucuses, and the AFT-Professional Staff Congress's New Caucus exhibit some of the characteristics of a new type of counterpublic within the labor movement. None has forged itself entirely out of protest but has tried to put forward an alternative vision for the labor movement. Although the leading figures in these movements have socialist origins, their rhetoric and program are thoroughly trade unionist in the American sense: the labor movement advocates the broad social welfare state and is opposed to racism and sexism. At the heart of their conception is simple class solidarity, combined with a fervent commitment to what I have called radical (as opposed to procedural) democracy.

In what sense are the rank-and-file union movements and those local union leaders affiliated with it a counterpublic? Even if none of them has undertaken a wide-ranging critique of the prevailing practices of the trade union bureaucracies, it is their participatory or radical democratic practice that inevitably opposes the cliental conception of the liberal labor movement that constitutes and explains their successes. Although they have occasionally been co-opted by the liberal labor leadership when, under rank-and-file goading, it awakens from its slumber, some (like TDU) have survived setbacks, built a membership organization, and continued to fight for a new unionism. Whether most of the others born of protest are able to emulate this persistence remains to be seen. What is evident, however, is that the new insurgency means to change the face of labor and bring it back to the future, back in the sense that the movement involved large sections of rank-and-file workers prior to the New Deal.

16

THE NEW MEN OF POWER

THE LOST LEGACY OF C. WRIGHT MILLS

1

There are few contemporary academics who, during their lifetimes, match—let alone aspire to—the stature of C. Wright Mills as a public intellectual. For almost fifteen years, beginning with the 1948 publication of *The New Men of Power* and ending with his untimely death in 1963 at age forty-seven, Mills was among America's best-known social scientists and social critics. Although not exactly a household name, he was widely known among the politically active population as well as within wide circles of academic and independent intellectuals. Despite a broad grasp of the social world, he did not present himself as an "expert," which, in American television and print journalism, has become synonymous with what we mean by "intellectual." In a word, he was not a servant of power; he was, instead, in the sense of the seventeenth-century English radical, a ranter. Much of his work recalls, in addition, the pamphlets of the decades of the American Revolution, where the address of numerous and often anonymous writers was to the "publick" as much as to those holding political and economic power. Like these predecessors, his writing was always erudite, even scholarly—but Mills's intent was entirely subversive of contemporary mainstream ideologies.

Mills exemplified a vanishing breed in American life: the radical intellectual who is not safely ensconced in the academy. He adhered to none of the mainstream parties nor to those on the fringes of mainstream politics. Although it is true that he was a figure of his own time (his main work was done in the 1940s and 1950s, when issues of sex, gender, and ecology were barely blips on the screen), his position was congenitally critical—of the Right, conservatives, liberals, the relatively tiny parties of the Left, and especially members of his own shrinking group, the independent leftists. Like one of his heroes, the economist and social theorist Thorstein Veblen, himself a pariah in his chosen discipline, Mills was "in but not of" the academy (to paraphrase a famous aphorism of Marx). Unlike Veblen, whose alienation from conventional economics was almost total, Mills was, for most of his professional career, a sociologist in his heart as much as his mind. The scholarship of *The New Men of Power* is firmly rooted in the perspectives of mainstream American sociology at the end of World War II. It uses many of the tools of conventional social inquiry: surveys, interviews, data analysis, and charts, and takes pains to stay close to the "data" until the concluding chapters. What distinguishes Mills from mainstream sociology is that he adopted the standpoint of radical social change, not of fashionable sociological neutrality. From this standpoint, at the height of the so-called McCarthy period, he fearlessly named the system of domination from within one of its intellectual bastions, Columbia University, and distanced himself from the ex-radicals among his colleagues who were busy "choosing the West," otherwise giving aid and comfort to the witch hunters, or neutering themselves by hiding behind the ideology of value-free scholarship. Anticommunist to the core, towards the end of his life he was, nevertheless, accused of procommunist sympathies for his unsparing criticism of the militarization of America and his spirited defense of the Cuban revolution.

In the light of his later writings, which, to say the least, held out little hope for radical social change, *The New Men of Power* occupies a somewhat ambiguous place in the Mills corpus. Written on the heels of the general strike of industrial workers in 1946 and the conservative counterattack embedded in the Taft-Hartley amendments to the National Labor Relations Act, this study of America's labor leaders argues that, for the first time in history, the labor movement, having shown its capacity to shape the political economy, possessed the practical requisites to become a major actor in American politics as well. As both "army general and a contractor of labor," a machine politician and the head of a social movement, the labor leader occupies contradictory space.[1] By 1948, with the publication of the first edition of *The New Men of Power,* buoyed by American capitalism's unparalleled global dominance, a powerful conservative force was arrayed against labor's recently acquired power and, according to Mills, had no intention of yielding more ground without an all-out industrial and political war. Yet he found union leaders curiously unprepared for the struggle. Even as their cause was being abandoned by liberal allies, let alone belittled and besmirched by their natural enemies among the corporations and their ideological mouthpieces and right-wing and conservative politicians, union leaders remained faithful to the Democratic Party and the New Deal, which was rapidly fading into history. In fact, Mills and his collaborator, Helen Schneider, found that the concept of a labor party had declined from the perspective of most labor leaders whereas a decade earlier, the apex of industrial unionism, a majority had favored the formation of such a party, despite their practical support of the Democrats.

The ambiguity comes in when the subsequent writings are considered. By the mid-1950s, Mills had abandoned hope that the labor movement was capable of stemming the tide of almost complete corporate capitalist domination of American economic, political, and cultural life. Discussion of the labor movement's social weight is largely absent in *White Collar*, published in 1951, only three years after *The New Men of Power*;[2] *The Power Elite*, which appeared in 1956, consigned organized labor to subordinate status within the commanding heights of national power.[3] In Mills's view, the moment had come and gone when unions could even conceive of making a difference in power arrangements. Whereas in 1948 Mills's address was, chiefly, to the labor leaders themselves—it was both a careful sociological portrait of these new men of power and an attempted dialogue with them—the subsequent works do not have a labor public in mind. To the contrary, his intended audience shifted to other intellectuals and to a generally anticorporate public, largely composed of middle-class individuals.

In the absence of social movements capable of making a genuine difference in power relations, these studies were directed to the largely "liberal center" for whom Mills never ceased to have mixed feelings. The liberals were a necessary ingredient of any possible grand coalition for social change, but this center was marked by "looseness of its ideas," an attribute which led it to "dissipate their political attention and activity."[4] In the wake of the failure of the labor leaders to face the challenge posed by the rightward drift of American politics, the hardening of corporate resistance to labor's economic demands, the freezing of the political environment by the Cold War, and the virtual disappearance of the Left, especially the independent Left, Mills's public shifted decisively until the late 1950s, even as his political position remained firmly on the independent, noncommunist Left.

The central category which suffused Mills's social thought and to which he returned again and again was that of power, especially the mechanisms by which it is achieved and retained by elites in the economy and in social institutions. This is the signal contribution of the Italian social theorist Vilfredo Pareto to Mills's conceptual arsenal. In Pareto's conception, elites (not classes) constitute the nexus of social rule. To derive his conception of power, Mills focused neither on the labor process, the starting point for the Marxists, nor on the market, the underlying institution for Weberians. In essence, Mills was a state theorist. The elites were, for Mills, always institutionally constituted. He recognized the relative autonomy of corporations but, consistent with the regulation era of advanced capitalism, as early as *The New Men of Power*, he argued that the state had become the fundamental location of the exercise of economic as much as political power. For example, in *The Power Elite*, his most famous and influential work, three "institutional orders" which were closely linked but spatially and historically independent—the military, the political directorate, and the corporate—constituted together what others might, in Marxist vocabulary, describe as a ruling class. Except it isn't a "class" either, in the sense of those who share a common relationship to the ownership and control of productive property, or as in Weber's conception, groups who share a common interest in gaining access to market opportunities for employment and to acquire goods. The power elite was an *alliance* of the individuals who composed top layers of each of the crucial institutional orders and whose relative strength varies according to historical circumstances.

In the immediate post–World War II period, Mills detected the autonomous power of the military as, increasingly, the driving force in the alliance, just as the political elite occupied that position during the 1930s slump, when the provision of social welfare attained an urgency—lest by neglecting the needs of the underlying population, the system might be endangered. Needless to say, the corporations, the holders of what he calls "big money," are by no means ignored. After all, they remain the backbone of the entire system. Naming the power elite as the only "independent variable" in American society, Mills was obliged to revise his earlier estimation of the labor movement. Barely eight years after designating the labor leaders "new men of power" who had to choose whether to lead the entire society in the name of working people and other subordinate groups, he designated them a "dependent variable" in the political economy. Accordingly, he lost hope that working people and their unions would enter the historical stage as autonomous actors, at least until a powerful new Left of intellectuals and other oppressed groups emerged.

2

Mills did a considerable portion of his work with, among others, Hans Gerth, whose powerful mind was never matched by a body of equally compelling written work. In some respects, including *The New Men of Power*, Mills gave an English-language voice to Gerth's ideas. These ideas, a complex synthesis of Marx, Max Weber, and Vilfredo Pareto, introduced a wide range of concepts into the study of modern institutional life. Crucial to Gerth and Mills's understanding of how modern institutions work was Weber's theory of bureaucracy, read through the pejorative connotation of its system of rules and occupational hierarchies as inimical to democratic decision making. Rather than viewing bureaucracies as necessary institutions to make complex industrial societies work more efficiently, as Weber argued, Gerth provided Mills with the idea that bureaucratic control of institutions entailed domination, which Robert Michels extended to socialist organizations in his classic *Political Parties.* For Michels, the mechanism of domination was the leadership's monopoly over the means of communication. Mills saw the development of the labor movement as a series of highly institutionalized bureaucracies that, in contrast to his preferred model of unions—voluntary, democratically run, and rank-and-file controlled organizations—were rapidly mutating into oligarchies of power.

Mills's dissertation, *Sociology and Pragmatism,* completed in 1943, was an explicit attempt to draw the implications of European sociological theory for the United States.[5] He himself exemplified that connection. For pragmatism, there is no question of intrinsic "truth," if by that term we designate the possibility that truth may be independent of the context within which a proposition about the social world is uttered. The truth of a proposition is closely tied to the practical consequences that might, under specific conditions, issue from it. Practical consequences may be evaluated only from the perspective of social interest. There is no "win-win" thinking here. In the end, Mills adhered to the notion that whether a particular power arrangement was desirable depended on whose ox was being gored.

He drew heavily from the concept of ideology as interpreted by Karl Mannheim, whose major work, *Ideology and Utopia,* is, in part, a critique of the Marxist designation of the proletariat as a universal class and particularly of Georg Lukacs's argument that, having adopted the standpoint of the proletariat, in relation to knowledge, it had no interest in reproducing the mystifications which buttress bourgeois rule. Marxism can penetrate the veil of reified social relations to reveal the laws of motion of capitalism and, therefore, produce truth. Mills was much too skeptical to buy into this formulation; Mannheim's relativism was more attractive and corresponded to his own pragmatic vision. Accordingly, knowledge is always infused with interest, even if it occurs behind the backs of actors. Mills, however, leaned towards ideology as an expression of intentionality and this characterization is particularly applicable to the labor leaders who are the subjects of *The New Men of Power.* Lacking an explicit ideology does not mean that the labor leader can dispense with the tools of persuasion. According to Mills, these were the tools of a "practical politician" rather than of an ideologue. Mills's employment of the word "rhetoric" described how leaders persuaded and otherwise justified to their constituencies policies and programs that may or may not have been in their interest.

Mills was also a close reader of the political and social thought of John Dewey, perhaps America's preeminent philosopher of the twentieth century and one of the leading figures in the development of pragmatism. From Dewey and from his interlocutor, Walter Lippmann, whose debate on whether there was a chance for the genuine democratic society and governance in America was among the most important intellectual events of the 1920s, Mills derived the concept of the "public" or, in his usage, "publics." By the time Lippmann's *Public Opinion* appeared in 1921, many intellectuals expressed doubts that the ideal of the public as the foundation of a democratic polity, which made decisions as well as conferred consent, was at all possible in the wake of the emergence of mass society with its mass publics and massified culture. Lippmann argued, persuasively to many, that a public consisting of independent-minded individuals was decisively foreclosed by the end of World War I. For a society of citizens making the vital decisions affecting the polity, in the sense of the Greek city-state, he held out no hope. The public was shortsighted, prejudiced, and most of all, chronically ill informed. Although defending the claim that the elite of experts, which came into its own with the consolidation of the modern state and the modern corporation, was as desirable as it was inevitable in complex societies, Lippmann retained a trace of his former socialist skepticism. He wanted a democratic public to force political leaders to obtain consent on a regular basis and, through the ballot, to pass judgment on their quasi-sovereign actions. Thus, democracy was conceived negatively, as the barrier against authoritarian, technocratic rule.

Deeply affected by this powerful argument against participatory democracy, John Dewey was moved to respond. *The Public and Its Problems* (1925) is, for all intents and purposes, the most penetrating case for an active polity and for radical democracy any American has written.[6] With Dewey, Mills held that the promiscuous use of term "democracy" to describe the plebiscite and other mechanisms by which consent is achieved by representative political institutions is unwarranted. For Mills, the institutions of the liberal state still need, and solicit, the consent of the governed, but Congress and the executive branch are increasingly beholden to the holders of institutional power and not their electors, except insofar as the public refuses to confer consent to policies which they perceive to be contrary to their interests and, as in the case of Social Security "reform," succeeds in staying the hand of legislators, at least for a time. Having entered into an alliance with the military and corporate orders, the political directorate becomes a self-contained body, undemocratic in both the process of its selection and its maintenance.

Dewey's concept of democracy recalls the New England town meeting in which the "public" was not a consumer of the work of active and influential people, but a participant, a decision maker, in the community's political and social life. In this respect, it is important to recall Mills's "Letter to the New Left" (1960), whose main ideas were first enunciated in the *The New Men of Power*.[7] "Letter" outlined the principles of participatory democracy on the basis of Dewey's concept of the public, and was perhaps the single most influential document in the early history of the Students for a Democratic Society. SDS's program, enunciated in the famous *Port Huron Statement,* was constructed around the concept/demand for "participatory" democracy in which "ordinary people" would control the "decisions that affected their lives." It presupposed the same distrust of the state and its branches that Mills evinced years earlier. But unlike 1948 when, notwithstanding its de facto expiration, the New Deal still inspired broad support for the ideology best expressed in Herbert Croly's *Promise of American Life* (1909), which Mills names as the most important work of liberal statism, two decades of militaristic statism and the appearance of a new generation of political activism made Mills's libertarian appeal more audible.

3

For most of his academic career, Mills taught sociology at Columbia University. He produced social knowledge but was also an intellectual agitator. He was deeply interested in advancing the science of sociology as a means toward giving us a wider understanding of how social things work. From the late 1940s when Mills (at age thirty-three) and Helen Schneider produced this landmark study of the American labor union leaders, he remained a close student of social movements; his writings span analyses of the labor movement, the student Left, the peace movement, and others. He swam, intellectually, against the current, yet unlike many independent leftists who saw only defeat in the postwar drift toward militaristic-corporate political economy and despaired of relevant political practice, he was above all a practical thinker whose interest was always to discover the chances for leftward social change. Consequently, even when he was the most descriptive of, say, labor leaders, his eyes never strayed far from the questions of What is to be done? What are the levers for changing the prevailing relations of power? How can those at or near the bottom emerge as historical actors?

Mills was aware that to reach beyond the audience of professional social scientists he was obliged to employ a rhetoric that, as much as possible, stayed within natural, even colloquial language. Addressing the general reader as well as his diminishing audience of academic colleagues, Mills conveyed often difficult and theoretically sophisticated concepts in plain (but often visual) prose, described by one critic as "muscular." Perhaps most famously, he was a phrasemaker. For example, his concept of the "main drift" to describe conventional wisdom, first described in *The New Men of Power*, as well as centrist politics encapsulated in a single phrase what others have required paragraphs to explain. Instead of using the loaded term "crisis" or the technical dodge "recession" to describe conditions of economic woe, he employed the colloquial term "slump." He characterized the rise of industrial unions after 1935 as the "big story" for American labor, a term which encompassed history and common perception.

He was also a great taxonomist. His writings were suffused with "ideal types"—Weber's methodological prescription to fashion composite profiles against which to measure any particular instance of the type—arranged horizontally as well as vertically. For example, the models assembled in *The New Men of Power*—of the labor leader, of the various publics which he addressed and to which he was obliged to respond—gave a glimpse of Mills's lifelong approach to social knowledge: first, produce a composite profile of the subject. Then, provide detailed descriptions of the context within which the subject operates, and evaluate the relative salience of each element of this context to how the subject is shaped. Then, return to the subject (in this case, the labor leader), and unpack the composite to break down the different types of labor leaders. Finally, replace the labor movement in the larger political, economic, and cultural situations. To what end? In *The New Men of Power*, perhaps it was to find the alternatives to the main drift of union politics and ideologies. Needless to say, although a student of elites, Mills asked whether the democratic movement from below, of the rank-and-file union members, might succeed in overcoming the leaders' tendency toward conservative bureaucratic domination or even racketeering.

Mills wrote scholarly works, but in keeping with the style of a public intellectual, he was also a pamphleteer, a proclivity that often disturbed his colleagues and led some to dismiss him as a "mere journalist," one of the more odious forms of academic hubris. In fact, this dismissal may account for the sad truth that he has been virtually unread in social science classrooms since the late 1970s, has disappeared from many scholarly references, and is rarely discussed in the academic trade. In the last decade of his life, manifestos and indictments of the prevailing social and political order issued from his pen as frequently as sociological works. In fact, *The Power Elite*, which inspired a subdiscipline whose academic practitioners include G. William Domhoff, Ralph Nader, and a veritable army of "public interest" researchers, has always been controversial on theoretical grounds, but also, despite its often meticulous and comprehensive "data," for its clear democratic bias. In these days, when most leading members of the professoriat have retreated from public engagement except as consultants for large corporations, as media experts, or recipients of the largesse of corporate foundations and government agencies who want their research to assist in policy formulation, or confine their interventions to professional journals and meetings, Mills remains an embarrassing reminder of one possible answer, which may be exemplified by his colleague Robert S. Lynd's probing challenge to knowledge producers of all sorts in *Knowledge for What?* (1939).

Mills rejected the spurious doctrine according to which the social investigator was obliged to purge herself of social and political commitment. His values infused his sociological research and theorizing and he never hid behind methodological protestations of neutrality. Mills was, instead, a partisan of movements of social freedom and emancipation while, at the same time, preserved his dedication to dry-eyed, critical theory and dispassionate, empirical inquiry. An advocate of a democratic, radical labor movement he was, nevertheless, moved to indict its leadership, not by fulmination, but by a careful investigation of how unions actually worked in the immediate postwar period. Although a "man of the Left" in the late 1940s, Mills provoked his Left publics to outrage when he concluded that the "old" socialist and communist Left had come to the end of the road. By the late 1950s, as the frost of the Cold War melted a bit, he was loudly proclaiming the need for a New Left that had the courage to throw off the ideological baggage of the past, especially Marxist orthodoxy and Stalinism. Like Jean-Paul Sartre, whose *Critique of Dialectical Reason* appeared in 1960, he came to regard tradition, even radical tradition, as a political albatross. He never used Sartre's fancy term "practico-inert" to mark the encrusted habits that induce people to reproduce the past in the present but he was a persistent critic of the habituation of the Left to old ideas. A withering opponent of the communists in and out of the labor movement, sensing the impending doom of the Soviet Union after the opening provided by Khrushchev's revelations of Stalin's crimes at the 20th Communist Party Congress in 1956, he was among the first to urge the young to disdain their elders' preoccupation with the "Russian" question and instead attend with fresh eyes and hearts to the tasks at hand: to oppose U.S. intervention in the affairs of revolutionary societies and to establish the framework for a radical democratic society.

I have no doubt he was right, at least in the short or intermediate term, but he never made clear that he had been reared, politically, on the Russian question and forgot that those who ignored it were doomed to relive it, an eventuality he was never cursed to witness. That the New Left that, eventually, captured the imagination of an entire generation went awry may not be attributed exclusively to its refusal to address existing socialisms of the Stalinist variety. It was entirely disarmed, however, in the wake of the heating up of the war in Southeast Asia, when various Marxist ideologies became matters of urgent debate; most young leftists found themselves overwhelmed. They were moved by guilt as much as ignorance to confer uncritical support to the Vietnamese communists and even hailed the efforts of Pol Pot in Cambodia. By 1970, many reared in the New Left were no longer Mills's spiritual children; they all but renounced his democratic faith in favor of a "third world" dogma of national liberation at all costs. Ironically, Mills himself was not immune from such enthusiasms.

Mills was a leading figure in the sociology of "mass" culture that developed along several highly visible lines in the 1940s and 1950s. He observed the increasing homogenization of American culture and brilliantly linked some of its more egregious features to the decline of the democratic public. While his rhetoric was distinctly in the American grain, his views paralleled those of Theodor Adorno, Max Horkheimer, and Herbert Marcuse, the leading theorists of the Marxian Frankfurt School. Like them, he linked cultural massification to mounting political conformity associated with the emergence of fascism and other authoritarian movements in nearly all advanced industrial societies. These ruminations are present in *The New Men of Power* but are, perhaps, best articulated in *White Collar,* the second volume of his social structure trilogy. This pioneering study of the emergence of the new middle classes of salaried professional, technical, and clerical employees situated the spread of mass culture after World War I to their growing significance in advanced industrial societies.

Although little more than elevated wageworkers and, for this reason, deprived of the work autonomy enjoyed by the "old" middle class of self-employed farmers, small merchants, and professionals, the new middle class remained culturally tied to capital. Mills saw little hope for their mass unionization as long as mass culture—their indigenous culture—remained tied to the main drift of mass society. On the one hand, reared in images of American exceptionalism, they were the embodiments of the cultural aspiration for social mobility; on the other, their growth was a sign of professional proletarianization. Yet their eyes were fixed on the stars. Lacking a secure class identity, which is intrinsic to those engaged in the production and appropriation of things, as producers of "symbols" they were likely to remain an atomized mass, an oxymoron which signified the trap into which they were thrust, the "enormous file" of administration.

The book-length pamphlets were received as more than controversial; they were, in many minds, notoriously heretical for their tacit violation of academic insularity, and also because they broke from the main tenets of the Cold War consensus at a time when, under siege, political repression was still alive and well in the country. *The Causes of World War Three* (1958) is, in many respects, a popularization and application to the international scale of *The Power Elite*.[8] It depicts world politics in terms of the rivalry of two power blocs, one led by the United States and the other by the Soviet Union, both of which were governed by irresponsible elites whose conduct of the nuclear arms race threatened the existence of humanity. Written in a period when one could count the number of radicals with full-time appointments in American universities on one hand and when the preponderant ex-radicals had "chosen the West," this equalization of responsibility for the world crisis between East and West endeared Mills neither to the communists and their periphery for whom the Soviet Union was virtually blameless for the state of things, nor to Cold War liberals for whom any suggestion that the United States' foreign policy could contribute to the chances for the outbreak of World War III was as shocking as it was absurd.

Hidden in the pages of *The New Men of Power* is the influence of the one strain of Trotskyism which, after the war, declared that both camps were forms of a new antidemocratic, militaristic capitalism and boldly, but futilely, called for the formation of a "third" camp whose base would be a radicalized labor movement in alliance with other anticapitalist elements of the population. At the time of its formulation, the leading unions in every capitalist country were busy making deals with their own corporations and with the capitalist state, and the project failed. Mills's appeal to the "public," translated in this context as the middle-class liberal center, proved more effective because it corresponded to the emergence of a mass movement against the testing and use of nuclear weapons and for an end to the Cold War. Needless to say, the preponderance of American labor leaders, including Walter Reuther, the liberal president of the largest industrial union, the Auto Workers, were aligned with their own government's policies and were convinced that the price of demilitarization was nothing less than a new slump.

A self-declared independent leftist (which in *The New Men of Power* meant an anti-Stalinist, but unaligned radical), Mills had been influenced by Trotskyism early in his life. By the evidence of *The New Men of Power*, Mills carefully separated the still-influential communists from radicalism. The communists were influential precisely because the party had been an important vehicle for bringing militant workers into the New Deal and, during the war, played a major role in enforcing the wartime no-strike pledge and the government's drive for productivity. Whatever oppositional politics they evinced after the war was due, almost exclusively, to the chasm between the United States and the Soviet Union.

Despite the continuing influence of some aspects of Trotskyist thinking, he believed neither Trotskyism nor the relatively weak and fragmented independent Left had much chance of influencing the course of the labor movement that, for Mills, represented the best chance of resisting the drift towards authoritarianism and war, despite its warts. He was not able to offer a convincing alternative until much later when, in the wake of the growth of what he had observed in *The New Men of Power*, the social structure had been reconfigured by the war such that society was at once military and industrial. Whereas in 1948, Mills saw the labor movement as the site for resistance to the already congealed power elite of big business, the military, and the top political layer; in 1960, however improbable, he called for the formation of a "new" Left that could oppose the military-industrial-political complex, but not on the basis of the discredited (communist) or (ignored) Trotskyist alternatives.

Listen, Yankee: The Revolution in Cuba (1961), an exemplary instance of Mills's penchant for rowing upstream, was a fierce defense of the early years of Cuban revolution when, even for many anti-Stalinist radicals, it appeared that the regime was dedicated to raising living standards and was still open to a democratic society.[9] At a time when even liberals such as Senator Wayne Morse were vocal advocates of counterrevolution and supported the Kennedy administration's ill-fated Bay of Pigs invasion, Mills asserted the right of the Cuban people to determine their own destiny and sharply condemned U.S. policy in the Caribbean and Latin America. He excoriated liberals and conservatives alike for their support of antipopular regimes such as those of Batista in Cuba and Somoza's brutal Nicaraguan dictatorship, pointing out how the U.S. government had opposed democratic efforts by financing military counterinsurgency, especially against the Arbenz regime in Guatemala as well as Cuba's new revolutionary government. Although he had been a lifelong anticommunist, Mills saw the Cuban revolution as a harbinger of the long struggle of peasants and workers for liberation from colonialism and imperialism, and predicted serious future confrontations between the spreading insurgencies and the United States, which had become the main defender of the dictators under Democratic and Republican national administrations alike.

Indeed, for the decade of the sixties and beyond, Mills's provocative intervention seemed prescient. In Colombia, Douglas Bravo led a formidable armed uprising; Che Guevera led a band of guerrillas into the Bolivian jungle that, like the Colombian revolt, failed. With Cuba's material help, the Sandinistas in Nicaragua and the National Liberation Front in El Salvador were alive with revolutionary activity, and by the mid-1960s, the dormant Puerto Rican independence movement revived under a Marxist leadership that closely identified with the Cuban revolution. In the 1970s, Maurice Bishop organized a successful uprising in Grenada that openly aligned itself with the Cuban revolution, and Michael Manley's democratically elected left social-democratic government in Jamaica forged close ties with Cuba. However much he was smitten, Mills

framed much of his own discourse in terms of the significance of these events
for America's neocolonial foreign policy and for America's future. Lacking the
tools of discriminating evaluation, many young radicals not only gave their
unconditional support but enlisted as volunteers in Grenada, Cuba, and
Nicaragua's educational and health efforts.

With his mentor, Hans Gerth, he published a major social psychological
study in 1953, *Character and Social Structure*, which situated the self firmly in
the social and historical context that shaped and was shaped by it.[10] This work
is perhaps the premier instance of Mills's efforts to combine theoretical social
science with the distinctly American psychology of William James and George
Herbert Mead, but in these days—when the little boxes of the mind seem to per-
vade social thought—this book is, unjustly, largely unread. Mills's bold juxtapositions are simply too adventuresome for a social science academy for which
conventional wisdom seems to be the farthest horizon of possibility. His numerous essays covered the broad expanse of issues in American politics and culture, a range that has caused more than one detractor to complain that he is "all
over the place."

In this respect, Mills is a true scion of the great thinkers who founded the
social sciences. Their task was to provide a philosophical scaffolding to the disciplines, a project which Mills understood did not end with the canonical
works. As a pragmatist, he was acutely aware that theory requires constant
renewal and revisions and that, contrary to much current thinking, the problem
is not one of "applications" of received wisdom but to interrogate the wisdom
in the light of contemporary developments. Even as Mills borrowed concepts
such as "elite" from eminent forebears, for example, he invested new significance to the process of investigating historically situated elites. As a result, the
labor union elite and the power (ruling) elite display different characteristics,
although in *The New Men of Power* we can only see the first pass at the development of a new theory.

4

You might say that Mills's notion of labor leaders owed much to Machiavelli's
The Prince. Just as Machiavelli reminded the prince that the old rules of the feu-
dal oligarchy no longer sufficed to retain power but that a public had formed
which intended to call the ruler to account for his actions, in *The New Men of
Power*, Mills is in dialogue with a labor leadership increasingly attracted to oli-
garchical rule. His study admonished the leadership to attend to the postwar
shift that endangered their own and their members' power. Arguing that the
"main drift" was away from the collaboration between business and labor made

necessary and viable by the war, he suggested that labor leaders of "great stature" must come to the fore before labor was reduced. "Now there is no war," but there is a powerful war machine and conservative reaction against labor's power at the bargaining table.

> Today, knit together as they are by trade associations, the corporations steadily translate economic strength into effective and united political power. The power of the federal state has increased enormously. The state is now so big in the economy, and the power of business is so great in the state, that unions can no longer seriously expect even the traditional short-run economic gains without considering the conditions under which their demands are politically realizable.[11]

Top-down rule, which implied keeping the membership at bay, was, according to Mills, inadequate to the new situation where a military-industrial alliance was emerging, among whose aims was to weaken and otherwise destroy the labor movement.

How to combat this drift? Mills forthrightly suggested that the labor leader become the basis for the formation of a new power bloc. Rather than make deals on the top with powerful interests, he would have to accumulate power from the bottom. "If the democratic power of members is to be used against the concentrated power of money, it must in some way create its own political force. . . . the left would create an independent labor party" based on labor's formidable economic strength.[12] At the same time, Mills argued, it must enlarge its own base to include the "underdogs"—few of whom were in the unions. By underdogs, Mills did not mean those at the very bottom. They were, in his view, too habituated to "submission." He meant the working poor, the unskilled who were largely left out of the great organizing wave of the 1930s and the war years. He called for the organization of elements of the new middle class and the rapidly growing white-collar strata whose potential power, he argued, would remain unrealized unless they became organized.

One may read *The New Men of Power* with a number of pairs of eyes. At a minimum, it can be read as a stimulating account of the problems and prospects facing post–World War II American labor. It is descriptively comprehensive of the state of organized labor and the obstacles that it faced in this period. If Mills was mistaken in his belief that unions would have to become an independent political force to meet the elementary economic demands of their memberships, it may be argued that this limitation applies only to the first decades after the war. Unions did deliver, in some cases handsomely, to a substantial minority of the American working class. They organized neither the "underdogs" nor the new middle-class and white-collar workers who were all but ignored by the postwar labor movement, but forged a new social compact with large employers for their own members. For a third of the labor force in unions, and a much larger percentage of industrial workers, they succeeded in negotiating what may be called a "private" welfare state, huge advances in their members' standard of living, and a high degree of job security and individual protection against arbitrary discharge and other forms of discipline.

Ironically, this book is far more accurate in its central prognostication of labor's decline for the years since 1973. Labor has paid a steep price for its refusal to heed Mills's admonition to forge its own power bloc. Buffeted by economic globalization, corporate mergers, and the deindustrialization of vast areas of the Northeast and Midwest, and by the growth of the largely nonunion South as the industrial investment of choice, many unions have despaired of making new gains and are hanging onto their declining memberships for dear life. Labor is, perhaps irreversibly, on the defensive. In this period, union density—the proportion of union members to the workforce—has been cut in half. Collective bargaining still occurs regularly in unionized industries and occupations, and employers still sign contracts. But the last two decades are marked by labor's steady retreat from hard-won gains. In many instances, collective bargaining has yielded to collective begging.

As for the welfare state, corporations and their political allies have succeeded in rolling back one of its most important features, the provision of a minimum income for the long-term unemployed (pejoratively coded as "welfare" by post–New Deal politicians). Many who still collect checks are forced to work in public and private agencies for minimum wages, in some states replacing union labor. Social Security is on the block and privatization of public goods, especially schools and health care facilities, seems to be the long-term program of conservatives and many in the liberal center. As I write these lines, Puerto Rican labor organizations have called a forty-eight-hour general strike to support six thousand employees of the telephone company who have walked out in protest against the governor's announcement of the sale of the publicly owned service.

Backs to the wall, some labor leaders declared their intention to revive the all but somnambulant unions. They replaced the old leadership of the AFL-CIO and initiated some exciting organizing campaigns, especially among the underdogs. But, like their predecessors, intention is not matched by vision. Mills's program for combating the power elite, which has been organized labor's chief antagonist, and for developing a different strategy from the current drift toward retreat and accommodation, is nowhere better articulated than in *The New Men of Power*. It has been on the backburner of organized labor's agenda since the turn of the twentieth century when the prevailing power bloc began to take definite shape. It called for organized labor's political and ideological independence on the basis of a new conception of the labor movement: rank-and-file run, militant, and above all, oppositional and alternative to the main drift towards complete conservative hegemony. It argued that workers should "control" their own workplaces by, among other things, insisting on a significant voice in how major decisions are made. These would, by necessity, include decisions about where plants and other facilities should be built and by whom.

Mills recognized, as few labor leaders do, the importance of reaching out to the various publics that frame the political landscape. During the era of the social compact, union leaders saw no value in taking labor's case to the public during either strikes or important legislative campaigns. As junior partners of the power elite, they were often advised to keep conflicts in the "family." Labor leaders would rarely divulge the issues in union negotiations and, during the final stages of bargaining, often agreed to a press blackout. Only as an act of desperation, when an organizing drive or a strike was in its losing stage, did some unions make public statements. Following Mills's advice, one might argue that the public is always the third party at the bargaining table and the struggle to win it over has generally been won by management, especially for public employees' unions and unions in major national corporations.

To succeed, labor will have to see itself as no longer dependent on capital. It will have to cancel cooperative agreements by which, in return for short-term job security for a shrinking labor force, workers will have to cede more power to management. Mills's call for the creation of a new labor party may appear to have been decisively defeated by historical conditions that led to union shrinkage and by labor's own fateful decision after the war to remain loyal to the Democratic Party, even as it suffered the consequences of the steady retreat of the party from its brief moment of modern liberalism. In the early days of this millennium, there are signs, however tentative, that some in labor's middle and even top leadership are receptive to a new political stance. For the first time since 1924, some unions formed a labor party that, so far, does not enjoy the support of the AFL-CIO leadership and the new regime is, at least, no longer hostile to the proposal. After years when the strike became almost arcane, labor is, haltingly, rediscovering the value of direct action to win its demands and to defend itself against further deterioration of wages and working conditions. The late 1990s through early 2001 have seen a wave of militancy not matched since the early 1970s.

These events are reason for bringing back Mills's *The New Men of Power* to a new generation of readers. Perhaps more to the point, the issues addressed deserve a hearing at a time when unions sorely lack the strategic intelligence that Mills provides.

NOTES

1 No Time for Democracy

1. Etta Kralovec and John Buell, *The End of Homework: How Homework Disrupts Families, Overburdens Children and Limits Learning* (Boston: Beacon Press, 2001).

2. Henri Lefebvre, *The Explosion: Marxism and the French Revolution,* translated by Alfred Ehrenfeld (New York: Monthly Review Press, 1969).

3. Karl Marx and Frederick Engels, "The Communist Manifesto" in *Karl Marx, Frederick Engels: Collected Works,* vol. 1 (New York: International Publishers, 1975), 208–9.

4. Donna Haraway, *Simians, Cyborgs, and Women: The Reinvention of Nature* (New York: Routledge, 1991).

5. Marx and Engels, *The Communist Manifesto,* 10.

6. *Financial Times,* 11 November 2000.

4 Thinking Beyond "School Failure"

1. Paulo Freire, *The Pedagogy of Freedom* (Lanham, Md.: Rowman & Littlefield, 1998).

2. Freire, *The Pedagogy of Freedom,* 38.

5 Violence and the Myth of Democracy

1. Pierre Bourdieu and Jean-Claud Passeron, *Reproduction in Education, Society and Culture* (Thousand Oaks, Calif.: Sage Publications, 1977).

2. Paul Fussell, *Great War and Modern Memory* (New York: Oxford University Press, 1989).

3. Hannah Arendt, *The Human Condition* (New York: Harcourt, Brace and Jovanovich, 1968).

4. Wendy Kaminer, "Clinton for Senate?" *The Nation,* 9–16 August 1999, 4.

5. For the classic statement of this position see Oscar Lewis, *La Vida: A Puerto Rican Family in the Culture of Poverty—San Juan and New York* (New York: Random House, 1966).

6. Jay McLeod, *"There Ain't No Makin' It,"* 2d ed. (Boulder, Colo.: Rowman & Littlefield, 1997).

7. Thomas Hobbes, *The Leviathan* (London: Penguin Classics, 1990).

8. Albert O. Hirschman, *Exit, Voice, and Responses to Decline in Firms, Organizations, and States* (Cambridge, Mass.: Harvard University Press, 1970).

9. Jessie Klein and Lynn S. Chancer, "Masculinity Matters: The Omission of Gender from High-Profile School Violence Cases," in *Smoke and Mirrors: The Hidden Context of Violence in Schools and Society,* edited by Stephanie Urso Spina (Lanham, Md.: Rowman & Littlefield, 2000).

10. See Stephanie Spina, "When the Smoke Clears: Revisualizing Responses to Violence in Schools," *Smoke and Mirrors.*

7 Education for Citizenship

1. Antonio Gramsci, *The Open Marxism of Antonio Gramsci,* translated by Carl Marzani (New York: Cameron and Kahn, 1956).

2. Antonio Gramsci, *Selections from the Prison Notebooks of Antonio Gramsci,* edited and translated by Quintin Hoare and Geoffrey Newell Smith (New York: International Publishers, 1971).

3. Gramsci, "Notes on Italian History" in *Selections.*

4. Gramsci, *Selections,* 27.

5. Gramsci, *Selections,* 37.

6. Gramsci, *Selections,* 37.

7. Gramsci, "The Modern Prince" in *Selections,* 332–33.

8. Gramsci, "The Modern Prince," 333.

9. Gramsci, "The Modern Prince."

8 The Double Bind of Race

1. Richard Wright, *Black Power: A Record of Reactions in a Land of Pathos* (New York: HarperPerennial, 1995).

2. Paul Gilroy, *The Black Atlantic: Modernity and Double Consciousness* (Cambridge: Harvard University Press, 1993).

3. Richard Wright, *White Man, Listen!: Lectures in Europe* (New York: HarperPerennial, 1995).

4. Richard Wright, *The Color Curtain: A Report on the Bandung Conference* (Jackson, Miss.: Banner Books, 1995).

9   Race Relations in the Twenty-First Century

1. Vincent Bugliosi, "None Dare Call It Treason," *The Nation*, 5 February 2001.

2. William Julius Wilson, *The Declining Significance of Race: Blacks and Changing American Institutions* (Chicago, Ill.: University of Chicago Press, 1984).

3. John W. McWhorter, *Losing the Race: Self-Sabotage in Black America* (New York: Free Press, 2000).

4. Paul E. Willis, *Learning to Labor: How Working Class Kids Get Working Class Jobs* (New York: Columbia University Press, 1981).

5. Scott Malcomson, *One Drop of Blood: The American Misadventure of Race* (New York: Farrar, Straus and Giroux, 2000).

6. Thomas C. Holt, *The Problem of Freedom: Race, Labor and Politics in Jamaica and Britain, 1832–1938* (Baltimore, Md.: Johns Hopkins University Press, 1992).

7. Thomas C. Holt, *The Problem of Race in the 21st Century* (Cambridge, Mass.: Harvard University Press, 2000).

8. Holt, *Problem of Race,* 121.

10   Between Nationality and Class

1. David Dent, "The Million Man March," *Black Renaissance/Renaissance Now* 1, no. 2 (fall 1996).

2. W. Lloyd Warner, *Social Class in America: A Manual of Procedure for the Measurement of Social Status* (New York: Harper, 1960).

3. *Oxford English Dictionary* (London: Oxford University Press, 1978).

4. Barry Bluestone and Bennett Harrison, *The Deindustrialization of America: Plant Closings, Community Abandonment, and the Dismantling of Basic Industry* (New York: Basic Books, 1982).

5. Nathan Glazer, Daniel Patrick Moynihan, and Daniel Bell, eds., *Ethnicity* (New York: Free Press, 1970).

6. Steven Steinberg, *The Ethnic Myth: Race, Ethnicity, and Class in America*, 2nd ed. (Boston: Beacon Press, 1989).

7. William Julius Wilson, *When Work Disappears: The World of the New Urban Poor* (Cambridge, Mass.: Harvard University Press, 1996).

8. Paul Gilroy, *The Black Atlantic: Modernity and Double Consciousness* (Cambridge, Mass.: Harvard University Press, 1993).

9. Karl Popper, *The Open Society and Its Enemies* (London: Routledge and Kegan Paul, 1952).

10. H. T. Wilson, *The American Ideology: Science, Technology and Organization as Modes of Rationality in Advanced Industrial Societies* (London: Routledge and Kegan Paul, 1977).

11. Samuel Brittan, *The Role and Limits of Government: Essays in Political Economy* (Minneapolis: University of Minnesota Press, 1983).

12. Ulrich Beck, *The Risk Society* (Newbury Park, Calif.: Sage Publications, 1992).

13. Richard J. Herrnstein and Charles Murray, *The Bell Curve: Intelligence and Class Structure in American Life* (New York: Simon & Schuster, 1996).

11   Globalization and the State

1. Ralph Miliband, *The State in Capitalist Society* (London: New Left Books, 1969).

2. Michael Hardt and Tony Negri, *Empire* (Cambridge, Mass.: Harvard University Press, 2000).

3. Nicos Poulantzas, *State, Power, Socialism* (London: Verso Books, 2001).

4. Herbert Marcuse, *Technology, War and Fascism: The Collected Papers of Herbert Marcuse*, vol. 1, edited by Douglas Kellner (London: Routledge, 1998).

5. Marcuse, *Technology*, 67.

6. Marcuse, *Technology*, 80.

7. Marcuse, *Technology*, 81.

8. Marcuse, *Technology*, 82.

12   Capitalism and the State

1. Herbert Marcuse, *Technology, War and Fascism: The Collected Papers of Herbert Marcuse*, vol. 1, edited by Douglas Kellner (London: Routledge, 1998).

2. For a representative collection of writings by the key figures in the councilist tradition see *New Essays* (five volumes) (Westport, Conn.: Greenwood Press, 1970). Here, one may find commentaries on world politics, economic theory, and the Left by Paul Mattick, Anton Pannakoek (perhaps the leading theorist of the movement), and Karl Korsch. Dwight Macdonald was among the sympathetic intellectuals who contributed to their journal. See also Karl Korsch, *Revolutionary Theory*, edited by Douglas Kellner (Austin: University of Texas Press, 1977).

3. Paul Mattick, *Critique of Marcuse: One-Dimensional Man in Class Society* (London: Merlin Press, 1972). Marcuse once told me that in his opinion this book was the best critique of his work.

4. *Under the Banner of Marxism* was the theoretical journal of the Communist International.

5. Quoted in Rolf Waggershaus, *The Frankfurt School: Its History, Theories and Political Significance*, translated by Michael Robertson (Cambridge, Mass.: MIT Press, 1994), 4.

6. Paul Piccone, the long-time editor of the quarterly *Telos*, first used this phrase as a description of the demise of the New Left in the early 1970s. It quickly became the mantra of the group surrounding the journal.

7. The phrase was coined by the Swedish historian Goran Palm. See *The Flight from Work*, translated by Patrick Smith (Cambridge: Cambridge University Press, 1977).

8. Marcuse, *Technology*.

9. Marcuse, *Technology*, 266.

10. Herbert Marcuse, *Reason and Revolution: Hegel and the Rise of Social Theory* (Atlantic Highlands, N.J.: Humanities Press, 1988), 3.

11. Herbert Marcuse, *One Dimensional Man: Studies in the Ideology of Advanced Industrial Society* (Boston: Beacon Press, 1964).

12. Georgi Dimitrov, *The United Front against Fascism: The Fascist Offensive and the Tasks of the Communist International in the Fight for the Unity of the Working Class against Fascism* (New York: Workers Library, 1936). Dimitrov was the general secretary of the Communist International. This pamphlet is the text of Dimitrov's speech at the Seventh World Congress of the Communist International in 1935. It announced a fundamental shift of policy from that of class struggle to the multiclass effort to combat fascism and war. It marked the end of the period of communist anticapitalist militancy.

13. Paul Goodman, *Growing Up Absurd: Problems of Youth in the Organized System* (New York: Random House, 1960).

14. Herbert Marcuse, "Some Social Implications of Modern Technology" in Marcuse, *Technology*. See also Martin Heidegger, *The Question Concerning Technology and Other Essays*, translated by William Lovitt (New York: Harper and Row, 1977).

15. Marcuse, *Technology*, 44.

16. See Henri Lefebvre, *The Explosion: Marxism and the French Revolution*, translated by Alfred Ehrenfeld (New York: Monthly Review Press, 1969).

17. Max Horkheimer, "The Authoritarian State" in *The Essential Frankfurt School Reader*, edited by Andrew Arato and Eike Gebhardt. (New York: Urizen Books, 1978).

18. Marcuse, *Technology*, 218.

19. Marcuse, *Technology*, 222.

20. Marcuse, *Technology*, 219.

21. Alfred Sohn-Rethel, *Intellectual and Manual Labour: A Critique of Epistemology* (London: Macmillan, 1978); see also Harry Braverman, *Labor and Monopoly Capital: The Degradation of Work in the Twentieth Century* (New York: Monthly Review Press, 1975).

14   On Union Democracy

1. Steve Fraser, "Is Democracy Good for Unions?" *Dissent* (summer 1998).
2. Fraser, "Is Democracy Good?"
3. *Los Angeles Times*, 5 July 1998.

16   *The New Men of Power*

1. C. Wright Mills, *The New Men of Power* (New York: Harcourt, Brace, 1948), 6.
2. C. Wright Mills, *White Collar: The American Middle Class* (New York: Oxford University Press, 1951).
3. C. Wright Mills, *The Power Elite* (New York: Oxford University Press, 1956).
4. Mills, *New Men of Power*, 19.
5. C. Wright Mills, *Sociology and Pragmatism: The Higher Learning in America* (New York: Oxford University Press, 1976).
6. John Dewey, *The Public and Its Problems in the Later Works of John Dewey*, edited by JoAnn Boydston (Carbondale: Southern Illinois University Press, 1982).
7. C. Wright Mills, "Letter to the New Left" in *Power, Politics and People: The Collected Essays of C. Wright Mills,* edited by Irving Louis Horowitz (New York: Oxford University Press, 1964).
8. C. Wright Mills, *The Causes of World War Three* (New York: Simon & Schuster, 1958).
9. C. Wright Mills, *Listen, Yankee: The Revolution in Cuba* (New York: McGraw-Hill, 1961).
10. C. Wright Mills and Hans Gerth, *Character and Social Structure: The Psychology of Social Institutions* (New York: Harcourt, Brace, 1953).
11. Mills, *New Men of Power*, 260–61.
12. Mills, *New Men of Power*, 261.

INDEX

AAUP. *See* American Association of University Professors

abortion rights, 26

academia: future of, 42–44; labor in, 29–44; unionization in, 22, 33–34, 39–41, 43–44, 69, 212–14

access: civil rights movement and, 24–25; to higher education, 89, 91

administration: and alternative education, 60; of unions, 215–17; and violence, 85–86, 172–73

admissions policies, 95–96; exclusive, 90, 94, 96; open, 92, 153

Adorno, Theodor, 119–20, 178–79, 192, 199–200

The Aesthetic Dimension (Marcuse), 182

aesthetics, Marcuse on, 182, 184, 193

affirmative action, 125–36, 140–41, 147–48

AFL-CIO. *See* American Federation of Labor and Congress of Industrial Organizations

African Americans: and Civil Rights movement, 24–26, 125–27, 186; current status of, 125–36; nationalism, 122–23; term, 116, 137–38, 146–47; unions and, 235–36; Wright and Gilroy on, 113–24

African diaspora, term, 116–17

AFT. *See* American Federation of Teachers

agency, 120

The Age of Imperialism (Magdoff), 162

agricultural societies, and time, 5–6

alternative high schools, 59–61, 71

Althusser, Louis, 107, 165, 167

American Association of University Professors (AAUP), 33–34, 39, 44

American Federation of Labor and Congress of Industrial Organizations (AFL-CIO), 17, 21, 174, 209–10, 219, 226

American Federation of Teachers (AFT), 39, 44, 212–14

Americanism, 142

American Medical Association, 21

American Pie, 83–84

anarchism, 19–20, 27, 165

Anderson, Perry, 105

And Then, 47
anticolonialism, Wright on, 113–14
anti-intellectualism: among blacks, 130–32;
    and Marcuse, 182; school reformers
    and, 71
anti-Semitism, in academia, 34
Arendt, Hannah, 76, 79, 183
Aronson, Karen, 96
art, 141, 173; computers and, 204;
    Marcuse on, 193; *Village Voice* and, 50
Ashcroft, John, 127–28
assimilation, 140–41, 143, 150
Association for Union Democracy, 214
authoritarianism: Horkheimer on, 193;
    Marcuse on, 185; Poulantzas on,
    167–68
autonomy, Freire on, 67
avant-garde, versus bohemians, 52

Babbitt, Milton, 52
bachelor's degree, 90
Beats, 45–46
Beck, Ulrich, 154
Bell Atlantic/Verizon, 21, 99–100
Bell, Daniel, 145, 179, 186
Benedict, Ruth, 34
Benjamin, Walter, 117–18, 120, 192–93
Berkeley Free Speech Movement, 91
Bernstein, Eduard, 180
Bishop, Maurice, 250
black: term, 116. *See also* African
    Americans
The Black Atlantic (Gilroy), 115–24
Black-Bloc, 161
Black Boy (Wright), 114
Black Panthers, 133
Black Power (Wright), 113, 116
Black Reconstruction (DuBois), 120, 122
Black Renaissance, 137
blacksmithing, 29–30
Bloch, Ernst, 192
Bluestone, Barry, 144
Boeing strike, 21–22
bohemians, 45–56;
    current status of, 54
Bond, Julian, 24
Bookchin, Murray, 38

Bourdieu, Pierre, 107
Bowen, Barbara, 55
Braverman, Harry, 195
Bravo, Douglas, 250
Britain, privatization in, 166
Brittan, Samuel, 151
Brotherhood of Electrical Workers, 21
Brotherhood of Sleeping Car Porters, 122,
    126, 149
Brownmiller, Susan, 49
Brown University, 96
Brown v. Board of Education, 126
Buell, John, 4
Bugliosi, Vincent, 127
Bukharin, Nicolai, 105, 193
bureaucracy, Weber on, 243
Bush, George W., 127–28

California State University, 41
Cameron State University, 100
capital: definition of, 4; Marcuse on,
    11–13; and working class, 168
capitalism: and bohemians, 46, 55;
    corporate, 38–39, 170; cultural
    significance of, 12–13; definition of, 4;
    and education, 69; Gilroy on, 119–24;
    globalization and, 159–75; and higher
    education, 44; history of, 13–14;
    Horkheimer on, 193; Marcuse on,
    10–11, 170; Mills on, 241;
    restructuring of, 135; and state, 177–96
Carey, Ron, 218, 226–27
Carr, C., 51
Carter, Elliot, 52
Carter, Stephen, 131
Castro, Fidel, 175
caucus, 219–20
The Causes of World War Three (Mills),
    248–49
Cedar Bar, 48
Central Labor Council, 235
Chancer, Lynn, 81
Character and Social Structure (Mills and
    Gerth), 251
child-rearing, 3–4
citizenship: education for, 99, 103–10;
    limits on, 20

City College of New York, 93
City University of New York, 30–32,
35–36, 41–42, 95–96, 101, 219
civil disobedience. *See* direct action
civility, 141
Civil Rights Act, 24, 127
Civil Rights movement, 125–27, 186;
direct action in, 24–26
civil society: Gramsci and, 103–4;
Habermas on, 179; labor movement
and, 14; race and gender issues in,
140–41; voting and, 9
class: versus ethnicity, 137–55; versus race,
129–36
Classes in Contemporary Capitalism
(Poulantzas), 162
classics, Gramsci on, 107–8
class size: in alternative schools, 60; in
higher education, 42
Cliff, Jimmy, 138
Clinton administration, 23–24, 74, 77, 147,
153
clock time, 4–5
Coleman, Ornette, 52
The Color Curtain (Wright), 116
Columbia University, 96, 184, 240, 245
Columbine High School, 74, 78–79, 81–82
comedy films, 82–83
Communications Workers of America, 21,
100
communicative action, Habermas on, 179
Communist Parties, 14, 164–65, 180, 195,
221; DuBois and, 122; Mills on, 247,
249–50
compromises: in education, 69–71; of
feminist movement, 26–27; Freire on,
70–71; of Green Parties, 17–18; of
labor movement, 14–15, 24, 173–74,
210–12; of professoriat, 35
computers: bohemians and, 54; social
effects of, 202–4; and time, 6–7
condos and phony co-ops, 48–49
conflict resolution, 73–88
conformity: higher education and, 139–40;
schooling for, 62, 69, 132; tenure
process and, 35
consciensization, 71

consent: Gramsci on, 106–7; options for,
79; and social reproduction, 169
consumer expectations, 8–9
consumer society, and time, 6, 37
contracts, 7–8, 216–17
corporate capitalism, 38–39; Marcuse on,
170
corporations, 167; and education, 61–65,
70, 132; and higher education, 39–40,
92, 94, 97–102; versus law, 9; Mills on,
242; science and, 203; and state, 187;
Wright on, 115–16
councilists, 178
critical education, 70; challenges to, 101
Critical Theory, 177–78, 184–85, 190–91.
See also Frankfurt School
Critique of Marcuse (Mattick), 178
Croly, Herbert, 245
Cuba, 175; Mills on, 250–51
culturalism, Steinberg on, 145–46
cultural significance: of capitalism,
12–13; of technology, 202–5; of
workday, 36
curriculum debate, 89–91, 98–102

Davis, Charles, 114
Davis, Leon, 236
The Declining Significance of Race
(Wilson), 129
The Deindustrialization of America
(Bluestone and Bennett), 144
De Landa, Manuel, 31
Delaney, Martin, 117
Deleuze, Gille, 180
Dell, Floyd, 48
democracy: corporations and, 9; Freire on,
65; future of, 27; Gramsci on, 106, 108;
Mills on, 244–45; myth of, violence
and, 73–88; Poulantzas on, 167–68;
time and, 3–27; unions and, 209–24,
226–27
Democratic Party: and African Americans,
122–23, 126; and labor unions, 174
Denning, Michael, 43
Dent, David, 137–38
Derrida, Jacques, 179–80
Dewey, John, 244–45

Dialectic of Enlightenment (Horkheimer and Adorno), 119–20, 199–200
Diallo, Amadou, 81, 236
dialogue, Freire on, 64
DiFazio, William, 42
difference: Adorno on, 120; creation of, 4; ethnicity and, 142; and institutions of world order, 174
Dillon, C. Douglas, 187
Dimitrov, Georgi, 185
direct action, 14, 165; anarchism and, 19–20; in unions, 215, 235; in United States, 8–9, 141
disadvantaged populations: admissions policies and, 96; and alternative education, 60; and curriculum, 99; endless labor and, 37–38
DiSapio, Carmine, 49
disruptive students, 85–86
distance learning, 101, 204
divided subject/object, 199–200
Dijksterhuis, E. J., 205
Dodge, Mabel, 48
The Dom, 53
Domestic Workers Union, 149
Domhoff, G. William, 246
domination, Critical Theory on, 191
Dominicans, 150
dot.comism, 6
double consciousness, 117, 119, 121–22; of Enlightenment, 119–20
double shift, 26
drug wars, 77
DuBois, W. E. B., 116–17, 119–22, 134
Dulles, John Foster, 187
Dumont, Louis, 7
Duncan, Isadora, 48

Eastman, Max, 48
East Village, 50–51
The East Village Other, 53
ecology movements, compromises of, 17–18
Edison Project, 95
education: for citizenship, 99, 103–10; current status of, 61–67; Freire on, 59–72; Goodman on, 187–88; Gramsci

on, 103–10; privatization of, 39; racial disparities in, 127, 130–31
educational reform: Freire on, 66–67; Goodman and, 187–88
Eisenhower, Dwight, 187, 210
elections, 9; 2000, and race relations, 127–28. *See also* voting
Elman, Richard, 94
end of history, 11–12; Freire on, 65
end of ideology, 145
"The End of Utopia" (Marcuse), 10–11
Engels, Friedrich, 16
Enlightenment, 199–200; Gilroy on, 119–24
epistemology, 197–206
equality of opportunity, 138, 151
Eros and Civilization (Marcuse), 182
ethics: Freire on, 67; of war, 75–76
ethnicity, 137–55; and American culture, 138–41; beyond, 151–55; and class, 145–50; definition of, 142–43; new concept of, 142–44
Ethnicity (Glazer, Moynihan, and Bell), 145
The Ethnic Myth (Steinberg), 145–46
Europe: higher education in, 41; and Kosovo, 86–88; unions in, 221–22
evaluation, 68
everyday life, 3; in academia, 30–36; of bohemians, 47; and Civil Rights movement, 186; Marcuse on, 178; of unionism, 234
existentialism: and Civil Rights movement, 186; and Freire, 65–66; and Wright, 115, 118
exit, 79–82, 88
experiment, 197–98

Fabre, Michel, 115
facts, Freire on, 68
family life: Goodman on, 187; state and, 77–78
Farrakhan, Louis, 137, 146
fascism: Horkheimer and Adorno on, 119–20; Marcuse on, 169–70, 185, 193
fatalism, Freire on, 63, 65
Feiffer, Jules, 49

feminist movement: compromises of,
26–27; Marcuse and, 193
film, Marcuse on, 193
Filmore East, 53
Foley, Thomas, 211
Ford, Henry, 12
Fordism, 134–35
Ford system, 6
Foucault, Michel, 180, 188
France: direct action in, 165, 221–22;
higher education in, 41; privatization
in, 166
Frankfurt School, 167, 177–80, 189, 192.
See also Critical Theory
Fraser, Steve, 210–11, 222
freedom: academic, 33–34; bohemians and,
47; Clinton administration and, 77;
Freire on, 64, 71–72; Marcuse on, 11,
181, 185–86; Mills on, 247; rhetoric of,
9–10
Freire, Paolo, 59–72
Freud, Sigmund, 177
Fromm, Erich, 65
Fukuyama, Francis, 11
Fuller, Steve, 199
full-time jobs, 38
funding, for higher education, 89, 92
Further Selections (Gramsci), 104
Fussell, Paul, 75–76
future: of academia, 42–44; of bohemia,
55–56; of democracy, 27; possibilities
for, 4, 15–20, 27, 192; of public higher
education, 155; of race relations,
135–36. *See also* hope

Gaines, Donna, 84
gang films, 82
Gans, Herbert, 145
Garvey, Marcus, 117
Geller, Stanley, 49
Gem Spa, 53
General Electric, 210
General Motors, 217, 230
gentrification, 48–49
Germany, 75, 182–83
Gerth, Hans, 242–43, 251
Ghana, 113, 122

GI Bill, 93
Gilroy, Paul, 115–24
Giroux, Henry, 107
Giuliani, Rudolph, 172
glass ceiling, 27, 142
Glazer, Nathan, 143, 145
globalization: and revolution, 18; and state,
159–75
Godoff, Elliot, 235
Goldberg, Arthur J., 209
Gold, Ed, 49
Gold, Tami, 55
Goldwater, Barry, 127
Good Life: Freire on, 71–72; Marcuse on,
11–12
Goodman, Paul, 178, 186–88
Gore, Al, 19, 127–29
Gorz, Andre, 15–16
Gould, Stephen J., 200
grade inflation, 96
graduate assistants, unionization of, 22,
40–41, 43–44
Graham, Bill, 53
Gramsci, Antonio, 103–10, 167
Great Books program, 96
Great Refusal, 64
Green Parties, 159; compromises of, 17–18
Greenwich Village, 45–56
Grossman, Henryk, 193
Grosz, Elizabeth, 31
Growing Up Absurd (Goodman), 186–88
The Guardian, 53–54
Guevara, Che, 250

Habermas, Jürgen, 179
Hacking, Ian, 197
Hanson, Norwood, 197
Haraway, Donna, 13, 190
Hardt, Michael, 161, 166
Harrington, Michael, 49
Harrington, Stephanie, 49
Harris, Townsend, 93
Harrison, Bennett, 144
Haywood, Big Bill, 48
healthcare: labor conditions in, 55;
privatization and, 39; rhetoric on, 10;
unionization in, 20–21, 204, 234–35

health maintenance organizations, 39, 221
Hegel, G. W. F., 103, 205
Heidegger, Martin, 182–84
Helms, Jesse, 141
Hentoff, Nat, 49
Henwood, Doug, 166
Herrnstein, Richard, 131, 155
heteronomy, 42, 171–72
higher education, 89–102; class issues and,
    153–54; corporatization of, 39–40, 94,
    97–102; in Europe, 41; public, 90,
    92–98, 155; recommendations for, 102;
    restructuring of, 43; and social mobility,
    139–40
Hilferding, Rudolph, 162, 193
Hirschman, Albert O., 79
history, 191–92, 197–206; end of, 11–12,
    65; Gramsci on, 109; possibility of
    change in, 3–27
Hoare, Quintin, 104
Hochchild, Arlie, 26
Hoffa, James P., 227
Hoffman, Abbie, 53
Holocaust, 75, 182–83
Holt, Thomas, 133–36
homework, 4
homophobia, and school violence, 81–82
Hook, Sidney, 62
hope: for academia, 42–44; for education,
    Freire on, 63–64; Marcuse on, 192–93,
    195–96. See also future
Horkheimer, Max, 119–20, 178, 182, 191,
    193, 199–200
horror films, 82–83
Hospital Workers Union Local 1199,
    234–36
Howe, Irving, 34
Hudson Institute, 92
Human Genome Project, 70
humanism: Freire and, 66; Wright and, 114
humanities, 42, 70, 89–90, 97–100;
    Gramsci on, 107–8
human rights issues, 23–24; and warfare,
    87
Hussein, Saddam, 87
Husserl, Edmund, 200

identity: Marcuse on, 181; race and,
    113–24
identity politics, 137–55
ideological apparatus, 107, 165–68, 174
Ideology and Utopia (Manheim), 243
ideology, end of, 145
ILA. See International Longshoremen's
    Association
IMF. See International Monetary Fund
imperialism, new, 161–62
independent bookstores, 47
industrial civilization: and bohemians, 46;
    and education, 61–65, 70; and time,
    5–6
Institute for Social Research. See Critical
    Theory
insurance, unions and, 220–21
integration, 122–23
Intellectual and Manual Labor (Sohn-
    Rethel), 205
intellectual moral bloc, Gramsci on,
    109–10
intellectuals, 177, 239; versus academics,
    55; endangered, 132; teachers as, 36,
    44, 64
intellectual workers, unions among, 22
intelligence, measurement of, 200
international business organizations, 160;
    Seattle protesters on, 20
internationalism, 160, 162
International Longshore and Warehouse
    Union, 19
International Longshoremen's Association
    (ILA), 215
International Monetary Fund (IMF), 18,
    74, 87–88, 160
Internet: bohemians and, 55; and time, 6–7

Jackson, Jesse, 24, 118, 123
Jackson, Michael, 118
Jacobs, Jane, 50–51
Jacoby, Russell, 177
James, C. L. R., 118–19
jazz, 52, 141
Jews: culture of, 145–46; diaspora of,
    116–17

jobs, 38, 98, 171; good, last in America. *See* academia; race and, 129
Johnson, Joyce, 45–46
Johnson, Lyndon B., 127
Jospin, Lionel, 164

Kaminer, Wendy, 77
Kant, Immanuel, 197
Kennedy, Ted, 127
Kerr proposal, 90–91, 99
King, Martin Luther, Jr., 123
Kirscheimer, Otto, 167
Klein, Jessie, 81
Knowland, William, 133
Knowledge for What? (Lynd), 247
Koch, Ed, 49
Kosovo, 74, 86–88
Kralovec, Etta, 4
Kuhn, Thomas, 201–2

labor: academic, 29–44; bohemians and, 46–47, 54–55; computers and, 203–4; Gramsci on, 106; Marcuse on, 11–12; and NAFTA, 23–24; state and, 167; time and, 5–6, 21–22, 37; without end, 36–38, 63; women and, 26; youth and, 86
laboratory life, 198–99
labor law: enforcement of, 24, 171; reform of, 22–23, 220
Labor-Management Reporting Disclosure Act, 210, 214
labor movement: bohemians and, 55; compromises of, 14–15, 24, 173–74, 210–12; dependency of, 173; Marcuse on, 186, 195; Mills on, 240–41, 251–54; and stress, 17; and workday, 5–6. *See also* unions
Labor Parties, 14, 164
Laclau, Ernesto, 179
Lady from Shanghai, 229
land grant colleges, 93
law: and compromise, 26–27; Marcuse on, 169
lean production, 230

learner: Freire on, 63; in transmission theory of knowledge, 62
Learning to Labor (Willis), 132
Lefebvre, Henri, 4, 178, 192
Left: and ethnicity, 152–53; Freire on, 65; future of, 27; Mills on, 247; Seattle protests and, 160–61; and unions, 225–26, 235
Lenin, V. I., 189, 193
Lewis, John, 24
liberal arts, 89–90, 100; Gramsci on, 107–8
Linden Assemblers, 229–36
Lion's Head, 48
Lippmann, Walter, 244
Listen! (Wright), 116
Listen, Yankee (Mills), 250
litigation, versus law, 9, 171
Littleton, Colo., 74, 78–79, 81–82
London, Jack, 133
London protests, 160–61
The Long Dream (Wright), 115
Louima, Abner, 81
love, Marcuse on, 182, 193
loyalty, 79, 87–88
Lucy, Autherine, 126
Lukacs, Georg, 189
Lynd, Robert S., 247
Lynd, Staughton, 22–23

Macdonald, Dwight, 183
Machiavelli, Niccolò, 105, 110, 251–52
Magdoff, Harry, 162
Mailer, Norman, 49
main drift, 246
Malcolmson, Scott, 133–36
Mallet, Serge, 16
Maloney, Joseph, 210
management: professors as, 43; scientific, 5–6; and technology, 38; Wright on, 115–16
Manhattan Institute, 92, 95
Manley, Michael, 250
Mannheim, Karl, 243
Marcuse, Herbert, 10–15, 38, 53, 169–70, 177–96

Marcuse, Peter, 194
Marxism: Derrida and, 180; discourse
    after, 179; in disrepute, 179; Freire and,
    65; Gramsci and, 103–5, 109; Marcuse
    and, 177, 185, 189; Mills and, 242;
    Wright and, 114–15, 122
Marx, Karl, 12–13, 16
Marzani, Carl, 103–4
masculinity, and school violence, 81–82
mass culture, Mills on, 248
mathematization of nature, 200
Mattick, Paul, 178
McClelland, James, 210
McDonald, Heather, 95
McLeod, Jay, 78
McSorley's, 51
McWhorter, John W., 129–32
Mead, Margaret, 34
mechanical reproduction, Marcuse on,
    192–93
The Mechanization of the World Picture
    (Dijksterhuis), 205
media, and higher education, 92, 95
mediation, 80–81, 84–86
Meredith, James, 126
mergers and acquisitions, 167, 172, 203
Merton, Robert, 199
method, 205–6
Michels, Robert, 243
middle class: conflict resolution in, 78–79;
    new, 139
Miliband, Ralph, 161, 164
military, Mills on, 242
Millet, Kate, 45
Million Man March, 123, 137–38, 146
Mills, C. Wright, 14–15, 178, 186–87, 189,
    239–54
Milosevic, Slobodan, 74, 86–88
miseducation, 187–88
modernity, 12; DuBois on, 120; Gilroy on,
    119–24; Wright on, 113–14, 116
The Modern Prince (Gramsci), 110
modular production, 230–31
Montagu, Ashley, 200
Montgomery, David, 43
Moore, Barrington, 7
morality, education and, 188

Morgenthau, Henry, 187
Morrell Act, 93
Morrison, Toni, 118
Mouffe, Chantal, 179
Moynihan, Daniel Patrick, 143, 145
multiculturalism, 98–102
multinational corporations. *See* corporations
Mumford, Lewis, 190
Murray, Albert, 118
Murray, Charles, 131, 155
music: avant-garde, 52; black, 118;
    computers and, 204

NAACP. *See* National Association for the
    Advancement of Colored People
Nader, Ralph, 246
NAFTA. *See* North American Free Trade
    Agreement
National Association for the Advancement
    of Colored People (NAACP), 121, 126
National Education Association (NEA), 39,
    212–13
nationality, and class, 137–55
National Labor Relations Act, 22–24,
    216–17, 237
National Writers Union, 55
nation-state, 162, 164
Native Americans, 133–34
Native Son (Wright), 114
nature, mathematization of, 200
NEA. *See* National Education Association
Negri, Tony, 16, 161, 166
Neill, A. S., 188
neoimperialism, 161–62
neoliberalism, 160, 164–65; Freire on, 63,
    65; Green Parties and, 159; labor and,
    23–24; student movement and, 101
Neumann, Franz, 53, 167, 182
Neumann, Tom, 53
New Deal, 24–25, 122, 237
Newfield, Jack, 49
New Left: Marcuse and, 178; Mills on, 247
The New Men of Power (Mills), 239–54
new social movements, 179–81
New York City: Board of Education,
    59–60; Greenwich Village, 45–56;
    police in, 172–73

New York Intellectuals, 46, 55, 178
New York Municipal Employees District
    Council 37, 226–27, 233–34
New York Painters District, 214
Nichols, Mary, 49
Nietzsche, Friedrich, 68
nihilism, in teen films, 83
Nixon, Richard, 127–28, 148
nonviolence, 80–81
North American Free Trade Agreement
    (NAFTA), 23

Oakland, Calif., 133–34
objectivity, Freire on, 68
Office and Professional Employees Union, 21
Olin Foundation, 40, 62
One Dimensional Man (Marcuse), 10–11,
    184, 188–89
onto-history, 197–206
open admissions, 92, 153
The Open Marxism of Antonio Gramsci
    (Gramsci), 103
open society, 138–39, 151–52
Operation Dixie, 210
Oppenheimer, Joel, 49
opposition: exit option and, 79–82; tenure
    and, 34–35
organization model of unionism, 226
The Outsider (Wright), 114–15

Padmore, George, 122
Palmer, R. P., 13
pan-African movement, 122
Pareto, Vilfredo, 241–42
Parks, Rosa, 126
parties: of government, 14, 164, 180;
    within unions, 219–20
Partisan Review, 178
patriarchy, Goodman on, 187
Patterson, Orlando, 119
Pedagogy of Freedom (Freire), 63, 65–67, 70
Pedagogy of the Oppressed (Freire), 61
peer review, 35
pessimism, Freire on, 63, 65
philosophy of praxis, 192; in disrepute,
    179; Gramsci on, 109; Marcuse on,
    178, 184

philosophy of science, 197–206
physicians, unionization of, 20–21, 204
Piccone, Paul, 181
Pickering, Andrew, 198–99
police, in United States, 76–77, 168, 172
political localism: globalization and, 20;
    Gramsci on, 105; Marcuse on, 181–82;
    and warfare, 76–77
Political Parties (Michels), 243
politics: bohemians and, 48–49; Gramsci
    on, 110; Marcuse on, 181; Mills on,
    248–49; science and, 201; Wright on,
    113–14
Pollock, Frederick, 167, 193
Popper, Karl, 151, 198, 205
popular culture, 141; Marcuse on, 193
Port Huron Statement, 245
positivism, 198
poststructuralism, 179–80
Poulantzas, Nicos, 161–75
Powell, Colin, 128
power: challenges to, 7–8, 40; versus
    comfort, 12; ethnicity and, 152; Mills
    on, 239–54; science as, 206; versus
    violence, 73–74
The Power Elite (Mills), 186–87, 241, 246
pragmatism, Mills on, 243
printing, 29–30
privatization: globalization and, 166; of
    higher education, 92, 94–100
The Problem of Freedom (Holt), 134–35
professoriat: compromises of, 35;
    disappearing, 30, 32, 40, 94; distance
    from students, 42–43
progressivism, Freire on, 65
Promise of American Life (Croly), 245
protests: consumer expectations in, 8–9; of
    Marcuse, 53; Seattle, 4, 9, 18–19,
    160–61; in student movement, 91
public: Gramsci on, 109–10; Mills on, 244,
    249
The Public and Its Problems (Dewey), 244–45
public good, higher education as, 89–102
public higher education: attacks on, 90, 92,
    95, 98; future of, 155; history of, 93–98
Public Opinion (Lippmann), 244
public sphere, unions as, 225–38

Quaderni (Gramsci), 103–4
questioning, Freire on, 64
Quine, Willard, 197

race: versus class, 129–36; versus ethnicity,
    137–55
race relations: chasms in, 127; and criminal
    justice system, 168; current status of,
    125–36; unions and, 235–36; Wright
    and Gilroy on, 113–24
racism: Gilroy on, 118–19; London and,
    133; McWhorter on, 129–32
radicalism, 186, 249; in unions, 211
Rampersad, Arnold, 114
Randolph, A. Philip, 122, 126, 149
rank and file, and union democracy,
    214–17, 226, 237–38
Rarick, Pat, 210
The Rat, 54
Reagan, Ronald, 17
reason: Horkheimer on, 191; Marcuse on,
    185
Reason and Revolution (Marcuse), 184
Rebels with a Cause, 125
recess, 62–63
reflection, Freire on, 64
Regents Examinations, 60–61
Reich, Wilhelm, 187
religion, in United States, 140
rent control, 45, 48–49, 166
repression apparatus, 165
reproduction, 3; break in, 4; consent and,
    169; disruption of, 20; mechanical,
    Marcuse on, 192–93
reproductive theory, 107
Republican Party, and African Americans,
    126–28
research universities, 41–42, 90–91, 93–94,
    96–97
resistance, in education, 107
respect, in education, 60–61
Reuther, Walter, 210, 249
revolution: current status of, 165;
    globalization and, 18; Gramsci on, 105;
    Marcuse on, 184; Marx on, 13;
    preconditions for, 7–8, 88

rhetoric: of freedom, 9–10; Mills on,
    243–46
Rice, Condoleezza, 128
Right, and education, 92
rights: discourse on, 23–24; voice as, 80
Rivera, Dennis, 236
Rockefeller, David, 51
Roe v. Wade, 26
Roosevelt, Franklin D., 24, 93, 126
Ross, Andrew, 30
Roth, Robert, 47
Rubin, Robert, 187

Sacher, Arnie, 47
Sahlins, Peter, 45
Sanger, Margaret, 48
São Paulo, 66, 68
Sartre, Jean-Paul, 65, 115, 247
Savage Holiday (Wright), 115–16
scarcity, artificial, 12, 37–38, 69, 192
Schlesinger, Arthur, 17
Schmidt, Benno, 95
Schneider, Helen, 241, 245
Schoenkopf, Sarah, 49
scholarship, Marcuse on, 183
Schonfeld, Frank, 214
school: discipline in, 80–81, 85–86,
    172–73; Goodman on, 187–88; state
    and, 107
school failure, 59–72, 107
school violence, 78–79, 81–82
science: Critical Theory on, 191;
    Enlightenment and, 120; Freire on,
    67–68; Gramsci on, 109; in higher
    education, 40; logics of, 197–98;
    Marcuse on, 11; philosophy of, 197–206
scientific management, 5–6
Scream, 82–83
Seafarers and National Maritime Unions,
    229
Seale, Bobby, 133
Seattle WTO protests, 4, 9, 18–19,
    160–61, 174
Selden, David, 212
*Selections from the Prison Notebooks of
    Antoni Gramsci* (Gramsci), 104

self, Freire on, 67
separatism, 130
Service Employees International Union,
    21, 150, 219, 226
Servicemen's Readjustment Act, 93
service model of unionism, 233–36
sexuality: bohemians and, 48; policing of,
    77–78, 188; in teen films, 83–84
Shelburne museum, 29–30
Sherover, Erica, 193
Sinclair, Upton, 133
Sitkoff, Harvard, 122
slackers, 15–16, 46–47
slavery, Gilroy on, 119–24
Sloan, John, 48
slump, 246
social change, possibility of, 3–27
Social Class in America (Warner), 142
social constructionism, 199
socialism, 164; current status of, 165;
    Marcuse on, 195; status of, 38
Socialist Parties, 14, 133, 164–65
social mobility, 151; civil rights movement
    and, 24–25; higher education and,
    139–40
social time, 4–5, 12
Sociology and Pragmatism (Mills), 243
Sohn-Rethel, Alfred, 195, 205
Soviet ideology, Marcuse on, 178–79, 185
Soviet Union, 183; collapse of, 17
space, and social change, 3–27
speedup, 14, 55
Spiegelman, Robert, 38
Stalinism: Marcuse on, 178–79, 185; Mills
    on, 247
standardized testing, 62
state: capitalism and, 13–14, 177–96; and
    family life, 77–78; globalization and,
    159–75; Marcuse on, 12, 185; Mills on,
    242; and school, 107
State, Power, Socialism (Poulantzas), 162, 167
Steinberg, Steven, 145
stress, labor movement and, 17
strikes: Boeing, 21–22; in Seattle, 4; UPS,
    218, 226–27; Verizon, 21; without legal
    framework, 24–25

student movement, 62, 91; Marcuse and,
    178, 189; and neoliberalism, 101
Students for a Democratic Society, 125,
    245
subjective time, 4–5
sundial, 5
surplus repression, 12
surveillance, 76–77
Sweeney, John, 226
Sweezy, Paul, 162

Taft-Hartley Amendments, 22–23, 210,
    217
Taylor, Frederick Winslow, 5
TDU. See Teamsters for a Democratic
    Union
teachers: and alternative education, 59–61;
    bohemians as, 54–55; Freire on, 63–67;
    in transmission theory of knowledge,
    62; unions of, 21, 39, 212–14, 233
teacher work, 39–44; characteristics of, 36;
    future of, 42–44; political economy of,
    36–42
Teamsters for a Democratic Union (TDU),
    214, 226, 238
Technics and Civilization (Mumford), 190
technology, 191–92, 201–6; and culture,
    204–5; management and, 38; Marcuse
    on, 10, 13, 185, 189–90; unions and,
    37; and warfare, 75–76
teenagers: boredom of, 86, 132; movies for,
    82–84; violence among, 78–79, 81–82
tenants' movements, 48–49
tenure, 22, 33–35
Textile Workers Union, 210
third tier institutions, 90–91, 97–98
Thurmond, Strom, 126
time: academic labor and, 32–34; and
    democracy, 3–27; experience of, 6–8
tracking, Gramsci on, 106
transmission theory of school knowledge,
    61–63
Transport Workers, 215, 226–27, 238
Traweek, Sharon, 198–99
Trilling, Lionel, 34
Tronti, Mario, 15–16

Trotskyism, Mills on, 249–50
Truman, Harry S., 76, 126
Turner, Doris, 236
Twelve Million Black Voices (Wright),
    114–15, 122
Typographical Union, 220

UAW. *See* United Auto Workers
UFT. *See* United Federation of Teachers
undergraduates, and research, 99
unemployment, 37–38, 146
unions: in academia, 22, 33–34, 39–41,
    43–44, 69, 212–14, 233; competetion
    among, 219, 221–22; democracy and,
    209–24, 226–27; and education,
    99–100; and ethnicity, 143–44,
    148–50; history of, 209–10, 227–28;
    and internationalism, 19–20;
    members' bill of rights, 210;
    membership in, 232–33; Mills on, 15,
    248; of physicians, 20–21, 204; as
    public sphere, 225–38; reform of,
    recommendations for, 218–22,
    252–54; and technology, 37. *See also*
    labor movement
UNITE (Union of Needle Industries and
    Textile Employees), 23, 150
United Airlines, 21
United Auto Workers (UAW), 44, 210–12,
    217, 226, 249; Local 595, 229–36
United Farm Workers, 150
United Federation of Teachers (UFT), 213
United Parcel Service (UPS): strike, 218,
    226–27
United States: anti-intellectualism in, 132;
    conflict resolution in, 73–88; direct
    action in, 8–9, 141; ethnicity in,
    138–41; ideological apparatus in,
    165–68, 174; post-Soviet, 160;
    privatization in, 166
United States foreign policy, 74–75; on
    Cuba, 175; human rights issues and,
    23–24; and trade, 171–72
United Steelworkers, 173–74
University of California, 91, 96, 99, 192
University of Chicago, 96

University of Paris at Saint Denis, 41
UPS. *See* United Parcel Service
utopia, Marcuse on, 10–11, 186

Van Arsdale, Harry, 235
Verizon/Bell Atlantic, 21, 99–100
Vico, Giambattista, 199
victimology, 130
Vietnam Syndrome, 87
Village Voice, 49–50, 53
violence, 73–88; definition of, 73; in teen
    films, 84
vocationalization, 39–40, 99–100, 153–54;
    Gramsci on, 106
voice, 79–80, 88, 169, 171; in schools,
    84–86
Voselka, 53
voting, 9, 14, 169; African Americans and,
    125–36; in unions, 215
Voting Rights Act, 24, 127

Wales, unionization in, 228
Wallach, Ira, 187
Wall, Rochelle, 50
warfare, 75–76, 87; Mills on, 248–49
Warner, W. Lloyd, 142
Washington, D.C. protests, 160–61
Weber, Max, 177, 190, 242–43, 246
welfare reform, 147, 160, 164–66, 168
welfare state, 14, 128
Welles, Orson, 229
Weltfish, Gene, 34
Westbeth, 51
Western Marxism, 105
West Village, 50
When Work Disappears (Wilson), 146
White Collar (Mills), 241, 248
White Horse, 48
White Man (Wright), 116
whites, and ethnicity, 148–49
Williams, Eric, 119
Williams, Raymond, 118, 227–28
Willis, Paul, 107, 132
Wilson, H. T., 151
Wilson, William Julius, 129, 146
Wilson, Woodrow, 121–22

wireless industry strike, 21
Wolf, Dan, 49
workday, 5–6, 36–37, 173
Workers Party, 66
working class: and bohemians, 47–48;
    capital and, 168; international, 162;
    Marcuse on, 15; new, 16–17. *See also*
    labor movement
World Bank, 160
World Trade Organization (WTO), 160;
    protests of, 4, 9, 18–19, 160–61, 174

Wright, Richard, 113–24
WTO. *See* World Trade Organization

Yale University: Afro-American Studies
    program, 113–14; Graduate Assistants
    Union, 43
Yudice, George, 30
Yugoslavia, 74, 86–88

Zangwill, Israel, 140
Zionism, 117

ABOUT THE AUTHOR

Stanley Aronowitz lives in Manhattan, where he is Distinguished Professor of Sociology and Cultural Studies at the Graduate Center of the City University of New York.

Critical Perspectives Series
General Editor, Donaldo Macedo, University of Massachusetts, Boston
A book series dedicated to Paulo Freire

Chomsky on Miseducation
   Noam Chomsky

Critical Education in the New Information Age
   Manuel Castells, Ramón Flecha, Paulo Freire, Henry A. Giroux, Donaldo
   Macedo, and Paul Willis

Critical Ethnicity: Countering the Waves of Identity Politics
   Edited by Robert H. Tai and Mary L. Kenyatta

Debatable Diversity: Critical Dialogues on Change in American Universities
   Raymond V. Padilla and Miguel Montiel

Imagining Teachers: Rethinking Gender Dynamics in the Classroom
   Gustavo E. Fischman

Immigrant Voices: In Search of Educational Equity
   Edited by Enrique (Henry) T. Trueba and Lilia I. Bartolomé

Latinos Unidos: From Cultural Diversity to the Politics of Solidarity
   Enrique (Henry) T. Trueba

Pedagogy of Freedom: Ethics, Democracy, and Civic Courage
   Paulo Freire

Pedagogy, Symbolic Control, and Identity, Revised Edition
   Basil Bernstein

A Sanctuary of their Own: Intellectual Refugees in the Academy
   Raphael Sassower

Sharing Words: Theory and Practice of Dialogic Learning
   Ramón Flecha

Forthcoming

Ideology Matters
   Paulo Freire and Donaldo Macedo

Paulo Freire and the Social Imagination: From Dreams to Praxis
   Maxine Greene